THE HEART OF CATHOLIC SPIRITUALITY

To Brendan and Philippa
who gave great glory to God
in life and in death

The Heart
of Catholic Spirituality

FINDING A VOICE THROUGH THE CENTURIES

Thomas Lane CM

PAULIST PRESS
NEW YORK / MAHWAH, N.J.

First published in 2000 by
THE COLUMBA PRESS
55A Spruce Avenue, Stillorgan Industrial Park,
Blackrock, Co Dublin

Cover design by Ray Lundgren

Library of Congress Cataloging-in-Publication Data

Lane, Thomas, CM.
  The heart of Catholic spirituality : finding a voice through the
centuries / Thomas Lane.
    p. cm.
  ISBN 0-8091-4143-4
  1. Spirituality—Catholic Church. 1. Title
  BX2350.65 .L37 2003
  248'.888'22—dc21

                                            2002155195

Published in the United States of America in 2003 by
Paulist Press
997 Macarthur Boulevard
Mahwah, New Jersey 07430
www.paulistpress.com
Printed and bound in the United States of America

Contents

Preface 7

1. Images, Icons and the Trinity 11

2. The Trinity Tell Us Who They Are 21

3. Coming to the Father 30

4. Follow You More Nearly 37

5. Spirit of the Living God 45

6. Do God's Will 55

7. Be Transparent 66

8. Keep Fanning the Flame 75

9. Have a Heart 84

10. Salvation Revisited 93

11. Church of a Sacrificing God 107

12. A Church Always Interceding 116

13. Making Our Home in the Lord's Word 125

14. Bake Before You Break 133

15. From Lecture to *Lectio* 143

16. The Consecrations of Christians 150

17. Can These Consecrated Bones Live? 160

18. Called and Calling   169

19. Being Really Present   177

20. Emptying and Filling   187

21. Discerning the Body   198

22. Preached or Directed?   207

23. At the Shrine of the Lamb: Knock Calls   217

24. Miraculous Indeed: A Medal Speaks   225

25. Old Oak, New Branches: St. Vincent Lives   233

26. A Beautiful Millennium   242

Index   252

Preface

We come into this world with a cry and we leave it with the remains of a cry. In the time in between we go through a whole range of other cries. Not all of them are cries of pain or of grief but each expresses something of our human limitations. The poet who said that we are like "an infant crying in the night, an infant crying for the light, and with no language but a cry" was indulging in poetic license but he was alerting us to the fact that, even when we have left the things of a child, we cannot leave the fragility of being human. This fragility accompanies us even when we cry with joy and when we raise the cry of victory.

As we read the scriptures, we can identify with people who, in their longing for God, knew what it was to give many cries from the heart. The gospels tell us of the cries of the Lord and the cries of people who rejoiced at his coming. His presence in the womb of his mother made St. Elizabeth give a loud cry of joy (Luke 1:42). On the feast of Tabernacles, he himself cried out "let anyone who is thirsty come to me" (John 7:37). His loud cry at the tomb of Lazarus (John 11:43) included sadness at the reality of death and gladness at his own victory over it. There were cries of rejoicing when he entered into Jerusalem (Matt 21:9, 15). His cry at his own death was the cry of one who had personally struggled with the great enemy and who was giving his last gasp as he gave up his spirit (Mark 15:37; Matt 27:50). Even in this cry there was a note of confident self-surrender (cf. Luke 23:46). Through all his cries, the Lord brought us a freedom in which we can now gladly cry "Abba, Father" (Rom 8:15).

Since the days when Pope John XXIII was calling for a new Pentecost, we have been a church of many cries. There have been cries of gratitude and delight at the many fruits of the Second Vatican Council. There have also been cries of surprise, disappointment, anger. There have been cries in response to hopes unrealized, to decline where people had expected new growth, to death where people had looked for life. Not all the cries can be easily heard by the human ear. Some can be picked up only by a special kind of listening. Undoubtedly some of the more painful cries have been good for us. As "new-born infants" (1 Pet 2:2) we need to do some crying if we are to keep healthy. The whole church today is groaning in the labor pains of some new birthing (cf Rom 8:22).

No matter what forms this birthing will take, it will remain true that we exist for the purpose of giving glory to God. There was a serenity about the song of the angels as they praised God and said "Glory to God in the highest heaven" (Luke 2:14) on the night the Savior was born. There is not always the same serenity about the various ways we say "glory be to God." As well as being an expression of a desire to praise God, it can be an importunate call for help. It can express shock, dismay, bewilderment. All the chapters of this book are attempts to capture some of the tones of some of the cries of "glory be to God" that are coming from Christians today.

For practical reasons I have, in recent years, been writing out the full text of my addresses to various groups and keeping the text beside me when I am speaking. I have also kept the texts of articles I have written for various periodicals. Some of my colleagues have been encouraging me to collect some of these for publication. As I did the collecting, I saw the need to write some new chapters and to rewrite much of the existing material.

My involvement with priests, seminarians and religious for most of my priestly life gives an obvious coloring to a lot of the material; so do my Vincentian interests. But I like to believe that, in my choice of topics, there is nothing that does not have immediate implications for all the baptized. I am seeing ever more clearly that all Christian spirituality is effective and credible to the extent that it is baptismal. This was already dawning on me in the limited parish ministry in which I became involved in my days of seminary teaching. It became clearer and clearer during my part-time work in Bonnybrook parish, Dublin, in recent years.

The chapters are not essays in theology and spirituality. They have no footnotes, no cross-references. They are my attempt to express for busy readers some of what I was gleaning from my own reading since the days when my main work was teaching theology. When *A Priesthood in Tune* was published in 1993, some of my friends said they would have liked a more personal approach in some of the chapters. I hope that I have not gone to the other extreme this time.

In the first draft of the chapters, I attempted to be consistent in the use of inclusive language. I soon found myself bogging down in my attempts to use a language that is still in the making; I hope I will continue to learn. In quoting from the gospels, I tend to write as if we always have the very words of Jesus and the exact historical settings in which he spoke them. Something similar applies to the way I quote from the Old Testament. I am aware of the scholarly questions that this raises and I respectfully refer the enquiring reader to the learned commentaries.

Over the past year, Margaret Doyle has been patiently gathering the fragments, typing and re-typing, and putting up with my foibles and changes of plan. Thanks again, Margaret. Thanks too to Sr. Assumpta, FMDM, Fr. Kevin Rafferty, CM, Fr. Eugene Duffy, and Fr. Andrew Faley, who read the full text and made very valuable criticisms and suggestions. May they and all of us meet where all the cries will be cries of joy.

Thomas Lane CM
Feast of St. Vincent
27 September 2000

SOURCES

Chapters 8, 17, 18 are based on various talks to religious.

Chapters 13 and 14 are based on talks at the Intercession for Priests, All Hallows College.

Chapter 25 is based on talks to conferences of the Society of St. Vincent de Paul.

Chapters 19, 21, 23 are based on talks to various parish groups.

Chapters 22 and 24 are based on reflections with my Vincentian colleagues and with communities of the Daughters of Charity.

Chapter 11 is an adaptation of a review article in *Doctrine and Life* (Ian Bradley, *The Power of Sacrifice*, DLT 1995).

Chapter 20 is an adaptation of a review article in *Doctrine and Life*, (Dermot Power, *A Spiritual Theology of the Priesthood*, T & T Clark, 1998).

Chapters 3 and 16 are adaptations of articles in *Doctrine and Life*.

Chapter 10 is an adaptation of an article in the Vincentian *Colloque*.

Chapter 24 is an adaptation of an article in the *Newsletter of the Daughters of Charity*, Irish Province.

All the articles are used with permission.

ACKNOWLEDGMENTS

Biblical texts are from *The New Revised Standard Version*, copyright © 1989, by the Division of Christian Education of the National Council of the Churches of Christ in the United States of America.

Chapter 2: the title, and some of the approach, were prompted by Anne Hunt's *The Trinity and the Paschal Mystery* (Liturgical Press, Collegeville, 1997).

Chapter 4: For the first three images I have drawn heavily (sometimes by paraphrase and even direct transcription) on: Wright, Norman T., *Jesus and the Victory of God* (SPCK, 1996), Meier, John P., *A Marginal Jew* (Doubleday, 1991, 1998), and Rousseau, John J. (ed.), *Jesus and His World* (SCM, 1996).

Chapter 15: My principal sources are:

De Verteuil, Michel, *Your Word is a Lamp for My Steps* (Veritas, 1996),

Pennington, Basil, *Lectio Divina* (Crossroad, 1998), and

Martini, Cardinal Carlo, *Lectio Divina and Vocation in Life* (*Spirituality*, Nos. 15, 16).

Chapter 19: In my approach to real presence, I have been helped a lot by Regis Duffy's *Real Presence* (Harper, San Francisco, 1982).

Chapter 26: I have drawn a great deal on two books by Fr. John Navone, SJ: *Towards a Theology of Beauty* (Liturgical Press, Collegeville, 1996); *Enjoying God's Beauty* (idem, 1999).

CHAPTER 1

Images, Icons and the Trinity

A few years ago, I preached a Lenten retreat in a parish in the United States. In the course of the first day, there was a gathering of parishioners in the community center and I was introduced to many of them. I couldn't help noticing a man who was rather stilted in his movements but whose face was strangely radiant. Eventually he came up to me, reached out his hand and said, "Father, my name is Harold. I want you to know that you are talking to the happiest man in the world." He then told me his story. As a young man, he was reluctantly enlisted for service in the war in Vietnam. Every morning he woke up angry with God, angry with the government of his country, angry with life generally. Then, one day, he was, literally, blown to pieces. All the most modern wonders of surgery were made available for him and a new Harold emerged. He received new hands, new feet, and quite a variety of implants. When the day came for him to walk his first step, he found himself crying out, "Isn't it wonderful to be part of God's creation? I'll spend the rest of my life giving glory to the Father and to the Son and to the Holy Spirit." It was obvious that he had never looked back. His pastor later told me that he was God's gift to the parish.

In the decades when Harold was giving new glory to God after his dramatic conversion of heart, he was expressing in his day-to-day living what many learned writers were saying about two topics, the Trinity and the Christian call to continual conversion. At first sight, the two would not seem to be related. They are, in fact, closely and essentially related. The daily call to conversion is a call to getting our energies of knowing and loving into an ever-clearer focus. Christian conversion is a redirecting of our minds and hearts into the flow of knowing and loving that takes place between the three divine persons.

From many directions we have been receiving invitations to this redirecting. Pope John Paul II gave us a large body of teaching in preparation for the third Christian millennium. He expressed a wish that the mystery of the three divine persons should be continually reflected in our lives. This is why he wished that the relationships between the divine persons should be the under-pinning of our understanding of his other writings. His first encyclical was on the Son who is the redeemer of humankind. Later he wrote on the Father who is rich in mercy. Later again he wrote on the Holy Spirit who is the Lord and giver of life. In im-mediate preparation for the new millennium, he wished that one year be dedicated to the Son, the next year to the Holy Spirit, the next to the Father. The millennium year would celebrate the whole mystery of the Trinity. As helps into the mystery of the Trinity, he drew attention to the importance of the experience of people like Elizabeth of the Trinity, the Carmelite sister whose life was lived in the aura of Father, Son and Spirit. At the same time, those who look into the Irish and Celtic traditions of spirit-uality have been encouraging us to re-read such prayers as the eighth century *Lúireach, Lorica,* Breastplate of St. Patrick, with its descriptions of the five energies, the five expressions of *neart* that come to us from our life in the Trinity, and ancient prayers like *An triúr is sine, an triúr is óige, an triúr is tréine,* the "three who are oldest, youngest, strongest."

A growing number of Christian writers are giving their at-tention to this mystery of the Trinity. They are telling us that the greatest message of the church's teaching on the Trinity is that the life that unites the three divine persons is also our life. They are reminding us that all Christians are called to be living icons of the Trinity. They show how the life of Father, Son and Spirit keeps overflowing into our lives. Our call to be icons of the Trinity, to let the divine persons' knowing and loving of each other flow into our knowing and loving, thus becomes for us the good news of the Trinity. It is our call to move in divine circles.

The Call to be Living Icons

Icons have had an interesting history. In the Jewish-Christian story there has been a tradition of a love of icons and a tradition of the breaking of icons. We have had one tradition telling us to be iconophiles and one telling us to be iconoclasts. In a sense, we are all called to be both. We are made as icons, images of God and, in this sense, we cannot but love and respect every person and every thing that carries the stamp of their maker. On the other hand, truly religious people have always recognized the limitations of images. The reason is that there has been a constant temptation to worship the image rather than the God of whom it is the image. This has not been just a theoretical possibility. It was one of the continuing realities in the history of a people who alternated between being faithful and unfaithful to the God who is always faithful. The decision of God which is expressed in the first page of the Bible and described by the priestly authors six centuries before Christ was to make humans in God's own image and likeness (Gen 1:26). With that start, humans were to share in God's kingship by exercising dominion over creation in God's loving and merciful way. Since humans were the high point of God's creation, carrying in them something of everything else in creation, they were invited to see to it that everything in creation would truly give glory to its maker. The second account of creation, which follows fast on the first, tells of the breakdown of the working out of what it is to be an icon and what it is to have dominion. It is a graphic story of icon-loving and icon-breaking.

Six centuries after the writing of the Genesis account of our call to be icons, Christians were told that Jesus Christ is the icon of the invisible God (Col 1:15). They learned that their vocation is to be icons of Christ (Col 3:10; 2 Cor 3:18). In our own day, people have a whole new realization of what it is to be an icon. This realization has come to us in both secular contexts and religious contexts. In the secular contexts, we hear the word used in the world of sport, of cinema, of theater, and even in the world of computers. It would appear that these new uses of the word have followed on the renewed interest in religious icons. This, in turn, is related to the new opening up to us of the religious and artistic treasures of Russia.

The Icon of the Three
Of all the Russian icons that have fascinated people in recent years, it is significant that pride of place must go to one of Andrew Rublev's that comes from the beginning of the fifteenth century A.D. It is particularly significant that, even now, this is variously called "the hospitality of Abraham," "the icon of the three angels" and "the mystery of the Trinity." It is beyond controversy that the original inspiration for this icon is the story in Genesis, chapter 18, about the visit to Abraham and Sarah by the

three unnamed guests. In the background of the table of hospitality at which the three are sitting are the oak tree, the mountain
and the house. The whole icon evokes for us the fact that as generations of covenant people heard the story of what happened
beside the oak of Mamre, near the house of Abraham and Sarah,
in the shadow of the ancient mountain of God, each generation
interpreted it in the light of the nuancing that came with each
new event of religious history.

As Christians came to ponder the story, they began to wonder whether there was some hint here of the three guests, the
three divine persons, who are both the hosts and the guests of
those who follow Jesus Christ. This wondering gained impetus
as the Christian centuries moved on. It reached a significant
stage when St. Augustine asked why it was that Abraham saw
three and adored one. Those who painted or, more correctly,
wrote new icons carried the wondering further. If you look at
Rublev's icon for the first time, you may well find yourself asking a number of questions: Are these three men? or three
women? or three angels? or the three divine persons? Is it all
about the visitors that came to Abraham and Sarah or is it about
our relationship with the Trinity and with each other? The
Christian can answer yes to each of these questions. That is part
of the genius of religious icons. They keep revealing layers of
meaning. More important, this is the genius of the mystery of
the Trinity: what is taking place between the three divine persons has implications for all people and indeed for the whole of
creation. It has special and urgent implications for us humans,
made as we are as images, icons of the Trinity. Wherever there
are human beings in relationships that are authentically human,
you have a reflection of what is going on eternally between
Father, Son and Spirit. The divine persons keep calling us into
the circle of their knowing and of their loving. It is not by chance
that the Rublev icon portrays the three at the table in the shape
of a perfectly drawn circle. The whole icon is an invitation to us
to keep moving in the right circles.

Circles of Friends
A circle has many things to say to us. It can, in contrast to the
straight line, be seen as a symbol of eternity; the line has a beginning point and an end point, but the circle has no beginning
point and no end point. It may be for this reason that it is such a

prominent symbol in many ancient cultures. The pre-Christian, pre-Celtic burial place in Newgrange, County Meath, presents us with a very thought-provoking image in the spiraling shapes of the three circles that open into one another. Whatever its deepest meaning, it is not unrelated to the protective circles that people made around themselves and to the religious "rounds" that were later to become a feature of the Celtic religious world and that, in turn, influenced the various descriptions of people "doing their rounds." The nimbus or halo that came to be associated with Christian sainthood was a reminder that the holy person had stepped from the world of passing time into the world without beginning or end.

The triple spiraling in Newgrange reminds Christians to live their lives in three circles that keep intersecting with and flowing into each other all the time. We live in the circle of our families, friends and neighbors. Each of us could name several of the people and events that link us intimately with the family into which we were born, and with the wider community. The second circle in which we live as Christians is the circle of disciples of Jesus Christ. It is not widely recognized that in the gospel according to St. Mark (3:34) Jesus and his disciples are described in circle language. The context is the occasion when Jesus was told that his mother and his brothers were outside, wishing to speak to him. In a way that certainly sounds peremptory, Jesus asked, "Who are my mother and my brothers?" Then, pointing to the circle of disciples around him, he said, "Here are my mother and my brothers. Whoever does the will of God is my brother and sister and mother." There is a sense in which we are here at the very heart of the gospel. The account of the incident should never be interpreted without referring to another gospel scene in which Jesus looks toward Mary and John and says, "Woman, here is your son...here is your mother" (John 19:26, 27). Between what Mark described and what John described, Mary had so walked the whole path of discipleship that she had found her unique place right in the center of the circle of disciples.

The third circle in which Christians move is the circle of the Trinity. That is the deepest meaning of the three at table in Rublev's icon. In the Genesis account, the three unnamed visitors are the ones who receive hospitality. In the icon they are the ones who are offering hospitality. The Father raises his creative, life-giving hand. The Son, in a cloak tinged with red, reaches his hand toward the nourishing contents of the redemptive cup. He is gently asking us can we drink of the whole range of cups, sweet and bitter, from which he himself drank (cf. Matt 20:22). The Holy Spirit, in garments that suggest the flow of living water, invites us into the inner riches of what the table-altar has to offer. There is a vacant place for the unnamed guest. Between Abraham's time and Rublev's time, the one teacher of Christians had said that "those who love me will keep my word and my Father will love them, and we will come to them and make our home with them" (John 14:23). The same teacher had said, "Listen! I am standing at the door, knocking; if you hear my voice and open the door, I will come in to you and eat with you, and you with me" (Rev 3:20). There is room at the table of the three divine persons for all of us and for all the circles that comprise our families and friends. There is room for every man, woman and child who has been made as an icon of the God who is three in one and one in three.

The three circles in which we live our lives as Christians keep intersecting with one another. This is why the spiraling circles of Newgrange have a special appeal for those who accept the revelation of the triune God. In the gospel according to St. John, some prospective disciples asked Jesus, "Rabbi, where are you staying?" and Jesus replied, "Come and see" and "they remained with him that day" (1:39). Christians can see themselves as called individually by name and invited to stay with the Lord all day every day. Full Christian living involves moving in the three interconnecting circles, dwelling in and being at home in all three. It also involves a readiness to give and receive hospitality at many tables. This is why a crucial question for the Christian is, "How am I at table?" There is no end to the possible answers to this question.

Speaking of Persons

The language of the New Testament about the relationships between Father, Son and Holy Spirit is a warm and intimate language. The Father speaks of his Son as "the beloved with whom I am well pleased" (Matt 3:17). The Son continually speaks about his Father in the language of love, intimate knowledge and trust. The relationship between Son and Father is most intimately expressed in the Gethsemane cry in which the Father is addressed as "Abba, my own dear father" (Mark 14:36). The

Holy Spirit is the one through whom the love of the Father has been poured into our hearts (Rom 5:45). This is the friend in need who comes from the Father at the request of the Son (John 14:16, 17). Being initiated into the life of the Father, Son and Spirit involves being plunged, baptized into their names, their persons (Matt 28:19).

Before the mystery of the three divine persons was eventually put into some formal words by Christians, a good deal of clarification of religious language had taken place. As a legacy of this clarification, we are fortunate today to be able to talk about three divine persons really distinct and equal in all things. As we reflect on this, we may be surprised to learn that the New Testament doesn't talk about three divine persons. The New Testament language about Father, Son and Spirit is very personal, but none of the three is called a person. That is the language of a later time. To safeguard the personal nature of Father, Son and Spirit, learned Christians, paradoxically, came to use very impersonal language. Drawing on the scholarly language available in their times, they described persons in terms of words like *substance, nature, relations*. One might say that the warmest and most personal of these words is *relations*. But even that very personal word came to be used in impersonal ways. It would be easy today to be critical of and impatient with this use of abstract language as a way of expressing the most personal of realities. But the clarity it engendered served the great purpose of providing a clear and systematic doctrine of the Trinity that has served the church in good stead. The debit side of the legacy is that many Christians have tended to look on the very words Blessed Trinity as a conundrum to be puzzled over rather than as the source and origin of all personal love, the loving source from which we come, in which we continue to be enveloped and to which we return.

The Personal Touch

Today the language of persons is getting a new prominence. We realize, in a variety of senses, that there is nothing like the personal touch. Many thinking people have been exploring what it is that constitutes a person. Arguably, it is in our relationships with other persons that we become persons; I am most a person when I link the three words *I-you-we*, and see them as inseparable. As we look at the three divine persons in this perspective we come to realize that before the church saw the need to speak in abstract, academic language about the three divine persons, the books of the New Testament spoke of Father, Son and Spirit in language that is intimacy itself. In that perspective, our every experience of knowing and loving is the overflowing into us of what is going on in the Trinity from all eternity; everything that is going on in the Trinity is there for our sharing. Here lies the essence of the graced life. The divine persons keep surprising us by offering us a share in their life. The immanent life of the Trinity is not a sealed-off world. The gracious God, the God of grace, is ever ready to pour the divine life into all our relationships. The "immanent" Trinity is the same Trinity that is ever active in God's "economy" of salvation.

An Emerging Language
The language we use to describe the relationships between the three divine persons is coming to be drawn more and more from the way we observe people communicating with each other in the variety of situations in which they find themselves. Allowing for the limitations of human language and the fact that all our language about God the creator is only by analogy with what happens in his creatures, we see the divine persons in terms of community. We are discovering again that what we always called the missions of the three divine persons are the story of one loving person inviting another loving person to go on an errand of love and mercy in the name of a cause that is dear to both of them. What older writers described in puzzling, abstract words we see as a union of love whereby each of the divine persons is so taken over by the love of the others that each keeps living and moving in the others.

St. Augustine was one of the first to see clearly that the Genesis story about the three unnamed guests had its fullest meaning in the three divine persons coming to dwell in the house of the Christian and inviting the Christian to dwell in their house. He described the very nature of the three divine persons in terms of knowing and loving. The Son, the Word, is the Father's knowledge of himself from all eternity. What God knows is so infinitely perfect that it is a distinct person. The Father and the Son love each other in such an infinitely perfect way that their love is a distinct divine person, the Holy Spirit. Augustine kept drawing on the workings of the human mind and heart in a way that provided him with analogies for probing the mind and heart of God. His probings have been a help to the church ever since. Few Christian teachers have written so powerfully about human knowing and loving as did Augustine. It was he who summed up the aim of all our knowing and loving in his cry to the Lord, "Would that I might know you; would that I might know myself." It was he too who said to the Lord, "late have I loved you" and who dared to say, "love, and do what you wish!" In his writings, he kept asking what it is to know and what it is to love. He knew, partly through his own checkered experience of knowing and loving, that all human knowing is authentic to the extent that it leads to authentic loving. For him, every glimpse of true knowing and true loving is a new glimpse of the mystery of God. He gave us many new insights into the reasons why the Son of God is called the Word, the *Logos* of God, and why the Spirit is seen as the love uniting Father and Son.

The Search Goes On

As we revisit today the mystery of the three-in-one and one-in-three, we are helped enormously by the searchings and probings of people like St. Augustine. We are also aware of the limitations of these searchings and probings. We are reminded that God made humans in God's own image and likeness. We also recognize the danger that we could, in turn, make God into our own image and likeness. We realize that God is beyond words, beyond images. That is why Christian thinking has to learn when images help and when images fail. The great advances in our investigations into the workings of the human mind and heart since the time of Augustine provide us with new gateways into the mystery of the inner life of Father, Son and Spirit in whose image we were all made. For this we thank God. There is need to keep deepening and purifying the images that help us know and love God. To think of the divine persons as occupying a kind of cozy corner in heaven and keeping a kindly eye on those made on earth in their likeness would be a caricature of the inner life of God and it would be of no benefit to us, but this should not keep us from seeking new glimpses into the mystery of mysteries. As the divine persons keep inviting us to go on probing all the words that express authentic human knowing and authentic human loving, the real test of our probing is the extent to which we are helped to know and love ourselves, to know and love each other, to know and love Father, Son and Spirit, in the world which they continue to love. We are helped to become real persons and to become really personal. We are helped by people like St. Thérèse of Lisieux, the new doctor of the church, who saw the loving fathering and mothering she had experienced in her own family as so many manifestations of the mystery of the Trinity. We are helped by new saints like Edith Stein whose whole life got a new focusing and energizing as she read about the workings of the Trinity in the life of St. Teresa of Avila.

To be true icons of the Trinity and to live and love in their circle calls daily for many kinds of conversion. It calls for a change in the ways we think, a change in the ways we love, a change in the ways we remember, a change in the ways we feel, a change in the ways we behave, a change in the ways we approach the mystery of God. This is the way to the kind of happiness that Harold found by being broken and remade. Into this happiness, Father, Son and Spirit are continually calling us. In this happiness, we keep giving glory to the Father, the Son and the Holy Spirit, by knowing in the way they know, loving in the way they love, and doing in the way they do.

CHAPTER 2

The Trinity Tell Us Who They Are

Which is the most basic of all our Christian prayers? The obvious answer is the Lord's Prayer, which Jesus himself taught us. A case could also be made for the way we call on the Father, Son and Holy Spirit as we make the sign of the cross with our right hand, over our foreheads which protect our thoughts, over our lips which speak these thoughts, and over our breasts which protect our hearts. The thought of this was very strong in my mind as I directed a Holy Week retreat for seminarians in Rome in the year of the Holy Spirit that led up to the new millennium. It was also the year of Luke, the evangelist of the Holy Spirit. I had just finished reading a new scholarly book on the Trinity and the paschal mystery. The thesis of the book is that it is in the dying and rising of Jesus, and in the ascension and pentecost that are of a piece with them, that the Father, Son and Holy Spirit tell us who they really are. The message became more and more alive as the week went on.

In the course of the week, we received copies of the Pope's Holy Thursday letter to priests. The topic was the Holy Spirit in the lives of priests. The letter was written in the form of a verse-by-verse meditation on the *Veni Creator Spiritus* hymn. Our retreat began with the Palm Sunday welcome of Jesus as king into Jerusalem, the city of the king and of the temple. It was clearly his attitude to both kingship and the temple that was to cost him his life on Good Friday. As the week progressed, I was keenly aware of the use of all four Servant Songs, on Monday, Tuesday, Wednesday, and Friday, to interpret who he was and what he was doing. With the introduction of the betrayal theme on Tuesday and Wednesday, I looked out more and more for the variety of ways in which Jesus lovingly handed himself over for us and was handed over in betrayal. The same gospel word is used for these two actions of handing over. My preparing for the retreat conferences and meditations made me focus on all the readings in the Lucan cycle, but I also found myself moving into the other cycles. The more I entered into the unfathomable riches of the week, the more I came to realize that it is in the paschal mystery above all that we discover why we call God Father, why, on God's instructions, Mary's child was to be called Jesus, why the Holy Spirit is the life-breath of both Father and Son, why all three divine persons bared the secrets of their hearts most of all at the time when they were never so united but when they were to all appearances on the verge of falling apart.

Abba, Father

As I searched for the image of God the Father that throws most light on Holy Week, I found myself going outside the Lucan year and re-reading the pages of Mark. Some years ago, the German lover of the scriptures, Joachim Jeremias, wrote that if all the Christian memory were to be obliterated, and all the Christian records were lost, we could reconstruct the essential message of Jesus if we were assured that the most intimate word by which he addressed God had been rediscovered. That word is *Abba*, which seems to be best translated "my own dear Father." It is Mark, and he alone of the four evangelists, who tells us of the Abba cry of Jesus (Mark 14:36). It was his cry when he was doing four things that are very difficult for every human being to do: he was facing a cruel and undeserved death; he was acutely aware of the suffering this would entail; he was praying in a state of turmoil; he was searching to do the Father's will as it manifested itself through events. In all four, he was drinking from the bitter cup from which he had invited his disciples to drink.

Years after the Jeremias book was written, I heard Fr. Jerome Murphy O'Connor, OP say that no English translation adequately captures the shattered state of Jesus as described by Mark. Fr. Jerome spoke of a man who was his classmate many years ago and who was outstanding at Greek. Later he became a very successful psychiatrist. When they happened to meet a few years earlier, Fr. Jerome asked him if he would read the Greek text of Mark's account of the agony, word by word, and describe what state he thought Jesus was in. He did as he was asked and said, "It is a powerful description of a man in my clinic on the verge of a nervous breakdown." I don't think either Fr. Jerome or the psychiatrist was saying that Jesus had a nervous breakdown.

But they were both clear that he at least showed the symptoms. In this falling apart, did the Abba, Father, say yes to the plaintive request of Jesus? On the face of it, the answer is no. Yet the Letter to the Hebrews tells us that "he was heard because of his reverent submission" (6:8). Is there any better entry than this into the mystery of the Father of love? This is the same Father who sends the Spirit of his Son into the hearts of all his children, enabling them to cry "Abba, Father" (Gal 4:6) and to be made free. It is the same Abba, Father who gives us the Spirit of adoption, assuring us that we are beneficiaries of the last will and testament of Jesus, making us "heirs of God and joint heirs with Christ" (Rom 8:17). In this great saving process, we have the whole Trinity fully active in a way of loving and saving that only they could have designed and only they could have carried out.

He Descended into Hell

None of the scriptural readings in all the liturgy of Holy Week states that Jesus descended into hell. And still that teaching has always been a distinctive part of the Apostles' Creed. On Holy Saturday in the year of Luke and of the Holy Spirit, I was more aware than ever before that we are dealing here with a very powerful symbol. I was more touched than ever by the second lesson in the office of readings as it described the saving work of Jesus continuing after he had breathed his last. He brought the good news to all who were in the depths of Sheol, of Hades, of "hell." This was fully in character for the Son who out of his own depths had cried "Abba, Father." I have always loved the ways in which the Anglo-Saxon imagination portrayed the harrowing of hell between Jesus' death and resurrection. My Celtic ancestors gave their own coloring to what they called the *Argain Ifrinn*. For both imaginations, the sojourn of Jesus in Sheol was a very active sojourn.

Hans Urs von Balthasar, in line with Karl Rahner, has enriched theology by giving his own very different approach to the descent into hell. It is so different that it could be seen as contradicting the Holy Saturday homily, the Anglo-Saxon harrowing and the Celtic *Argain*. In these three, Jesus is very active in the world of the dead. In the Balthasar-Rahner emphasis, Jesus descends into the lowest depths of all human experience and human God-forsakenness, wherever it would carry him. With all their differences, the two approaches bring home to us the implications of the total self-emptying of Jesus and the fact that all humankind and indeed the whole of creation have benefited from this emptying. The traditional representations of the harrowing depict a very active Jesus, bringing good news into all the world of death. In the Balthasar approach, Jesus has become so drained and emptied that he ceases to be active; indeed, his descent is the last word in passivity. The self-emptying of Jesus had become so total that, in the words of St. Francis of Assisi, his obedience was the obedience of a corpse. In both the harrowing approach and in the Balthasar approach, the descent of Jesus is good news for all. In both, there is nothing and nobody, none of our Auschwitzs, none of our Gulags, that has not benefited from the obedience of Jesus unto death, the obedience that was his total self-surrender. In both, the Abba Father has indeed heard the cry of Jesus who has become, for all who obey him, the cause of eternal salvation (Heb 5:9). Nothing in heaven, on earth or under the earth will be the same again. The Father has sent his Son into hell; the Spirit accompanies him, uniting Father and Son in the separation of separations. This is heady language. Here, indeed, are God's glory and beauty at their best. Here is the setting for the new "seeing" of Jesus to which Balthasar keeps calling us.

The Spirit: From Heaven to Hell, and Back
In the year of St. Luke, we had been hearing a lot about the Holy Spirit. According to Luke, the Spirit came on Mary at the conception of Jesus; the Spirit appeared at the baptism of Jesus; the Spirit led Jesus into the desert; the Spirit was on Jesus as he pronounced his great mission statement in the synagogue; the Spirit made Jesus rejoice in his Father and thank him; the Spirit enabled Jesus to drive out demons. As we entered into the liturgy of Holy Week, in the year of Luke, I couldn't help asking what ever had happened to the Holy Spirit. The voice of the Spirit seemed to have been strangely muted. As I searched the pages of Luke's gospel, I became aware of the apparent absence of the Holy Spirit. As I read the Pope's Holy Thursday letter, and followed his meditation and reflection on the verses of the *Veni Creator*, I noticed that he gave all of Luke's significant references to the Holy Spirit, but again there were no Holy Spirit texts for the Holy Week events. But, no, there were. There were two great texts, though neither of them was from Luke. The Pope quoted the text from Hebrews which says that, in his sacrifice, Christ offered himself "through the eternal Spirit" (9:14). He also picked

out the text from Romans which says that if the Spirit of him "who raised Jesus from the dead" dwells in us, he "who raised Christ from the dead" will give life to our mortal bodies also (8:11). He also drew our attention to the introduction to the same letter in which Paul presents Jesus Christ Our Lord as being "declared to be Son of God with power according to the Spirit of holiness by resurrection from the dead" (1:4). It dawned on me that it is these powerful texts from Romans that best interpret Luke's silence about the work of the Holy Spirit during the suffering and dying of Jesus. They also cast light on the only further reference to the Holy Spirit before the end of Luke's gospel. This is the rather shy wording of the assurance of Jesus that he was sending on his apostles "what my Father promised" (24:49). At the time of the dying of Jesus and his descent, the Spirit is active as the basic, unnoticed breath of life, as the air that makes breathing possible, rather than as the wind and the fire.

There is no shyness about the action of the Holy Spirit when we come to the pages of Luke's Acts of the Apostles. In the very first chapter, Jesus is recorded as telling his apostles not to leave Jerusalem because it is there they would be "baptized with the Holy Spirit" (1:5). In this they would "receive power" (v. 8). It is in the very act of promising this baptism and this power that Jesus was "lifted up" (v. 9). A process had been set in motion which would be completed in the explosion of the activity of the Holy Spirit at Pentecost when they were "filled with the Holy Spirit" (2:4). Out of that filling came the "boldness" that enabled Peter to preach so often and so effectively, in the name of Jesus, as is so beautifully illustrated in the first reading of the morning Mass on Easter Sunday in the year of Luke.

The Spirit revealed in the suffering, dying, rising, ascending and Spirit-sending of Jesus, as portrayed by Luke, is the Spirit who reveals the Abba Father's most characteristic way of hearing the "loud cry and tears" (Heb 5:7) of those who beg to be delivered from death. This is the Spirit of Jesus the Suffering Servant who has descended into every human hell. I am moved by Balthasar's teaching that the Spirit accompanied Jesus in all the stages and aspects of his abandonment and self-emptying, as the one bond that united Father and Son in the time of their apparent estrangement, separation and falling apart. This is the same Spirit whom, in a different perspective, the fourth gospel describes as being "given up" (19:30) as Jesus died. This is the Spirit who didn't abandon Jesus, the light of the world, in his darkest hour. It was in this very hour that the Spirit of God was most active, most present.

The Trinity's Way of Saving

So, is it any wonder that Balthasar and others teach that it is in the paschal mystery that the divine persons tell us who they really are? In all their apparent separations, the three divine persons are totally together, totally at one. This becomes clear especially in the rising of Jesus from the dead and in the sending of the Holy Spirit. To human eyes, the whole process is a strange way of being and staying together, a strange way of being and staying one. Is it any wonder that God has to keep reminding us that "my thoughts are not your thoughts, nor are your ways my ways" (Isa 55:8)? The way of the Father, Son and Spirit is to create out of nothing, to reveal greatness in littleness. This is the way in which they reveal the beauty and the profundity behind big words like their perichoresis, their circumincessions, and the other words that have been used to express the loving movement of union between them. It is in this loving union of both profundity and simplicity that people like St. Thérèse lived their lives.

As I was penning these reflections on Easter Sunday morning, I got a message from Dublin about the death of one of Thérèse's most ardent devotees. The message read "Fr. Pat died early this morning." It was both sad news and good news. What a beautiful time, I thought, for Pat to enter into this stage of the paschal mystery and for his charming lilt to become part of the great alleluia chorus! It was not the first time in the last twenty-four hours that I had heard the words "very early in the morning." Pat was once my classmate. We first met when we eyed each other on the train to Dublin. We felt we had something in common. "Are you, by any chance, going to the Vincentian novitiate?" he asked me. "Yes," I said. "And what age are you?" "Seventeen," I replied. "I envy you," he said, "giving your young life to God. I've wasted mine. I'm twenty-five." I was soon to learn that he would more than make up for the wastage. Living with somebody in close quarters sometimes brings its disillusionments. Over fifty years on, I say, with even more conviction, "Pat was a man of God." I know no Vincentian, no Daughter of Charity, no lay person who would not say the same. His priestly life gave us many glimpses of the Trinity of the paschal mystery. He brought the compassion and forgiveness of the Abba, Father into many broken lives. In his bicycle rounds to parishioners, he brought with him the name and love of Jesus Christ and, in doing so, he was never known to break a bruised reed or to extinguish the smoking flax. His ministry of the Spirit was to be a listening and sympathetic ear, morning by morning, day by day, as he accompanied people to the various valleys of death into which they had to descend. He never strove for or received any high office in the church he loved so much. He would not recognize himself in any word I have been saying. One of the great graces of my life was to have been influenced by such a great sacrament of the saving style of Father, Son and Spirit.

God-words

There are a number of words expressing basic human activities that have found new life in recent writing on the Trinity. They came alive for me in a very special way during the Holy Week retreat. From all of them I choose three pairs of words:

- descending and ascending
- emptying and filling
- giving and being given away.

I came to see these six words as the basic language of Holy Week and of the rest of the church's year to which the paschal triduum is the key. The language of giving, giving away and being given away had a special poignancy as the Holy Week unfolded. The Father gave his only Son as the great sign of his own eternal self-giving. Doing so involved the risk and the reality of the Son being "given over" (Matt 26:15) in betrayal. The life of Jesus was a life of many givings. As a result, the Spirit who raised him from the dead is ever-active in the giving of gifts to Christ's body which is the church. We are privileged to be sharers in all of this trinitarian giving and to be called to serve a God who is more than happy to receive.

Good News for All Creation

Today we are learning that all the elements in the periodic table, the elements that make up the universe, are interwoven with the hundred and fifty trillion cells that comprise the human body and that we are for the most part unaware of their existence until they present problems. We are more and more discovering our interconnectedness and our interdependence with all other beings, animate and inanimate. All of creation, inside us and outside us, has been touched by the paschal mystery. Through that distinctive phenomenon which is human consciousness, we are expected to make sense of it all. This involves us in the recognizing of many absurdities, many apparent contradictions. The world of our bodies contains many unexplored continents. We cannot even name some of these continents, just as we cannot count or name those of the known world; we used to say there were five but now there is talk of another one or two. There are parts of each of our lives into which the gospel hasn't been allowed to enter yet, just as there are areas of every Christian country, geographical or psychological, that are still uninfluenced by the gospel. But the gospel news remains good. The Savior whose journey we followed in Holy Week is still longing to enter into all our depths, all our hells, all our dyings, all our experiences of exile. In all of them, the Holy Spirit is our paraclete, our comforter, our advocate, our defender in all the "trials" and "law-cases" of life. In supporting Jesus in the stadium of his agony, and being ever helpful in the groanings of the world, of the church and of every believer (cf. Rom 8:26) the Holy Spirit turns contradictions and apparent contradictions into power points. As the "other" paraclete, the Holy Spirit reminds us that the Father too is our paraclete, as is the Son who asked the Father to send the Spirit (John 14:16).

Love the Love that Loves You
The divine persons who are continually descending and ascending, emptying and filling, giving and being given away, can be best described only in the language of love. This, of course, is nothing new, as the author of 1 John clearly taught (1 John 4:16). Since the time of the writing of that letter, we have drawn on many sources, many philosophies, many thought systems, to talk about God. All have had their value, but theology today is seeing more and more clearly that the best category to point toward God is that of Being-in-Love. Love, of course, doesn't exclude an emphasis on knowledge, but God's distinctive way of knowing is loving. This is why Balthasar argues, convincingly, that love alone is credible, that both "processions" within God are processions of love. This teaching opens up new vistas. It helps us to see that the best way of describing Jesus' vision of the kingdom of God is in terms of God's unconditional love. It illumines the possibilities in the call of the recent popes for the shaping of a new civilization of love. It makes full sense of St. Thérèse's eventual discovery that her full vocation was to be

love in the heart of the church. It gives new hope to every community founded to be "sisters" or "brothers" of charity. As the life of Mother Teresa of Calcutta showed us beautifully, it reinstates the spiritual and corporal works of mercy as the one topic that will be on for our final examination on judgment day. It exposes the glaring inconsistencies that often exist between our words and our practice when it comes to charity. It discloses the deepest meaning of the words of Jesus when he said that he came to cast fire on the earth (Luke 12:49); the fire was the fire of judgment but his own loving laying down his life for his friends (John 15:13) showed that costly love is the true criterion of judgment. It keeps transforming judgement into love. The irresistible dynamics of divine and human love are a key to testing the validity of the contents of Balthasar's *Dare We Hope that All Will Be Saved?* Far from being an easy book that takes us off the hook, it is an urgent call to all of us to be agents of the love that is costly and that burns, in an age when love-words are in danger of being debased.

A fourteenth century Flemish mystic, Jan van Ruysbrueck, gave us a wonderful program for Christian living: *Love the love that loves you.* He had no illusions about the cost of love. He saw our growth in love as the climbing of a ladder with seven rungs, some of them difficult. He knew that if you love somebody you will think and feel so highly about them that you are ready to promote their concerns, their well-being and their happiness, whatever the cost to yourself. This is indeed the eternal meaning of Holy Week.

Co-creators

Each of us is made in the image and likeness of Father, Son and Spirit. To be fellow-workers, co-creators with each of them is our great vocation in the making of a whole new world. It is a vocation of love resourced by the Father who, out of love, gave his only Son, by the Son who, out of love, laid down his life for his friends (John 15:13), by the Holy Spirit through whom that same love is continually being poured into our hearts (Rom 5:5). In the church's liturgical year, the Trinity's way of loving and saving is highlighted and celebrated in the season of the paschal mystery of the dying, rising and Spirit-sending. In the rest of the liturgical year, we keep harrowing the field in which the word of God is sown by the Sower who harrowed all the hells of our existence until the final filling of the granaries of the triune God.

CHAPTER 3

Coming to the Father

Over forty summers ago, I did some work in a parish in England while on vacation. Early on, the parish priest asked me if I would like to celebrate Mass with the Catholic boys at a center for pre-Borstal offenders. I accepted the invitation as an exciting challenge. I looked up the two readings and found that the gospel comprised the Our Father and the words that lead up to it and follow it. I then proceeded to read everything I could lay my hands on about the prayer that our Savior gave us. Sunday came and at the end of the Mass I felt I had delivered my words of wisdom with considerable success. As I was about to leave, I got word that one of the boys wished to speak to me. I wondered whether he wanted to congratulate me on my sermon or to seek my advice. I found that the atmosphere of the center was quite informal and that the boy was waiting for me in a reception room. As I entered, he raised his fist. It was clear that this was not a time for pleasant introductions. "Do you dare to tell me," he said, with anger flashing from his eyes, "that God is like my dad? I hate my dad; as long as I was at home he came in drunk every night; he made life hell for my mum; he did the most wicked things to me and my brothers and sisters; if your God is like that, you can keep him." Before I could catch my breath and stammer a reply, he had slammed the door and left.

As I look back on the experience now, I can say that I was fully right in believing in and preaching the fatherhood of God, but I was wrong, very wrong, in the manner in which I preached it. My words had, in fact, been a display of insensitivity. It was, I hope, a good learning experience. In my defense, let it be said that it was in the days before the *General Instruction on the Roman Missal* taught us that every celebration of the Mass is, of its very nature, to take into account the circumstances of the individual assembly. In recent decades, we have received many helps to develop the kind of sensitivity that makes this possible. We have been told that some of our images of God must either go or be refined, purified and nuanced. We have been alerted to the limitations of what some like to call authoritarian and patriarchal models of God. In evaluating and reassessing the models, we have been encouraged to explore the ones that help us approach God in the language and imagery of friendship and intimacy. We have been reminded of the difference between the power exercised by the rulers of the Gentiles and the power that pervades the kingdom of God as preached by Jesus. As we have been hearing of the traps in the language of power and patriarchy, we have, paradoxically, recognized more clearly our need of authentic father figures.

My encounter with the boy in the reception room coincided with the beginning of the short pontificate of the man we now call Blessed John XXIII. Was there a man, woman or child who, directly or indirectly, was not somehow enriched by rays from the living fatherhood of God during those years? It was a happy coincidence that, at about the same time, Joachim Jeremias was writing and lecturing about the "Abba" word of Jesus. In the meantime, those who have continued the same search have explored the word further. They have not interpreted it in exactly the same way, but all are agreed that it is a family word, a relational word, a word of intimacy, a word that evokes confidence and trust.

An Ongoing Journey

The year 1999 was the year Pope John Paul II designated as "the year of the Father." One hopes that it was a year of true return to the Father. Whatever way we chose to celebrate it, one hopes that we didn't simply take the attitude that "1997 was the year of Jesus Christ; 1998 was the year of the Holy Spirit; it's the Father's turn this time." Each of the years was, in fact, the year of the three divine persons. The Jesus of 1997 keeps directing all our living and all our dying toward doing the will of the Father. This is a program not for a few years but for all life's journey.

In recent years, we have received many reminders of the fatherhood of God. One is the eleventh-century miniature that sets the tone for the section on prayer in the *Catechism of the Catholic Church*. In it, Jesus is praying in a desert place. His eyes and his whole body are focused on the Father. A group of disciples is looking on and Peter is pointing to Jesus in a way that

says, "Watch how he does it." This is the Jesus who is with us always, from millennium to millennium, the same forever. Every
time we look toward him we look toward the Father (cf. John
14:9). He is the sacrament of the Father's loving-kindness. By
word and by deed, he has shown us the wonderful world we
have when the Father's will is done. This is why he preached the
kingdom of his Father and was put to death because of the way
he entered as king into "the great king's city" (cf. Ps 48:1). The
Spirit whom we celebrated in 1998 is the life-breath of both
Father and Son, enabling us to be part of the chorus of those
who, through, with and in the beloved Son, keep giving glory to
the Father. This is the Spirit whom we keep inviting to fill our
hearts and change us into a new creation. This is the friendly
Spirit, the Spirit who, as the special Paraclete, is on our side and
at our side in all life's testings and trials.

It is only from the table and circle of Father, Son and Spirit
that we can bring healing to what has been described as our
fatherless society. There are indications that the Oedipus myth
is alive in new forms. The pain of those brought up in orphan-
ages is being expressed in ways too many and too prominent to
need listing. Those brought up by adoptive parents have been
crying out to discover their biological parents. The boy to whom
I preached so insensitively was articulating what many felt then
and many are not afraid to put into words now. All the time, the
number of those tracing their family trees is growing. This is an
expression of genuine family pride; it can sometimes be an expression of insecurity within. There is much in all of this that
might need lancing every time we pray to God, our Father.

Three Helps
In searching for ways of discovering anew the fatherhood of
God, I have recently been helped by three writings. One is a
book on the parable of the prodigal son. The second is a short
work that highlights one aspect of the parable. The third is a pastoral letter that provides variations on the same theme.

The late Fr. Henri Nouwen's book, *The Return of the Prodigal
Son*, was first published in 1992. For many reasons it has become
one of the most popular, if not the most popular, of his many
books. The reasons include the fact that it is about his own
unfinished business and his hopes for the future. It was as he
prepared to go to again St. Petersburg for the making of a film

about the contents of the book that he himself died after a very
short illness. More poignantly, the reasons include the fact that
the whole book, which is an extended meditation on the parable
of the prodigal son, reflects much of Nouwen's own fragile and
restless story. There is the added factor that he presents
Rembrandt's picture as the artist's self-portrait. I must confess
that, until I read the book, the picture didn't help me much to
capture the message of the parable. I much preferred the movement of the loving embrace of father and son in Murillo's paint-
ing on the same topic. But, in his beautiful telling of Rembrandt's
sad history, and his explaining that the feeble, half-blind but loving old man is the same Rembrandt whom earlier self-portraits
depicted as proud and sensual, Nouwen helped me to discover
a whole new world. The story of Nouwen's association with the
picture has already become well known, from his seeing the
poster in France in 1983 to his visit to St. Petersburg and to the
ways the picture helped him to relate to mentally handicapped
people in the L'Arche community in Toronto.

One can only surmise what might have come about if Henri
Nouwen had lived for the making of the film. Even as things
stand, he was able to say that in the story of the return of the
prodigal son he saw all the gospel, all his own life, all the lives of
people he had known. The parable, he says, had become a window
through which he could enter the kingdom of God. In pursuing
the implications of the parable, Rembrandt's picture helped him
powerfully. He found new meaning in words like leaving, jour-
neying, returning, celebrating. In his own experience of each of
these four, he had learned what it was to identify with the elder
son as well as with the younger son. In identifying with both, he
discovered who the prodigal father is. Out of this grew his
excitement in discovering his own call to actually become that
father. Some of his readers have been surprised to find him describing Jesus himself as the prodigal son of the prodigal father,
and they have wondered whether there is here a certain straining
of imagery and language. A reason may be that, in our repeated
reading and hearing of the parable, we have unconsciously nar-
rowed our understanding of what it is to be prodigal. There is a
sense in which, in the incarnation, the Word of God did not
leave the Father's side. There is a sense in which he did. He did
empty himself of all his glory and he went into a far country. In
his return to the Father, he brought the whole of sinful humankind

back to the Father. He was the younger brother who, though sin-less, was made to be sin (cf. 2 Cor 5:21). He was the older brother who never ceased to be with the Father and who, unlike his counterpart in the parable, is more than willing to take part in the homecoming celebrations of any prodigal son or daughter who has strayed from the Father.

As Henri Nouwen's body was being laid into the earth in Toronto, his ninety-one year old father, to whom the book is dedicated and who himself died shortly afterwards, said mis-chievously, "I think Henri will stay put this time." The subtitle of the book is, significantly, *A Story of Homecoming*. The parable about God's prodigality is, on many levels, an ongoing invit-ation to homecoming, an invitation to love and be loved, an in-vitation to reconcile and be reconciled, in an atmosphere of home. It is an invitation to each of us as God calls us back by name. It is a loving invitation to the whole people of God to come home from their many self-imposed exiles.

A Pair of Hands

A recent book by a scripture teacher, Fr. Mauro Orsatti, has a beautiful title and a beautiful cover picture. The title is *A Father with the Heart of a Mother*. The cover picture is a detail from the same Rembrandt picture that inspired Henri Nouwen. It focuses on the hands of the father resting lovingly on the returned son. The author draws our attention to a very significant detail on which Henri Nouwen had also written. The right hand is the hand of a woman; the left hand is the hand of a man. The inside cover of the book, surprisingly, describes this as an anatomical error. I prefer to see it as one key to the message of the whole pic-ture. Those who have been exploring the treasures of the Bible's covenant language in recent times have been drawing our atten-tion to the fact that our mercy words are attempts to capture the compassion, the tenderness, the mother-love that were charac-teristic of the God of Israel. This new awareness provides the underpinning for our growing realization that God is beyond gender, a realization that has many implications for the words and the images we use.

The new interest in the father-love and mother-love of God invites us to read or recall some of the literature on the mother-love shown by the Father and by Jesus Christ, as described not merely in the Bible but in the works of some of the most orthodox of theologians and spiritual writers. One thinks of Anselm the theologian who addressed Jesus Christ as mother, of Julian of Norwich the mystic who spoke of the same Jesus as mother and sister, and of a pastoral man as theologically circumspect as Vincent de Paul who prayed that the priests and laymen of the Congregation of the Mission would "have a deep love for Jesus Christ who is our father, our mother and our all." Writers like these were talking directly out of their own experience of the mother-love of God and of God's beloved Son. It is in this context that we can best look at many gender issues that keep arising in the human family, in the church, in ministry.

A Pastoral

Many of the topics dealt with by Nouwen and Orsatti were put into good focus by Cardinal Carlo Martini in his pastoral letter for the diocese of Milan leading up to the new millennium. The pastoral was entitled *The Return to the Father of All*. Some commentators drew attention to one aspect of the letter, the fact that God is described in mother-language as well as in father-language. In this regard, the Cardinal was not, in fact, saying more than what has been said in much serious Catholic writing in recent years. His pastoral letter drew generously on teachings of Pope Paul VI and Pope John Paul II. Interestingly, he didn't quote what was perhaps the most explicit papal statement about the mother-attributes of God, at least in our days. Before the Angelus on September 10, 1978, Pope John Paul I talked to the gathered faithful about God and told them, "He is our father; even more he is our mother." In very recent times, Pope John Paul II has been equally explicit on this teaching.

Early in his pastoral letter, Cardinal Martini said that some may wonder why we speak of God as our father rather than as our mother. He then stated clearly that God is both mother and father. More than once in the letter, he spoke of God as father-mother. For didactic purposes, he did not elaborate further on the implications of this way of speaking. He related his teaching about our father-mother with ways in which he saw today's society as fatherless and as being shot through with the values of relativism, post-modernity and secularism.

It is in this setting that the Cardinal presented his description of life as a continual invitation to listen to the Father, to meet the Father, to be on continual pilgrimage to the Father. Since death is the last stage in that pilgrimage, he had moving words to say about how to face death in a death-denying culture. He invited us to keep probing what he calls the parable of the merciful father. His whole letter was an invitation to continual conversion toward God who is father and mother of all. In the heart of this loving and forgiving God, there is a special place for the poor. There is more than ample space in this great heart for both believer and unbeliever, for saint and sinner.

Our Place in the Our Father

Jesus told us to call nobody on earth our father, since we have only one father and he is in heaven (Matt 23:9). He told us that anyone who does the will of this heavenly Father is his brother and sister and mother (Mark 3:35). Though he told us that no one can come to the Father except through him (John 14:6), he made it clear, in his parables and ministry, that we are surrounded by people who are mirrors of the Father's loving-kindness and fidelity. The letter to the Ephesians invites us to recognize the one source of this mirroring. The source is the Father of our Lord Jesus Christ from whom all family, all fatherhood in heaven and on earth is named (cf. 3:15).

Every prayer to the Father is an opportunity to do some of this naming. It is a reminder that every man, woman and child is made in the image and likeness of God and called to be remade in Christ who is the image of the invisible God (Col 1:15). It helps us to see that, while allowing for the Lord's injunction, we can continue to dare to call people by the name of father. It reminds us of the many brothers and sisters and mothers of Jesus. Each of us is invited daily to compose our own version of the Our Father and to insert our own story into its petitions.

I sometimes wonder what became of my young visitor in the pre-Borstal reception room. In his anger that Sunday morning, he disclosed a little of his dream of what a father should be. I hope he is now the father of children who delight in their father's love and in saying the Our Father, and who are teaching or will teach the same to their children. In the spirit of Jesus Christ who was born of the Father before time began, may he and all of us continue to be born again of the Father.

CHAPTER 4

Follow You More Nearly

There was a time, and it was not so very long ago, when every religious library had a collection of lives of Jesus Christ. Candidates for priestly ordination or for religious profession were expected to be familiar with the contents of one or more of them. In recent years, innumerable new books have been written about the person and ministry of Jesus, but it is generally accepted now that to write a life of Jesus is an impossible task. While the old lives still have their value insofar as they provide many glimpses of our Savior and many insights into his message and ministry, most people today prefer to go direct to the gospels themselves and to the great variety of commentaries that throw light on their pages. In doing so, we are introduced to a whole series of portraits that highlight various aspects of the man who "went about doing good" (Acts 19:38).

We are introduced to a series of silhouettes that throw beams of light on the outline of his figure as he went about. Each portrait and each silhouette helps us, in the lovely words of St. Richard of Chichester, to know him more clearly, to love him more dearly, to follow him more nearly. The various portraits and silhouettes that are emerging in recent writing all ensure that the clearer knowing, dearer loving and nearer following will not be a kind of private discipleship; they all point to a Jesus who was for others because he was for his Father and who calls us to follow all his steps. Each is a new help to find the hidden treasure with a new joy and, having sought for good pearls, to keep finding again the one really precious pearl (Matt 13:44, 45). All of us have, in some way, already found the treasure and the pearl, but life turns out to be a continual process of finding, losing and finding again. In this finding, losing and re-finding, there is a daily newness, and sometimes a daily anguish, in answering the question "Who do you say that I am?" (Matt 16:15).

Image Enriches Image

Each gospel image of Jesus helps us to know him, to love him, to follow him. The various images enrich each other. Each of us needs some thread to stitch the images together and unify them. In the meantime, we need to pray that we'll love not just the image but the one of whom it is the image. The various images help us to follow Jesus in his whole journey, not just the sections of it that attract us. In helping us to follow Jesus on his whole journey, some writers present him in the garb of his Jewish origins and background. Others like to point out the influences from Greece and Rome that colored his teaching and lifestyle in his native Galilee. There is a variety of ways of presenting him as God's Wisdom, God's *Sophia*, and naming the influences that shaped his various wisdom utterances and the enigmatic questions by which he got people thinking and wondering. There are writers who like to stress the social and even revolutionary aspects of his message. There are those who would play down or even deny these and put the emphasis plainly and squarely on the spiritual and interior aspects. There are those who find various liberation categories as the best ones in which to present him. There are those who make much of the apocalyptic influences in his teaching. There are those who don't. All of this can be confusing and bewildering for those of us who were formed in the perspectives of Blessed Columba Marmion's *Christ in His Mysteries*. But patience will be rewarded if we keep searching for one ray of light, one new vision of the Lord, in each of the portraits, each of the silhouettes, each of the new perspectives.

It is becoming more and more clear that, while there is only one Lord and one faith, there is a sense in which each of the gospels presents a different Jesus. Thus, Mark sets out to highlight the fact that Jesus is the messiah, a messiah who calls his disciples to follow him by carrying the cross. Matthew presents Jesus as the new teacher, the new lawgiver for a new people, fulfilling all that was foreshadowed by the teachers and lawgivers under the old covenant. For Luke, Jesus is the prophet of God's compassion, bringing good news to the poor and liberty to captives. For John, Jesus is God's Word made flesh, inviting us to be fully alive. Out of the rich proliferation of portraits and silhouettes from all four gospels and from the riches of the rest of the New Testament, writers today are shaping new portraits and new silhouettes from the treasures without number that are in our Christian sources. They help us not just to take a front view of the temple which is Christ's body but to walk all around it, review its ramparts, that we may tell this generation and generations to come that such is our God (cf. Ps 48:12-14). The pages that follow dwell on three images that have been helping me to look at and admire God's temple which was and is the body of his Son incarnate. Each image has an important place in the New Testament. Each has been well written on by at least one contemporary writer. Each can provide new incentives to know the Lord, to love him and to follow him. Each can encourage us to keep going to him as our physician and Savior.

New King in a New City

The ministry of Jesus alternated mainly between his native Galilee and Jerusalem which the psalmist calls the great king's city (Ps 48:1). We will never know for certain how often Jesus actually visited Jerusalem. According to the accounts of his final journey there, he expressed both a hesitancy about going and a desire to go. In his gospel, Luke sees a special symbolism in the name of Jerusalem. He groups events in a way that highlights the prominence of the great king's city. In particular, he has the final commissioning of the apostles and Jesus' final farewell to them taking place in Jerusalem. He thus lays the foundation for the growing conviction of Christians that we are the new Jerusalem, the new city where God dwells with a new people. The importance of Jerusalem is that it was the city of the kings, the city in which God's own kingship was exercised by the human kings who somehow represented him. This brings us near to the basic message of Jesus. He came to bring the good news of the rule, the reign of God. This is what the three synoptic gospels tell us. St. John's gospel gives us the same message by telling us that Jesus brings us the life of a whole new age, eternal life. In Jesus, God's reign had come. In his words and in his works, he showed us the wonderful world we have when God's will is done, when God reigns, when things are done in God's way.

Jesus himself was the agent of the kingdom of God which had come and which would come more completely in the future. In his day-to-day ministering, the blind received their sight, the lame walked, the dead were raised (Matt 11:43). On Palm Sunday, he symbolically enacted the coming of God to the great king's city, Zion, his own city. He did what, in the best of Israel's

longings, the messiah was expected to do: he cleansed and restored the temple which had been the special dwelling place of
God in his own city. The enemy of Israel against whom he bat-
tled turned out to be not a warring country but Satan. The style
in which he set about rebuilding the temple and fighting Israel's
enemy was not the style of power and weapons but the style of
the Sermon on the Mount, the style of the Beatitudes, the style of
the Our Father, the style of the water-bowl and towel.

In his preaching and ministry, Jesus gave a new meaning to
the great symbols of God's relationship with the chosen people:
the glory of God, the law, wisdom, God's word, God's spirit. He
invited God's people to be salt and light, not for a section of
humanity but for the whole human race, the whole earth. Is it
any wonder that we celebrate a feast of Christ the King? This
feast did not take its present shape until the twentieth century. It
recently settled in a fitting place on the last Sunday of the
church's year.

The kingly attitude of Jesus toward Jerusalem and the temple
brought about his condemnation and his crucifixion. In his tri-
umphal entry into Jerusalem, Jesus overturned people's understanding of God's city, God's temple, God's kingship over both.
In his teaching, the temple became relativized. Its buildings
were about to become redundant. Jesus symbolically enacted its
destruction. His action in cleansing the temple evoked the
Maccabean reconsecration, the Hannukah. He invited his un-
sympathetic listeners to destroy the temple. He would himself
rebuild the temple. He declared himself to be the temple. He
prepared the way for the great teaching that we are the living
stones of the new temple which is his body (1 Pet 2:5). His last
supper had pointed to what and where the new temple would
be. As a result, Christians can truly say, "What a city we have
and on what a hill! What a temple we have! What a king we
have, and what a kingdom!"

The Lord of the Margins
Sometimes the title of a book is so eloquent that it suggests a
whole agenda for what follows and it even suggests a program
for one's entire life. Such is the title of a work which is still in the
process of being completed and which describes Jesus as a marginal Jew. The author lists six ways in which Jesus the Jew could
be described as marginal. The reader will, no doubt, be remind-

ed of other ways too in which he was marginal. He was insignif-
icant to national and world history; he died the ghastly death of
slaves and rebels; he marginalized himself in his lifestyle; some
of his practices and teachings, for example his celibate living
and his teaching on divorce, were marginal; at the final clash he
had very few people, especially people of influence, on his side;
he was a poor layman, from a rural culture, bringing disturbing
doctrines and claims to a sophisticated capital in which he had
no power base.

It would be a very rewarding exercise to re-read the whole
story of Jesus through the lens of marginality. In doing so, one
would recognize many forms of marginality from which Jesus
called people. In calling them, he brought them from the margins into the very center of the kingdom. He made them part of
"the circle of those about him" (Mark 3:34). He invited them to
full table-fellowship. He showed in his own daily practice what
he meant when he said that the first will be last and the last first
(Matt 19:30). This did not stop him from saving not just the obviously marginal people but every man, woman and child made
in the image and likeness of God. His obvious concern to save
the forgotten people on the margins was the striking sign of his
burning desire to save all. It is in this setting too that we can best
see the contemporary prominence of our call to have a preferential option for the poor. This option can no longer be seen as optional. It brings us not to the margins of the gospel but to its center. But it in no way means that salvation is for only one section
of the human race.

Jesus the Itinerant

Since the days when we confidently read the standard lives of
Christ, Catholics have gotten involved in questions about the
search for the historical Jesus. They have been hearing of the distinction between the Jesus of history and the Christ of faith.
They have been hearing of form-criticism and of the historical-
critical approach to the gospels. Documents emanating from the
Pontifical Biblical Commission have grasped many nettles about
the process by which the gospels came into being and they have
made statements that in days gone by would have caused a raising of eyebrows. We certainly have been experiencing a new
intellectual liberty but, if truth were told, we have also had our
moments of bewilderment. It can be disconcerting to find scholarly books that deal with the historical foundations of our faith

using a lot of words like *maybe, possibly, unlikely, we don't know.*
But it is often in a book emanating from radical gospel questions
that one finds a very moving portrait of Jesus. One such portrait
is of the itinerant Jesus in pages describing "a down-to-earth
Jesus." It treats as autobiographical some of the instructions
Jesus gave to his disciples and to his first missioners:

• He carried no purse, for he had no money.

• He wore no backpack, for he had no change of clothes, no
food.

• He carried no club, the weapon of the poor, for he turned
the other cheek and gave muggers the shirt off his back, de-
fenseless.

• He developed a circuit of three villages ... where he cured
sick people, laid out his thoughts ... motivated a few people
to abandon their customary lifestyle and join up with him.

• He would walk along the shore, catch an occasional ride on
a fishing boat, hike through the hilly terrain from house to
house, hamlet to hamlet, knocking on doors.

• He would say "Shalom" when someone opened the door
and, if received hospitably, would show the reality of the
ideal he kept talking about by the way he cared for the sick.

• He ate moderately or sumptuously, depending on what
was provided, but on leaving the next day or so, he would accept no provisions for the road, not because he was an ascetic
but perhaps because carrying one's own provisions through
the day might involve depriving those in need.

• He advocated an alternative lifestyle that presupposed a
different, utopian kind of world. By calling it the kingdom of
God, the reign of God, God ruling, he by implication de-
frocked the temple cult and the state religion.

• His abandon regarding practical matters of self-interest
came to expression as prayer, turning those matters over to
God to handle.

This portrait of the itinerant, down-to-earth Jesus is not a
complete picture. Its author did not intend it to be so. Many
readers would like to fill it in with many shades of color from
the gospel pages. Some would like to adjust some of its wording.
All would agree that it does put us in touch with a Jesus who is
real.

Call the Doctor

When they are praying to the Lord in private, it would appear that most people address him as "Jesus" or as "Lord." It is unlikely that anybody addresses him as "doctor." Yet, there is a good gospel foundation for addressing him in that way. Jesus spoke of himself as the physician who came to attend to those who are ill, not those who are healthy (Mark 2:17). He anticipated the objection of those who would say, "Physician, heal yourself" (Luke 4:23). In our daily lives we have ambivalent attitudes toward doctors. On one level they are people we want to keep away. At times of serious illness, we cry out for their services. We need the doctor on account of our human fragility. We need the doctor on account of our mortality. We need the doctor because we are continually in need of healing, on a variety of levels. The saints are people acutely aware of all these expressions of our human dependency. That is why they are quick to call on the healing power of the Lord, whether they call on him by the name of doctor or not.

Christian poets have helped us to recognize our dependency and our need of the earthly doctor's touch and the heavenly doctor's touch. One of them, who himself experienced this healing touch in a striking way, reminded us that "we were born in others' pain and perish in our own" (Francis Thompson). Another (T. S. Eliot) told us that the whole world is our hospital, endowed by the bankrupt millionaire. He described Christ our healer by such images as the wounded surgeon, the dying nurse. He talked of the dripping blood of our dying physician as being our only drink and his bloody flesh as being our only food. It is no surprise that the imagery of illness and healing has been strong in the Christian tradition and that it is getting a new prominence today in prayer groups and in other settings in which Christians become keenly aware of their dependence on the God who heals. It is well captured in the popular *Anima Christi* in which we ask the body of Christ to save us, his blood to inebriate us and the water from his side to wash us.

There are close links between healing and saving. The whole Bible is the story of a people who kept experiencing a saving God. They experienced him as continually saving the heavens and the earth. They experienced him in the saving events of history. In these events, he often reassured them about his saving and liberating presence after they had been wondering whether he had abandoned them. They experienced his saving presence in the reassuring words of the prophets when they were threatened with exile, in time of exile, and in the time after exile.

In the person and ministry of Jesus, people experienced God in ways that reminded them of the story of their ancestors and in ways that were entirely new. The very name of Jesus, commanded by God's angel, means saving. He came to save his people from their sins and from all the evils that were seen to be related to sin. He was the Christ, the anointed one who was the anointed priest, the anointed prophet, the anointed king, and who formed a people who would be priestly, prophetic and kingly. His disciples came to be called Christians, anointed people. They are a people for whom oil is important—the oil that comforts, the oil that strengthens, the oil that heals. Christians are ritually anointed by the saving, healing Lord at baptism, at confirmation and in time of sickness. Their servant-leaders are anointed when they receive holy orders. They are continually reminded that Jesus, their physician-savior, came to give them his peace and to leave them his peace

Keep Digging

We are people of the treasure, people of the pearl. We have found the treasure but we must keep digging in the field. We keep searching for pearls in the hope of finding the one precious pearl. Every new glimpse of Christ makes us ask the gospel question, "What sort of man is this?" (Matt 8:27) and it sends us on a new and great dig, a new and exciting search. It gives us new motives for clearer knowing. It gives us new motives for love that is dear in the two senses of affectionate and costly. It gives us new motives for a nearer following of our one and only teacher who is at the same time our king, our margin-person and our fellow-itinerant.

CHAPTER 5

Spirit of the Living God

During the first half of the twentieth century, concern was sometimes expressed that the Holy Spirit had become the forgotten
person of the Blessed Trinity, the forgotten Paraclete. At the Second
Vatican Council, a number of the bishops and their advisers
seemed to be in sympathy with this concern. The exchanges at
the Council and the new searchings into the church's history
helped to provide fresh perspectives on the role of the Holy
Spirit. One result was a call by the bishops for a better appreciation of who the Holy Spirit is in the daily life of the church, and
for a more explicit calling on the same Spirit in the revised rites
of the individual sacraments.

At around the same time, a growing number of prayer
groups were beginning to call on the Spirit of the living God to
fall afresh on them, on the whole church, on the entire human
family. In all of this, one couldn't help having the impression
that they were somehow making amends to the Holy Spirit,
making up for lost time. And still, it could be said that the place
of the Holy Spirit had been well established in the church's
prayer and worship. We recalled the special life-giving work of
God's Spirit every time we said the Angelus and the Creed. The
prayer, "Glory be to the Father and to the Son and to the Holy
Spirit" had been continually on our lips. At Pentecost time every
year we had the hauntingly beautiful hymn *Veni Creator Spiritus*
which dates back to the ninth century. In many seminaries and
religious communities, it formed the basis of the pre-Pentecost
novena and of the opening of periods of retreat and renewal.

In the years before the Council, the *Veni Creator* was a sum-
ming-up for many of the meaning of the coming of the Holy
Spirit. Pentecost Sunday with its ensuing octave gave prominence to the equally beautiful *Veni Sancte Spiritus*. Every day of
Pentecost week, it was the Sequence for the Mass and it was
often sung with a faith and devotion that befitted our welcome

for the "sweet guest of the soul." It might be argued that this memorable lead up to and following from the feast of Pentecost was a form of tokenism that, in practice, sealed off our full awareness of the Holy Spirit until the corresponding time next year. The reality is that, again in seminaries and religious houses, every prayer time, every spiritual conference, every religious lecture began with the shorter version of the *Veni Sancte Spiritus,* which was a beautiful synthesis of the great hymn and of the great Sequence. The three taken together managed to capture all that the New Testament and Christian tradition have to say about the Holy Spirit. The great hymn addressed the Spirit of God as the one who was especially active in the world's creation in the beginning and in the world's re-creation in Christ. The Sequence reminded us that the Spirit of God keeps healing us and gifting us. The shorter prayer drew our attention to the content of both hymn and Sequence. A prayer that was used effectively by many renewal groups during the recent year of the Holy Spirit distilled further the content of all three prayers. It said simply: "Spirit of God come into our hearts; make us your new creation."

The change, in recent years, in our awareness of the person and mission of the Holy Spirit could be described in terms of two significant developments. One is that the appreciation of the person and mission of the Holy Spirit has moved from the seminary and religious house into wherever baptized men and women are praying and worshiping. The other is that we have come to realize that Pentecost is not the only feast of the Holy Spirit. The annunciation celebrates the conception of Jesus by the power of the Holy Spirit (Luke 1:35). The baptism of Jesus celebrates a special descent of the Holy Spirit (Matt 3:16). The Jesus who was tempted in the wilderness was full of the Holy Spirit and led by the Spirit (Matt 4:1). The whole ministry of Jesus was the ministry of one filled with the same Spirit (Luke 4:1, 14; 18-21; 6:19). From the side of the dying Christ came the water that signifies the Spirit (John 19:34; cf. 7:38, 39). It was through the Holy Spirit that Jesus was raised from the dead (Rom 8:11). Thus raised up, he breathed his Spirit on his disciples (John 20:20). Out of that breathing comes the assurance that the Spirit of the risen Christ is with the church not merely at Pentecost time but always. One could say that every feastday, indeed every day in the Christian calendar, is a day of the Holy

Spirit. No wonder that we keep calling on the Holy Spirit to "come." This calling has implications not merely in the renewal of the liturgy but in every area of our Christian life. We call on the Spirit of God to come into each of our hearts, to make each of us into a new creation and an agent of a new creation.

Spirit, Breath, Air, Wind

The one whom we call on to come is Spirit. It could be said that spirit, and its equivalents, is one of the most elementary words in any language. Spirit is breath. As long as I breathe I am alive. When I cease to breathe I am dead. In the usage coming from the Latin languages, breathing is spiration. Variations on the word include respiration, inspiration, aspiration, spirituality. Reflecting on the richness of words like these is a good help for us to appreciate the fact that the most basic biblical metaphor for the activity of the Spirit of God is in terms of the breath of God, the *ruach* of God, God breathing. It comes as no surprise that the risen Lord gave the gift of peace and the gift of the forgiving of sins to his disciples in the act of breathing on them and saying "Receive the Holy Spirit." In that act of breathing, he was sending his disciples as the Father had sent him (John 20:21-23). His own eternal origin as Word of God was in the atmosphere of love that was of one piece with the eternal breathing forth of the Holy Spirit.

There is an intimate connection between our breathing and the air that we breathe. The presence of some people in our lives is like the experience of a breath of fresh air. The Spirit of God is the air, the atmosphere, the refreshing breath of God. It is not surprising that thinking about the woman on whom God breathed in a unique way prompted Gerard Manley Hopkins to compose a poem called "The Blessed Virgin compared to the Air we Breathe." The whole poem is pervaded by a freshness of imagery which, though it is applied directly to Mary, is really a celebration of the presence and action of the Spirit of God who came upon her and who comes upon all for whom she is mother.

The transition from breath and air to wind is easy. In his conversation with Nicodemus in the gospel according to John (3:8), Jesus talks of the wind that blows where it chooses. Drawing on that image, he makes the statement that "so it is with everyone that is born of the Spirit." Nobody can predict whether the action of God's Spirit, in our individual lives or in the whole of society, will, at any time, come in the form of gentle breathing, or refreshing air, or in the form of a strong wind. In the English language the best known poet of the wild west wind is Percy Bysshe Shelley. In the first line of his poem, the wind is the "breath of autumn's being." In a later stanza, the wind is addressed as "destroyer and preserver." It is the very same breath of autumn's being that both destroys and preserves. This is a salutary reminder to us that none of us can control the breathing of God. We are in particular need of the reminder today as we experience the falling apart of programs of renewal in which we had invested much of our energies.

Spirit of God

A result of the new interest in the person and role of the Holy Spirit is that many people are not quite sure how to address or speak about this divine person. In many circles, it is common practice to talk simply about "the Spirit." This growing practice has a lot to recommend it and it has strong biblical precedents. At this juncture of history, though, it also has its hazards. It can sometimes give the impression that the Spirit has somehow an autonomy and an independent existence without obvious connections with Father and Son. For this reason, it is usually advisable to situate the Spirit in a trinitarian context. This context is best expressed at the end of the eucharistic prayer when we say "through him, with him, in him, in the unity of the Holy Spirit..." The controversies between East and West about the procession of the Holy Spirit from the Son as well as from the Father have not yet been fully resolved. In ecumenical dialogue, various wordings have been suggested as ways of moving beyond the impasse. What all the formulae have in common is that they never separate Father, Son and Spirit. This provides a good model for all our speaking of God's Spirit. It is always good to use the extra word and to talk of the Holy Spirit, the Spirit of the Father, the Spirit of Jesus.

The Holy Spirit is the Spirit of the Abba Father, teaching us to probe the mystery of this uniquely intimate name for God. St. Paul gives us the lead in this work of probing, by teaching us that it is the Father who has sent the Spirit of his Son into our hearts, crying Abba, Father (Gal 4:6). The same St. Paul tells us that, as we say Abba, Father, the Spirit is bearing witness to our spirit that we are children of the same Father (Rom 8:16).

The Holy Spirit is the Spirit of Jesus who is the Father's Son and Word. Without the Holy Spirit we are incapable of saying "Jesus is Lord" (1 Cor 12:3). It was by the prompting of the Holy Spirit that the angel of God told Mary and Joseph that the name of the child was not negotiable. The reason was that he was the only one who could and would save his people from their sins (Matt 1:22). Later, in his work of saving, this Jesus came to be recognized as the Christ. He was the one anointed by the Father. The Spirit of the Lord was upon him, anointing him to bring good news to the poor (Luke 4:18). Thus anointed, he anoints all believers and he commissions them to anoint. In the unfolding of the saving work of Jesus the Christ, the work of the Holy Spirit is never separate from the work of the Father and the work of his saving Son. The mission of the Holy Spirit comes from both Father and Son. It is for this reason that God's Spirit was active in every stage of the mission of Jesus, from incarnation to resurrection and after. The Spirit of God was also active in every stage of the coming into existence and growth of the church. The church that came into existence was not called the church of the Spirit. It was the church of God (Acts 20:28). It was this church that Jesus called "my church" (Matt 16:18).

Come into Our Hearts
All the great prayers to the Holy Spirit invite this divine person to come into our hearts. As a symbol, the human heart has had a long history. Literature has given us many perspectives on it. Poets have been lyrical about it. Christian visionaries have described the interaction between our hearts and the heart of Jesus Christ. Some reflective writers have tended to oppose the heart to the thinking part of our make-up. Perhaps the most famous expression of all this is the statement that the heart has its reasons that the mind knows nothing about. Much popular language about the heart draws on this way of seeing things. For many, the heart has come to symbolize what is affective and loving about us, as against what is rational and cerebral. In this perspective, the biblical uses of the word come to some people as a surprise. In most of the Bible, the heart is primarily the place of our deepest thoughts, our deepest resolutions, our deepest memories, our deepest sensitivities, and the center where all these meet. But to stop there would be to oversimplify. Even the biblical meaning has its affective and loving resonances. When we ask the Holy Spirit to come into our hearts, we leave

the word open to all its shades of meaning, all the biblical nuances and all the other nuances that the word heart has collected over the centuries. Since the heart is at the same time the great center, the great meeting-point of all our sensing, all our knowing, all our loving, all our aspirations, all our desires, all our yearnings, we say simply "come into our hearts."

The Holy Spirit enables us to have a heart and to engage in a heart-to-heart communication with the God who is all-holy. Our holiness consists of sharing in the holiness of God. The Holy Spirit is the one who searches everything, even the depths of God (1 Cor 2:10ff). In introducing us to the inner sanctuary of God, the inner holy of holies, the depths of God's heart, God's holiness, the Spirit who is holy teaches us to pray, to reach out of our depths into God's depths. That is what St. Paul had in mind when he wrote that in our praying we are of ourselves helpless but the Spirit intercedes for us "with cries too deep for words" (Rom 8:26). The only person who by his once-for-all sacrifice entered the holy of holies of the Father's heart is Jesus who made that entry "through the eternal Spirit" (Heb 9:14). Ever since, he remains in that holy of holies making intercession for us (Heb 7:25). He keeps drawing our prayer and ourselves into that holy of holies. He thereby becomes the center of the whole communion of saints, that great network of holy persons, holy places, holy times, holy things.

A New Creation

We keep asking the Holy Spirit to make us a new creation and to make us into agents of a new creation. God the Father is the creator of the universe, the whole universe. His Son Jesus came to recreate a fallen world. The Holy Spirit, "finger" of the Father's creative and wonder-working hand, has been called the transcreator, continually transforming every person and every thing and enabling them to be part of that new creation. The activity of the Holy Spirit is not confined to the church. Today, more than ever before, we are being asked to recognize the action of the Spirit of God outside the church's visible boundaries. The Spirit of God keeps unifying and orchestrating the influences for good both inside and outside the church. The Holy Spirit has been described as the how of the work of creation and re-creation. The question asked by Mary at the time of the announcing of the new creation points to the Holy Spirit as the Father's how. Both

Mary's question and the angel's answer have endless implic-ations and applications: "How can this be...?" "The Holy Spirit will come upon you..." (Luke 1:35).

In the continual life-giving work of transforming everything and everybody into the new creation, the Holy Spirit of God keeps renewing the face of the earth and ensuring that all the seeds of the Father's goodness and of the good news brought by his Son keep bearing fruit. It is no wonder that the word *fruit* is a word especially associated with God's Spirit. The classic list of fruits of the Holy Spirit expresses this continual seed-sowing and seed-cultivating which is the work of the Holy Spirit. In particular, the Holy Spirit keeps making real and fruitful what was real and fruitful in Jesus who was filled by the Spirit of his Father.

Back to Basics
In renewing us and enabling us to bear fruit, the Holy Spirit keeps bringing us back to basics. The wise men and women in many ancient cultures liked to keep asking what were the basic ingredients that comprised the whole universe. The most recur-ring answer to this question was in terms of earth, air, fire and water. It is interesting that these four basics have continually been used as images to express the action and role of the Holy Spirit.

The creating activity of God was an interaction between the breath of God—the divine air—and the earth that was coming into being. In the beginning, the earth was a formless void and the Spirit of God, a wind from God, swept over the face of the waters (Gen 1:2). The psalmist acknowledged that when God takes away the breath of living things they die and return to the dust of the earth. But he also acknowledged that when God sends forth the divine Spirit, the divine breath, they are created and God renews the face of the earth (Ps 104:29, 30). It is no wonder that the church keeps reminding us that we are dust and into dust we will return. Physicists now tell us that the dust from which we came is stardust. Our dusty origins and our moving back to dust could sound like bad news, but they have been good news since, on the first Holy Saturday night, the body of Jesus which had gone, dead, into the earth was raised through the action of the Holy Spirit (Rom 8:11).

The Holy Spirit is symbolized by the basics that are earth and the air. God's Spirit is also symbolized by the basics that are water and fire. This is the Spirit who was active over the waters of creation (Gen 1:2), over the waters of Christ's baptism (Matt 3:16), and in the water that flowed from the side of Christ who is the new temple (John 19:34). The mission of Jesus was a mission of casting fire on the earth (Luke 12:49). The fire in question is the fire of judgment, the criterion of which came to be disclosed as costly love. This love has been poured into our hearts through the Holy Spirit who has been given to us (Rom 5:5). The Holy Spirit who came in the form of tongues of fire (Acts 2:3) enables us to show this love in what we say and in what we do, as we keep praying that the fire of divine love will be enkindled in us.

Church communities that were founded to be communities of charity remind us that the ideal that inspired their founders is a program for all followers of Jesus Christ. As the Daughters of Charity of St. Vincent de Paul probe their call to be "daughters of God's love," they become more and more clear that all God's children are called to be daughters and sons of that same love. They come to appreciate, more and more, the special place of the Holy Spirit in the life of their foundress, St. Louise de Marillac. As the members of the Society of St. Vincent de Paul read again the words of their founder, Blessed Frederick Ozanam, "I would like to embrace the whole world in a network of charity," they invite us all to be both makers and beneficiaries of that network. There is no end to the ways in which the love of God is being poured into human hearts through the Holy Spirit.

The Friendly Spirit
The most personal name of the Holy Spirit is the Paraclete. Jesus promised to send "another paraclete" (John 14:16). As the word comes to us in translation, it can be bewildering. In reality, it is one of the simplest of words. The Paraclete is, in every sense, the one who is on our side and at our side. As to the ways in which the Holy Spirit is both of these, the promise of Jesus to send the Paraclete implies three assurances.

Firstly, the Holy Spirit is a friend in need. Good friends bring us joy and surprises by the gifts they give us. This is why there is a long history of associating the Holy Spirit with the giving of gifts. According to the book of Isaiah, the promised messiah, because the Spirit of the Lord is upon him, would be gifted in a sixfold way (Isa 11:2). In the versions in which this list comes to us, there are seven gifts. The conventional six or seven express fullness, completeness, giving without limit. The Holy Spirit is at the same time God's gift and the generous giver of God's gifts. The source of all the gift-giving is the Father. Jesus his Son is the great gift of the Father. He is the great prophet of the Father. In preparing for his coming, the Holy Spirit had been speaking through all the prophets. Jesus the prophet alerted people to what was the will of the Father. He was, at the same time, God's Son and God's prophet. In forming a new messianic and prophetic community, he gave each member of the community power to be a daughter or son of God and to be God's prophet, God's spokesperson. For the shaping of this kind of community, the Holy Spirit keeps giving gifts so that the community becomes an everlasting gift to the Father, always reminding us of the fact that the community which is Christ's body is full of unopened and unused gifts. By a right use of the gifts of seeing and listening, we can learn to find ways of doing this opening and this using. In this way, we come to know and appreciate the gift of the Father that is Jesus his Son and the gift that is the Spirit. Jesus has told us that eternal life is knowing the Father and knowing Jesus Christ whom he has sent (John 17:3). It is in the atmosphere of the friendly and gift-giving Spirit of both Father and Son that we experience the knowing that leads to loving.

The second assurance of Jesus is that our friend in need is a good and patient teacher, alerting us to the meaning of all that Jesus said, and leading us into the truth. This leading into all the truth is a process that did not end with the death of the last apostle. It has not ended yet. It will go on until Christ will come again. It is a process that takes place in the whole church and in the life of every disciple.

By being our friend and teacher, the Holy Spirit is our advocate. The third assurance of Jesus is that this advocate will be always at our side. The word *advocate* evokes all the tensions that one associates with the law court. It suggests a theme that takes many forms in the scriptures and in Christian tradition. In law court imagery, the accuser is Satan, God is the just judge, the Holy Spirit is the advocate for the defense. Our advocate assures us of victory and of the fact that we will ultimately be vindicated and freed. In all of life's testings, symbolized by the law court, our advocate, who is also the Spirit of truth (John 14:17), teaches us what to say and how to say it (cf. Luke 12:13).

The law court imagery is closely linked with the battle imagery which has a particularly powerful expression in the extended metaphor in the Letter to the Ephesians (6:10-17). The letter ends with the appeal to "take the helmet of salvation, and the sword of the Spirit which is the word of God." The law court imagery and the warfare imagery capture something of the many forms of human brokenness in which the Holy Spirit comes to piece us together. They have been celebrated in the art and literature of many Christian cultures. The victory that is assured is described in imagery that is proper to each culture and in imagery that is common to all cultures.

In the Form of a Dove

The bird that has come to be most associated with the Holy Spirit is the dove. One must admit that the dove is not the most attractive or beautiful of birds. In fact, the dove could easily go unnoticed, unadmired, and even belittled on account of its naïve simplicity. The biblical authors were, no doubt, aware of this limited appeal of the image of the dove. The same awareness must have been shared by Jesus when he asked his disciples to be as innocent as doves (Matt 10:16). But perhaps it is in this being unnoticed, unadmired, that the real secret of the Holy Spirit lies. All of us know of the true friend whom we neither notice nor admire until he or she surprises us by showing themselves to be true friends who are quietly supportive in time of our real needs. In this perspective, maybe it is right to describe the Holy Spirit as the forgotten Paraclete, the unnoticed friend who is the truest of friends. Maybe it should be no surprise that the lover in the Canticle of Canticles chose the dove as the symbol of his loved one, his beautiful one, when he said:

Arise
My love, my fair one
My dove
Come
(Cant 2:10-14)

We would do well to pray these words as we keep calling on the friendly Spirit.

CHAPTER 6

Do God's Will

The story of the spiritual odyssey of Mother Teresa is now widely known. At the age of eighteen, an Albanian girl left for Dublin to join an order which owes its original inspiration to Mary Ward, the seventeenth-century woman whom Pope Pius XII described as incomparable and whose great dream is summed up in the inscription on her tombstone: "To love the poor, to live, die and rise with them." At her profession, the young Albanian disciple of Mary Ward chose the name of Teresa out of admiration for "the little Teresa of Lisieux." She proceeded to final vows and eventually became headmistress of a school in Calcutta. After about twenty years, she experienced a desire to continue to serve God in religious life but to go in quite a new direction. It took a few years before the Vatican approved of her living for a fixed period outside her religious community.

In the discerning that led to the shaping of Sister Teresa's future, four people entered in a special way into her life: a spiritual director, a missionary, a religious superior, and an archbishop. I wonder what each of us would have felt or suggested if we had been in the position of one of these. It would have been easy to say that it was clearly God's will that she remain in the way of life to which she had vowed herself. This would have been in line with an understanding of the will of God that was highly acceptable at the time. Now that Mother Teresa's life on earth is over and her story is told wherever the gospel is preached, she provides an interesting example of the struggle that might be involved for any of us in discerning the will of God for us now, even when, in some ways, that will has already been made clear.

In our best moments, we all wish to do the will of God. Every time we pray the prayer our Savior gave us, we say, "Thy will be done on earth as it is in heaven." In a sense, this invocation is the whole of the Our Father. When we say, "Hallowed be thy name," we are praying that the will of the all-holy God be done and recognized as being done. It is the same when we pray, "Thy kingdom come." In the second half of the Our Father we put the emphasis on our own need of what God wills for us. It is God's will that all of his children have sufficient bread today and tomorrow. It is the will of God our Father that we forgive each other, in imitation of his unfailing readiness to forgive us, his children. It is God's will that none of us will fall apart under the pressures of life's testings, especially the final testing. It is God's will that none of us will be damaged by what is evil in persons and in events. We know that it is God who always takes the initiative in bringing about the doing of the divine will. But God prompts us to keep on asking for new divine initiatives. God also invites us to be willing agents in carrying out the wishes that are dear to the heart of our God.

Three Texts
As we seek to know what is God's will for us at any given moment, there are three texts of scripture that can be particularly helpful. The first is an invitation to be, quite simply, like God. It is the call of Jesus to be perfect as our heavenly Father is perfect (Matt 5:48). The invitation to be perfect can be daunting. Perfection is not a very attractive word. Perfectionists can be off-putting people. But the call of Jesus, as expressed in Matthew's gospel, is an invitation to be ever more merciful, ever more forgiving, ever more loving. Jesus is drawing attention to the essential nature of the God we worship. In the Christian understanding, God shows limitless power most of all by having mercy on us and forgiving us (cf. Collect Prayer for the twenty-sixth Sunday of the year). As a result, it is God's will for us that we place no boundaries to our expressions of mercy and forgiveness. None of us can be content to say, "Thus far my mercy and forgiveness go and no further." The invitation to be perfect is an invitation to share in the nature of the God who is love unlimited, goodness unlimited, mercy unlimited, forgiveness unlimited. Its implications are well captured in the translation that reads, "There must be no limit to your goodness, for your heavenly Father's goodness knows no bounds" *(New English Bible).*

A second helpful text is St. Paul's direct statement that "this is the will of God, your sanctification" (1 Thess 4:3). Here again is an invitation to be like the God who is the source of all holiness, all sanctity. This is the holy God whose name we should be always praising and invoking. God is all holy because "he is light and in him there is no darkness at all" (1 John 1:5). There is a darkness and shadow that is a healthy part of everybody's psychological make-up. There is a kind of darkness that reveals God's majesty, as St. John of the Cross saw when he sang of the night that is more loveable than the dawn. There is also a darkness that is the equivalent of sin and the wilful and selfish falling short of the goodness of which one is capable. The sinful side of us is content to love darkness rather than light and to walk in darkness (cf. John 8:12). There is none of this kind of darkness in the God who is unconditional love. Love is God's very definition. God is love (1 John 4:16). It is God's will that we should be godly, holy, loving. In telling us that God's will for us is our sanctification, St. Paul draws particular attention to whatever defiles the human body which he elsewhere calls God's temple, and to whatever inclines us to defile the body of another person. The reason is that such behavior would be the negation of the love and sanctification that is God's will for us. Hence his wish, expressed in the same context, that we love "more and more" (1 Thess 4:10).

A third helpful text in our search for God's will is the one in which St. Paul expresses his wish that his readers will "discern the will of God—what is good and acceptable and perfect" (Rom 12:2). This is really a variation on the perfection text in the Sermon on the Mount and the text about God willing our sanctification. The new word here is *discernment*. We have no difficulty in seeing that God wishes us to do good. We need to keep learning how to set about doing that which is most good and most acceptable. We do God's will most perfectly when we discern what is most good and most acceptable every time we are called to make a decision. This is what St. Paul had in mind when he prayed that the love of the Philippians whom he loved so much would "overflow more and more with knowledge and full insight" (Phil 1:9). In this way they would determine not what is good but "what is best" (v. 10).

Imaging God's Will

God keeps inviting us to keep discerning and determining what is best. Has God made cast-iron decisions in determining what is best for us? Or is God's will for us continually in the making, in a way that does not determine any aspect of our free decisions? Has God written the script for the story of each of our lives in such a way that any deviation from it would be a deviation from the divine will? Is God like the architect who, having drawn up detailed plans for a building, would be shocked or angered if the plan were ignored or greatly modified without consultation? Are we capable of making a change in some great eternal plan? Did God's plan include details of my conception, my birth, my upbringing, the various decisions I have made, the decisions of others that affect my life, the events that affected me and are beyond my control? Most sensitive of all, perhaps, has God fixed the moment and manner of my death, in the way that seems to be envisaged in one of the hymns for Morning Prayer: "My destined time is fixed by thee, and death does know his hour. Did warriors strong around me throng, they could not stay his power?" (Thursday, Week 2). Has God fixed the exact moment when I will be called from life's departure lounge?

Whatever way we tend to answer questions like these, it is good to keep remembering St. Paul's salutary question, "Who can know the mind of the Lord or who has been his counselor?" (Rom 11:34). Within this perspective, great Christian minds have, over the centuries, probed into the meeting points between God's dominion over the whole of creation and the place of our freedom. The meeting points were explored most notably in the controversies between what came to be known as the "Thomist" school and what came to be known as the "Molinist" school. The Molinists put much emphasis on human freedom and on God's knowing of all that we do, all we will do, all we could do, all we might do. The Thomists stressed God's universal dominion. They were not satisfied to say that God knows and searches into our free decisions. They were unhappy with any suggestion that God is not the principal cause of everything that happens, even our freest decisions. We hear little today about these two schools of thinking, but the questions they dealt with continue to be raised in new forms. They will continue to be raised as long as human beings search for what constitutes God's will and how that will is manifested to us.

In the continual search for images to express their understanding of God's will, people have, over the centuries, tried to name the ways in which they see that will expressed. They have, for example, distinguished between what God positively wants and what God permits to happen. Nowhere has the topic had more practical implications than in the communities of men and women who are vowed to religious obedience. It would be easy to oversimplify the way God's will was seen to be linked with obedience, but some trends are recognizable. At least in some communities, there has been an emphasis on what came to be called blind obedience. The will of one's superior was a direct expression of the will of God. The will of God was expressed in a special way in what the rule of one community called the will or even the intimation of the superior. This fitted in well with a worldview in which whatever happened, even the greatest calamity, tended to be seen as the will of God. There was a type of calamity that was described simply as an act of God. In the same perspective, it was largely assumed that God had indeed written the script expressing the divine will for every detail of each of our lives. Going against the details of the great architect's plan for each of us would be acting against the will of God. God had fixed the exact moment when the number would go up for the birth and death of each of us. Between birth and death, people were encouraged to say "I would do this if I thought it were God's will for me." A life well lived was one in which one searched for what God had already decided.

There were many sources for this worldview. One source was in the way people understood the Bible. In the Old Testament especially, God tended to be described as the direct cause of everything that happened. There was little room for what later came to be called secondary causes. God directly controlled all natural events. God gave life directly. God opened the wombs of those who were fertile. God closed the wombs of those who were not. God had control of every aspect of human living and human dying, of all of what happened in the heavens, on earth, and in Sheol, the world of the dead.

Not the Gentile Way

As Christians in Europe listened to the message of the Bible, their understanding of God's dominion over the world generally and over people in particular were colored by the way they saw civil authority being exercised. Christian leaders, in turn, tended to see themselves as being privileged to share in God's direct dominion. The strongest expression of this conviction was what came to be known as the divine right of kings. This understanding of the divine right and of the thinking that led up to it left more than one mark on the way authority was exercised in some vowed reli-

gious communities and the ways in which they were encouraged
to understand the will of God. It cannot be denied that the understanding of both the nature of authority and of the will of God
sometimes was in the style of the "rulers of the Gentiles" rather
than in the style of Jesus Christ (cf. Luke 22:25, 26).

For many of the Christian centuries, the Bible was read and
authority was exercised in a setting in which the laws of nature
were seen as unchanging and fixed. This understanding of the
laws of nature further encouraged an understanding of the will
of God in terms of what is fixed and immutable.

A Changing World-picture

It is understandable that approaches to the will of God received
all these colorings throughout the centuries. In the past few centuries, and notably in the twentieth century, there has been a
changing worldview that affects our way of thinking and speaking about God's will. With the help of philosophy and with the
new insights of biblical scholarship, one can now more clearly
distinguish between various kinds of causes. We talk, for example, about primary causes, secondary causes and instrumental
causes. We recognize more and more clearly that the God of the
Bible exercised a dominion over creation in a way that involved
many secondary causes, all the strengths and all the weaknesses
of the human beings made in God's own image and likeness
(Gen 1:26). The expression of God's will bore all the marks of all
these strengths and all these weaknesses. Very often what is directly attributed to God in the Bible we would now attribute to
the interaction between the laws of nature which God designed
and the free decisions of both good people and people who were
not so good. We have the kind of understanding of history
that enables us to see clearly that those exercising authority
have always used a variety of models in their understanding of
the source and nature of that authority and that they sometimes
had the temptation to declare that what they themselves decided
was God's will. We recognize that there are some things in our
world that are fixed and unchanging. As physicists explore the
workings of the universe, they show us that there is much in the
laws of nature that is fixed and unchanging, but there is also
much that is unfixed, changing, unpredictable.

In our changing worldview, we are more and more coming
to realize that the universe God decided to create is a universe

unfinished, a universe continually in process of becoming itself. Even without taking sides on the creationist versus the evolutionary ways of looking at the universe, we cannot deny that many aspects of human life have been changing and evolving since human beginnings a million or so years ago. There is a continual unfolding of the resources of the universe, a learning to control what was regarded as uncontrollable, a learning that what for long we regarded as inevitable was not really so. There is a continual development in our understanding of what promotes human health and what damages it. Up to a short while ago, whole families were wiped out by tuberculosis, a disease that can now be easily cured. In this evolving state of knowledge, one would be slow to say that God had fixed the exact moment and manner of death's call to each of those who in the past were victims of a dreaded disease.

A Flawed Universe

We are coming to realize that God decided to make a universe that is, in many ways, flawed. The new millennium was ushered in by harrowing accounts of the occurrence of various monsoons, hurricanes, earthquakes. As we heard of the destruction of the lives and livelihoods of so many innocent people, we couldn't help wondering why, oh why? Over the centuries there have been many attempts to answer this disturbing question. For those who survived the disasters, their numb grief was amplified by the fear of pestilence and disease that might come from decaying bodies. Some wondered whether it continued to make sense to speak of a God of unlimited and unconditional love. Some wondered whether God really holds each of us in the palm of the divine hand. From a very different perspective, some wondered whether the disasters showed that God was angry and determined to punish the sins of people who refused to do the divine will. The questions and the answers continue. In the middle of it all, we are now informed simply that earthquakes are caused by underground faults. While we live in the assurance that God "has established the world" and that "it shall never be moved" (Ps 93:1), we are coming to see that God allowed for the consequences of laying flawed foundations. Why God decided to create in this way is not any clearer to us now than it was to the author of the Book of Job. All we can say is that the flawed universe comes from the God whose nature it is to be kenotic, self-emptying. One thing is certain. It is precisely in this flawed universe that God invites us to be perfect, to become holy, to discern what is the best way of thinking and doing, and to practice limitless goodness as we cope with many limitations.

A Universe of Freedoms

It is becoming clearer and clearer that God decided to make a universe in which nothing is more precious than freedom. The decision of God to create the universe was a free decision. In the interaction of the various laws of nature, God allowed for many freedoms. More important, it would appear that God wouldn't dream of making humans anything but free. God was willing to go ahead with a universe that would carry all the good and all the bad consequences of human decisions. We believe in and hope in and love a God for whom every human decision is precious and to be respected. It is in our understanding of the interaction between the various freedoms willed and encouraged by God that the greatest revolution is taking place in our understanding of the will of God today. If I believe today that the divine architect has fixed his plans for my life and my death, I do so in the realization that every detail of it leaves full space for what I freely decide. If I think that accidents and disasters are God's will, I do so because I believe in a God who was at ease in making a flawed universe and who allows for the interaction between the working of the laws of nature and the free decisions of people who do good things and bad. If I believe that any person I recognize as my superior expresses the will of God for me, I do so not with the option but with the obligation of taking part in the many forms of dialogue to which the church has been calling all of us in recent years. The fact that such dialogue was not always encouraged in the past doesn't dispense the whole church from searching together for God's will in the present.

Always in the Making

It is in this flawed universe, in this world in which every new generation gets new insights into what helps and what hinders health of mind, body and spirit, in this interaction of people's good decisions and not so good decisions, that God invites me to be perfect, to be sanctified, to discern what is best. I can be sure that I am not doing God's will if I try to control my own destiny in a way that bypasses the disclosing of God's invitations to limitless goodness in the events in which I am called to be part. Jesus himself allowed the decisions of others, and especially of the religious and political leaders of his day, to shape the unfolding of his Father's will for him. In the event, he had to undergo an undeserved and unjust death. Humanly speaking, he did not find the prospect of that death attractive. He begged his Father to let the bitter cup pass from him, and yet he prayed that things would happen as the Father wanted, not as he wanted (Mark 14:26). In the whole painful process, he was able to say that he was laying down his life of his own accord, that no one took his life from him (John 10:18). Is it any wonder that God made known to us the mystery of the divine will "according to his good pleasure which he set forth in Christ" (Eph 1:9)?

Jesus came to proclaim the good news of the kingdom of God. It is for the promoting of that kingdom that he lovingly and freely laid down his life. The kingdom of God is identical with the will of God. Both are an invitation to let our goodness know no limit because the heavenly Father's goodness knows no bounds. God's will for us has been described as God's dream of how each of us could express that boundless goodness. God's will for us is God's vision as to how each of us can become a man, or woman, or child of vision. God's will for us is that we allow new horizons of goodness to open up for us. God's will for us is that we do all for God's greater, indeed God's greatest glory. God is indeed the architect for the building of our lives, but not an architect who imposes a plan on us. In designing the plan and in helping us to carry it out, God is exquisitely sensitive to the freedom of all our decisions in the networking of the decisions of other people and in the unfolding of events.

The God Who Provides
The God whose will is always unfolding for us is the God who has provident care for us. God is the provident God, present in all things and active in all events. God is fully active even in the freest of our decisions, but in a way that totally respects our freedom. Every created agent is a co-agent with God. In every thing and every person I know and love there is space for God to be co-known and co-loved. God's providence is continually active in leading and guiding the whole of creation to the final renewal and re-creation that is its destiny (cf. Matt 19:28). God is continually at work in promoting this re-creation, through the action of

the Holy Spirit, involving what we have come to call secondary causes. In the activity of these secondary causes, we discover something of the reality of God's eternal law, of the laws of nature, of what has received the name of natural law. All the secondary causes bear the marks of God's decision to make an imperfect world and to allow the flawed and faulty decisions of people to be the agents of the unfolding of the divine plan and the divine will.

The Book of Wisdom praises God's wisdom as it reaches mightily from one end of the earth to the other and orders all things well (Wis 8:1). Jesus spoke touchingly about the way God clothes the lilies of the fields and he presented this as an image of God's providential care for the human family (Matt 6:28-30). It must be admitted that many sincere believers find it hard to recognize this providential hand in their own lives. Try as they might, they find it hard to see signs of the action of a loving, providential God. And still there are few, if any, who can find no signs at all, even in the most impossible of situations. The foundational experience that convinced God's people of God's providential care for them was the Exodus. Ever since, they have recognized the same providence in each new exodus in which they were involved. In the course of our own life, each of us gets at least one glimpse of God's providential hand in each of our messes, in each minor or major exodus we experience. From this glimpsing comes a deepening of our trust and of our hopes, in a way that makes sense of the assurance of Julian of Norwich that not merely will all be well and all manner of things be well, but that we will see for ourselves that all manner of things will be well. Our sense of hope and of trust, our assurance that God's providential hand is at work in good times and in bad times is strengthened as we contemplate the exodus of Jesus himself. God was never more present and active than in the course of that exodus, the exodus in which Jesus felt so forsaken. Here was the supreme manifestation of God's goodness that knows no bounds, of God's providence, of God's will.

Agents of God's Will

As we live our lives in the loving, nurturing, providential hands of God, we get continual intimations of what is God's will for us. At the same time, we learn that we are called to be free agents of the carrying out of that will. We learn the importance of the prayer of petition which will show us that the great eternal plan is always in the making and that our petitions and our decisions are a crucial part of it. What Fr. J. P. de Caussade (1675–1751) called self-abandonment to divine providence is not a call to be inactive. It is an invitation to dream new dreams as we enter into God's great dream for us. It enables us, in youth, in middle years, and in old age, to have new visions as we dream our new dreams (cf. Acts 2:17). The example of the Albanian girl whose signature tune became "You did it to me" (Matt 25:40) can motivate us to keep discerning the will of God, to do it, and to help others to know and do it.

CHAPTER 7

Be Transparent

At the completion of the filming of *Gandhi*, some elderly men who had known Mahatma Gandhi, and who made up part of the crowd in the film, paid a beautiful tribute to Ben Kingsley who played the title role. "You brought him back for us," they said. Gandhi himself had been known to tell Christian groups that, though he admired and loved Jesus Christ, he did not always recognize the master in the disciples. The elderly men were unwittingly using some of the words of the author of the Letter to the Hebrews: "May the God of peace, who brought back from the dead our Lord Jesus...make you complete in everything good" (13:20, 21).

All the baptized are called to express the presence of the Lord who has, once-for-all, been brought back from the dead. At the beginning of the third Christian millennium, the numerical strength of the baptized is impressive. There are about a billion Catholics and about half a billion other Christians. The downside of the story is that the number of Christians is not growing relative to the total world population. About half of the billion Catholics, largely on account of the growing number of priestless parishes, do not have easy access to the Eucharist. The sizable majority, perhaps up to eighty per cent in all, choose not to go regularly to the celebration of the Eucharist. This is notably true in Europe and in many of the countries that are conveniently classified as the first world. Concerned believers have recently been asking "Where have all the Catholics gone?" and they have been looking for a therapy and a program that will reverse the movement of the tide.

Which is the more alarming situation, the limited access to the Eucharist by half the Catholic population or the fact that so many of those with easy access do not bother to come to the table of the Lord? Our contemporary understanding of the parable of the mustard seed would seem to indicate that the second problem is the more serious. The parable is not so much an assurance of numerical strength as a call to let the seed of God's word grow into and influence all the areas of one's body, mind and spirit. It is a call to all believers to be transparent.

Transparency is a word that occurs a good deal in contemporary writing on the renewal of priesthood, of religious life, of Christian life generally. It is not a directly gospel word but it is a rather powerful summary of the message of many gospel words. Christians are called to be transparent with all the values of the gospel of Jesus who has been brought back from the dead. There are wrong ways and right ways of being transparent. I would be paying you no compliment if I told you that I could see through you. It would be worse again if I told you, in the words of a famous jibe, that deep down you are a very superficial person. The call to be transparent is not a call to look like Jesus. Even in our own day, there have been well-intentioned people who decided to dress as they would like to imagine that Jesus dressed and to copy details of a lifestyle that are more the creation of stage and film than a real imitation of Christ. One is reminded of the look-alike competition for the entertainer Charlie Chaplin. He himself surreptitiously entered the competition and he won third place. St. Paul invited his Christian readers to imitate him as he imitated Christ (1 Cor 11:1). This was an invitation to be transparent, not by copying external details but by clothing oneself with all the qualities of Christ (Col 3:12ff), with whatever is true, holy, just, pure, lovely and noble (Phil 4:8).

Be Magnanimous

The call to be transparent is a call to be magnanimous. The magnanimous person sets out to make the greatest use of the greatest things. Our God is the great God. As we praise God we say "How great thou art." The great God has put all the greatest things at our disposal. In Christ, the great God has "blessed us with every spiritual blessing" (Eph 1:3). This is why the Christian should never be satisfied with being or doing anything less than the best. Here we have a daunting program, so daunting that we can baulk at God's invitation and opt for what is more comfortable and what is only second best.

The great call to every Christian and to every Christian community is to be transparent with everything that Jesus Christ stands for, to be magnanimous in a way that is never satisfied with the second best. In a world in which people are continually receiving contradictory signals about what it is to be truly human, there is an urgent need to make Jesus Christ fully visible. In one of the Christmas prefaces, we express the desire that while we know God visibly in Christ we would be drawn into the love of what is invisible. As sacrament of the God who has become visible in Christ, the Christian community is called to let God's goodness and holiness be seen. Though Jesus Christ has warned us about the dire consequences of doing our good works in order to be seen and praised by people (Matt 6:2), he wishes us to be the light of the world, to be the city built on a hill, to be lamps, to let our light shine before others so that they may see the good we do and thus praise the Father in heaven (Matt 5:14-16).

We are called to be transparent with the whole mystery of Christ. There is a danger that each of us could worship and reflect what one might call a one-dimensional Christ. Unwittingly, we could worship and reflect a Christ whose meekness and gentleness are somewhat less than fully human. One could worship and reflect a Christ who is prodigal in his forgiveness in a way that blots out his "from now on do not sin again" (John 8:11). One could worship and reflect a Christ who is a social and political reformer in a way that obscures the fact that he is the prince of peace. The possible list of one-dimensional understandings of Christ is endless.

Christ the Sun

We can never afford to stop our searches into the immeasurable riches of Christ (Eph 3:8). We keep hoping that each search will lead us to find ways in which our daily life will be transparent with these riches. One image of Christ that can help us here is the one that envisages him as the sun. The image can help us to a new understanding of our call to being light, to being transparent. The prophet Malachi spoke of God sending his messenger ahead of him to clear the way. The Lord would enter his sanctuary like a refiner. The refining action of God would be like the sun of justice shining on God's people and bringing health in its rays (Mal 3:1-3; 4:20). In the Litany of the Holy Name, which has been a favorite prayer of many Christians, Jesus is addressed as the sun of justice. His person and his ministry were like the sun

shining in our darkness and putting us in touch with all the justice and holiness of God. In him, God makes all of us just and
holy. This image of Christ as God's sun shining in our darkness
has much to do with the connections between the summer and
winter solstices and the various stages of the church's liturgical
year.

The image of Christ as the sun can be particularly helpful in
our generation as we become more aware of our connections
with the solar system and its implications for us. We are more
and more realizing that our earth is but one of many planets in a
whole galaxy of planets and we are continually reminded of the
interconnectedness between our earth, the sun, the moon and
the stars. We are often reminded that our origin was in stardust
and that our destiny is in a world that reaches beyond the stars,
through the stars. We are used to calling Mary the morning star.
We are less used to the fact that her Son Jesus is the morning star
(Rev 2:28) whose brightness she introduced into the world. This
does not blur the fact that he is the sun of justice. Sun, moon and
stars symbolize our links with all the "constellations" that constitute the communion of saints, that intimate and undivided
union of holy persons and holy things, in the heavens, on the
earth and under the earth. The great eclipse of the sun that ushered in the new millennium was a new invitation to Christians
to look toward the heavens, in more senses than one. The diamond ring that will be remembered by many is a beautiful reminder that Christ is still wedded to his church which is the
woman clothed with the sun, with the moon under her feet, and
having on her head a crown of twelve stars (Rev 12:1).

For many centuries, Christians gave much importance to
the right orientation of church buildings. Ideally, the church
building, the house of the faithful, was to face the rising sun.
For Christians, the danger of disorientation is the urge in all of
us to turn in the direction opposite to the one along which
Christ our sun wishes to direct us. As the watchers of the heavens tell us that our earth has run more than half its course and
is likely to end one day in some form of fiery conflagration
when the sun becomes a "red giant" star, we are reminded to
live all our lives in the perspective of the last things. God is
love. Jesus, the sun of God's justice, is love. We have to learn
how to relate to the sun's rays. In his continual respect for our
freedom, God allows the possibility that instead of continually

availing ourselves of the healing that Malachi envisaged as
coming from the rays of God's sun, we could abuse the ways in
which God keeps radiating the divine love to us and keeps asking us to radiate it to others.

The Face of Christ
The great image of God is the face of Christ Jesus, the sun of
justice. We are all helped by the sight of faces that give us a
glimpse of the face of Christ Jesus. We are moved when we see
two people from hitherto hostile traditions looking into each
others' faces in a search for mutual understanding. One thinks
of the impact of the pictures of Pope John XXIII looking into the
eyes of Christian leaders of other traditions, of Pope Paul VI
beside the Patriarch Athenagoras, of Pope John Paul II reaching
out in a gesture of forgiveness at the man who had tried to be his
killer. The call to be a Christian is an invitation to be radiant, to
let something of the face of Christ, our sun, shine through our
faces. It is in this perspective that St. Paul (2 Cor 4:6) tells us that
the God who ordered light to shine out of darkness has made the
light to shine in our hearts too, so that we might radiate and
make known the glory of God as it shines in the face of Christ.
The same St. Paul stated that he had made an important decision
"in the person of Christ" (2 Cor 5:10). This is coming to be used a
lot as an apt description of the nature of ministerial priesthood.
A careful examination of the words St. Paul used reveals the fact
that he saw his decision as having been made in the presence of
Christ, before the face of Christ. One could say that every
Christian is called to live and act in the person of Christ, in the
presence of Christ, before the face of Christ. The program for
ministerial priesthood is one of enabling people, by the ministry
of the word, by the celebration of the sacraments, by pastoral action, to be Christ's face, his presence, his person, his glory made
transparent.

Over the centuries, some Christian preachers and teachers
have painted beautiful word-pictures of the world that was
opened up for the blind man who received his sight by the ministry of Jesus. He was fascinated by the figures of creature after
creature, of person after person. He then saw the unique face of
the Lord himself. Seeing the Lord's face put everything in perspective for him. Here indeed is a program for all Christians, at
all times. The daily call to conversion is a call to have our eyes

opened, to see the face of Christ, to see as he saw. Saints are people who allow God to open their eyes. By reading the lives of the saints, St. Ignatius of Loyola got a glimpse of the face of Christ. After some years of disbelief, St. Edith Stein stumbled on the life of St. Teresa of Avila. As she read it through the night, she suddenly found herself saying "This is truth!" She discovered the face of Christ, who is the way, the truth and the life, in the story of a woman whose heart had been transfixed by the love of Christ.

Mirrors

The call to see the face of Christ and to be the face of Christ is identical with the call to be transparent with Christ. It is the call to let our light shine before others (Matt 5:16), so that they may see our good works and glorify our Father who is in heaven. It is a call to be mirrors. In the Litany of Loreto, we call on Mary as mirror of justice. This is a worthy title for the woman who is mother of the sun of justice. With so great a mother and so great a divine teacher, there is no limit to the ways we can mirror the loving-kindness and the fidelity of God. As we search for ways of doing this work of mirroring, we have a rich treasury in the whole of the church's scriptures and the church's tradition. The Second Vatican Council put it very beautifully when it said (*Constitution on Divine Revelation,* 7) that tradition and scripture are like a mirror in which the church contemplates God until we see God face to face. The God we contemplate is Father, Son and Holy Spirit whom we cannot but love "when we see them reflected in looks that we love" (Thomas Moore, *The Meeting of the Waters*).

A Time of Eclipse

To go back to the image of Christ as the sun of justice. There is no doubt that, in our rather tired Western church, we are today experiencing a certain eclipsing of the sun. The eclipsing has been with us for some time now and there are indications that it will be with us for the foreseeable future. As with the disciples on the road to Emmaus (Luke 24:16), something is keeping people from recognizing the face of the Lord. In some places where we would wish to see the face of charity shining in the lives of people consecrated by baptism, by religious vows or by ordination, little light is forthcoming. It would be foolhardy and it could be judgmental to name exact reasons for this. Certain it is

that every member of the sinful church is always in need of re-
form and conversion. It is also certain that, in carrying out this
reform and conversion, the church must rid itself of ways that
do not reflect the spirit of the Beatitudes, of the Sermon on the
Mount, of the Our Father, of the washbasin and towel.

For convenience, it might be useful to name two areas of the
church's heritage that can blur our vision of the face of Christ.
One of these is our Constantinian heritage. There was great rejoicing among Christians when, by the decisions of the Emperors Constantine and Theodosius, Christianity became the official religion of the Roman empire. During the years that followed, the church has benefited in countless ways from these
decisions. But we cannot close our eyes to the debit side. The
main debit area would seem to be in the way power and authority have been exercised over the centuries. *Power* is a gospel
word. Jesus came full of God's power, the dynamic energy that
comes from God. It was this power that enabled him to heal, to
exorcise, and to have the wind and the sea obey him. He also
came as a man with authority. It was said of him (Matt 7:29) that
he spoke with authority and not like the official religious leaders
of the time. But he made it very clear that gospel power and
gospel authority are completely different from the worldly understanding and exercise of the two. The leaders in his saving
community which we call the church should be completely different from the rulers of pagan nations who rule over their people as lords. In the Christian community, the greatest must be as
the youngest and the leader must be as the suffering servant (cf.
Luke 22:25, 26). In the serving community which is the church of
Christ the Suffering Servant, power and authority have a whole
new meaning. One cannot help thinking that the decisions of the
two emperors, in spite of all our movements of renewal, continue to leave their mark on the ways Christians still give expression to power and authority.

Another area in which our Christian inheritance continues to
be blurred by non-gospel lifestyles is the coloring that comes
from the Renaissance. There are many reasons why Christians
should be deeply grateful for the Renaissance. Much of the
Christian humanism, of the search for the one, the good, the true
and the beautiful that we associate with the Renaissance is a
legacy and a treasure for which we can only thank God. But this
inheritance too has its debit side. The complex titles for office

holders and the lifestyle that up until recently we took for granted have tended to obscure the face of the Christ who humbled himself and emptied himself. Since the Second Vatican Council, there have been many calls for the equivalent of a new reformation in the church. There have been calls for a simplicity of lifestyle and a dismantling of some church structures that in today's society distort the true nature of gospel living. These calls are particularly effective when we see their message embodied in the day-to-day lives of leaders in whom much of the church's power and authority are seen as residing. Thank God we have lived to see many examples of changes in the exercise of power and authority and moves toward a simpler church lifestyle. To some people who thought that resurrection was an impossible dream, Jesus said "You know neither the scriptures nor the power of God" (Matt 22:29). As we rediscover the scriptures today and as we reassess our attitudes toward power, we can hope that we will get a new vision of the bridegroom of the church and new assurances that he is still wearing the diamond ring.

Much of the Constantinian and Renaissance legacy is, by force of circumstances, being dismantled before our eyes in the church today. But a vacuum has been created and many are unsure as to what kind of church lifestyle will replace it. It is encouraging that in the many forms of basic communities that are arising in the church there is a great simplicity, no triumphalism. One hopes that this return to gospel littleness will soon be the great characteristic of the wider and bigger Christian community.

Seeing Jesus: Seeing the Father
As we yearn for new epiphanies of Our Lord Jesus who has been brought back from the dead, we see the riches in his words that "whoever has seen me has seen the Father" (John 14:9). The transition from the lifestyle of a church strongly colored by the decisions of the emperors and by Renaissance ideals to a new following of the Christ who had nowhere to lay his head (Matt 8:20) has its bewildering moments and its humiliating moments. This is to be expected in what is essentially a journey back. We are not on a journey back in the sense that we want to restore church structures and practice as they were. The real journey back is one of revisiting and rediscovering the gospel

call to learn at the school of our unique teacher. In this school we will keep our eyes continually "fixed on Jesus" (Heb 12:2). Jesus had his eyes continually fixed on his Father. The focusing of our eyes on Jesus will ensure that the face of both Jesus and his Father will be reflected in our faces and in our demeanor. Both faces are the faces of compassion. There is no limit to the wells of compassion that are at our disposal in the heart of the God who is love, the God who shows omnipotence most of all by having compassion on us. True compassion is not patronizing or con-descending. When Jesus healed the sick, exorcised the possessed and raised from the dead, he showed that the kingdom, the reign, of the compassionate God had really come. The miracles of the compassionate Jesus lifted up hearts and showed people what they were really capable of.

In our call to be transparent with the compassion of God and to let the healing sun of justice shine through us, we give people a glimpse of what they can truly become.

CHAPTER 8

Keep Fanning the Flame

The Second Letter to Timothy (1:6) contains the makings of a program for all those who exercise what we now call ordained ministry in the church. Indeed it has something important to say to all who wish to be at the service of the kingdom of God. Timothy is invited to fan into a flame the gift of God that was received by the laying on of hands. The image speaks to every culture and to every generation. It is not of itself a religious or a Christian image. One of its best-known expressions was in the ancient Roman work of the vestal virgins at the temple of Vesta. Vesta was the goddess of fire. The work of the vestal virgins was to keep the fire lit. The accepted belief was that if the fire were allowed to go out there would be a great calamity.

The temple of Vesta was a round stone building. There are indications that in its original form it was a much simpler thatch building. Very likely the fire in question was the communal fire at the service of the people of Rome. This was in the days when fires were seen as especially precious and in need of constant and careful attention. They were hard to make and harder still to manage when they were made. In this setting, the work of those attending to the temple fires was the very basic but sensitive one of keeping the home fires burning. As time went on, this work took on all kinds of secondary symbolisms. The original simple work and simple lifestyle came to be surrounded by various forms of privilege as the centuries went by. The mystique surrounding what was originally a clear and unambiguous task took on new shades of coloring. At the best of times, the virgins were expected to keep their attention fixed on the task, not the privilege. There was a grave penalty for allowing the fire to go out, though, ironically, the temple itself went on fire at various times in history and all we can see today is what remained after such a temple fire. The penalty for loss of virginity was death.

Fire Going Out

The story of the vestal virgins provides an interesting parable for the church. In our church communities since the Second Vatican Council, there have been many instances of fires going out, of fires that were once strong but that are now only smoldering, as well as of new fires and new flames. Nowhere has the image of the enkindling of the fire and of keeping the fire burning been more appropriate than in the story surrounding the understanding of virginity in the church. In assessing the extent to which virginity is accepted or rejected in the church today, some might use the imagery of fire going out, some the imagery of smoldering. In the European and North American churches, there has been a dramatic fall in the number of people being consecrated in religious life, but we are hearing of new forms of the virginal vocation.

There has been a particular focusing of attention on priestly celibacy. In the words of a popular expression, it has been "under fire." Up to the time of the Council, it was common to quote the words of more than one pope and say that celibacy is the great jewel in the crown of the Catholic priesthood. Since then there has been a seismic change. Altered attitudes have resulted from a variety of factors. There has been a questioning as to whether the church's continuing practice of normally limiting the exercise of ministerial priesthood to those willing to be celibate was placing on the shoulders of some of them a yoke that is not easy and a burden that is not light (cf. Matt 11:30). This has been highlighted by the departure from active ministry of many who declared that they had reached this stage in their experience of the yoke and the burden. In the meantime, many began to question the church's right to place human laws about the requirements for ordination above people's right to the Eucharist. The celibacy requirement was the one most highlighted in this questioning. More recently, there have been shock tremors and even conflagrations by the coming into the open of sexual offenses of priests and religious officially committed to the virginal way of life. Celibates have been in the news for the whole spectrum of sexual misdemeanors, even the grossest. They are not immune to the effects of the sexual revolution. At a time when the sense of sexual sin has been weakened, celibates have sometimes become part of the sin. All of this gives a new poignancy to the Lord's words, "Let anyone among you who is without sin be the first to throw a stone" (John 8:7). There is a new need to cry for help to the Lord who "for our sakes was made sin though he knew no sin" (2 Cor 5:21).

Parallel Lines?
In dealing with the various fires and conflagrations that have been associated with this particular aspect of the living of virginity, there are two topics of concern that seem to be moving on parallel lines and that do not manage to meet. On the one hand, there has been a lot of arguing that the church has been damaged throughout history by negative attitudes regarding the human body and sexuality. Some would dismiss St. Paul's apparent dualism according to which he classified some parts of the body as noble parts and some as less noble parts (1 Cor 12:22ff). Some talk of the liberation we have experienced in recent decades by coming to see the goodness and beauty of human sexuality and they rejoice in the fact that the church has had her eyes opened, and has been teaching an increasingly positive attitude to sexuality and marriage. In the same perspective, there have been calls for a rethinking of the church's various injunctions and statements of "thou shalt not" in topics that concern human conception and the bringing to full term of life already conceived. There have been growing liberal trends with regard to such topics as one's sexual orientation, premarital sexual relationships and divorce and remarriage. There have been calls for tolerance and for the removal of any limits on how far we are entitled to go in such areas as human cloning and genetic engineering. Many have rejoiced that we are outgrowing a lot of sexual taboos inherited from less enlightened days. A result of all of this is that we have been experiencing what has been called the death of outrage, an atmosphere in which everything goes. What would have caused massive public expressions of offense and shock until quite recently would now cause less than the raising of eyebrows. The much publicized deviations from accepted moral standards of various prominent people in church and state have brought about a turning on its head of what St. Ignatius said about the saints: "These men can do it; these women can do it; why can't I do it?"

Even in the context of liberalizing trends like these, people express great shock and outrage at the news of the sexual abuse of young people, especially when the abuse is perpetrated by people in positions of great trust. They are right to express this shock and outrage. There is something exceptionally monstrous about the abuse of innocence. And still one wonders whether we have here been experiencing a kind of selective outrage. At the very same time when we have been hearing of adults who have abused the trust placed in them, there are reports of widespread sexual misdemeanors by young people. Arguably, these misdemeanors are as monstrous and as much destroyers of innocence as those that have been in the public news under the heading of abuse. What one hopes and prays for is that all the forms of the destruction of innocence will in the future be given equal attention. Certainly, there is an urgent need for new forms of exorcising all the evil spirits, personal and impersonal, that are destroyers of innocence.

In all the maelstrom that has been generated by recent discussions about what constitutes the use or abuse of human sexuality, one thing is becoming clear. What is at issue is not a search for an understanding of celibacy. Rather, the question at issue is what constitutes human and Christian chastity. Chastity is the regulating of sexuality. To this everybody is called. Virginity and celibacy are particular Christian expressions of chastity. They will not make any sense for the new generation unless they are placed in the setting of wonder at and respect for every human body, in all its fragilities and strengths, from conception to death. For the Christian, the human body is "something more exquisite still." It is nothing less than the temple of God. But, as we advance in knowledge, we are learning more and more that the stones that make up the temple of the body are taken from the whole of creation. We are learning how profound was the insight of St. Gregory the Great when he gave the reason why Jesus told his apostles to preach the good news not just to human beings but to the whole of creation. Each of us has the whole of creation in us, said St. Gregory. We have existence in common with the stones, life in common with the plants, feeling in common with the animals, intelligence in common with the angels. Today we are seeing more clearly what constitutes the stone in us, what constitutes the plant in us, what constitutes the animal in us, and what constitutes the angel in us. It is in the efforts to coordinate and regulate these four that the ongoing struggle with original sin resides. The struggle calls for continual movement on the ladder from earth to heaven and back. It gives rise to many moments of light as well as to various dark nights of the senses and of the spirit.

Shocks and Thrills
In our ongoing discovery of what we are and who we are, we experience many a shock and many a thrill. We may well wonder why God was so odd as to make such fragile yet fascinating images of the divine nature and to dwell in the fragile temples that are our bodies. In our shock as we experience our fragility, and in our amazement as we discover our resources, we will hopefully get new perspectives on what constitutes human chastity and Christian chastity. We will learn that we become chaste not by denying our affinity with the stones, the plants, the other animals, the angels, but by the kind of order that will do justice to all four. Nearly a hundred years ago, James Joyce wrote to his younger brother who had been shocked by a novel he had been reading. He told him that if he reached down a bucket into his own soul's depths, sexual department, he would draw up elements of such innocent people as St. Aloysius Gonzaga and elements of far less innocent people. He could have widened his range of search for the filling of the bucket. He needn't have limited the search to the sexual department.

With the help of the insights of people like St. Gregory and James Joyce, we can all reach down the bucket into our soul's depths. Nothing of what we find should surprise us or shock us. When we try to put all the pieces together, we should, instead of saying "how odd of God," lift our hearts and voices in praise of the God who is so loving as to enjoy being at home in us. In this lifting up of our hearts and voices, we discover the motivation for being chaste. This will require no denials, no repressions, no suppressions. What it will require is a continual cleansing of the temple and a re-ordering of our house as we give hospitality to so great a guest. In the process, we discover that celibacy is one loving expression of chastity. As we reach down into our depths, we think of the Lord who revealed himself when a woman talked of reaching a bucket into a well that was deep and who talked to her of a new temple that was coming into being. We remember that the same Lord revealed himself in the image of the fire which he came to cast on the earth (Luke 12:49). True chastity and true celibacy help us to fan the flames of that fire in the temples that are bodies of flesh.

A Higher State?
Christian chastity and Christian celibacy should not be afraid to
name all the elements that come to the surface when we reach
down the bucket. They do not call for a rejection of anything that
is human. As Christians, we are called to be builders. We are
called to build a worthy temple, a worthy dwelling place for the
Lord who has said that he is standing at the door, knocking and
inviting us to open the door to him (Rev 3:20). This opening of
the door requires that we evaluate all our urges, all our desires
in terms of what is worthy of our loving guest. It calls for a continual willingness to lose our lives in order to save them (Matt
10:39). It requires that we ask how our every human urge, including every sexual urge, can help us to love ourselves, to love
others, to love God. On the way we are helped by the experience
of chaste and celibate people who come across to us as being
truly human and truly loving.

In this context it is worthwhile raising the sensitive question
as to whether the living of the virginal life for the sake of the
kingdom of heaven is a higher state than the state of Christian
marriage. Many people today are surprised to learn that the
church has, in fact, given us an unambiguous teaching on this
topic. At the Council of Trent, it was clearly stated that the virginal state is, in fact, higher. The teaching is highly unacceptable
to many modern Christian ears, so unacceptable that the statement in the post-synodal document on the Consecrated Life
(1996) about the "objective superiority" of the way of life of
those consecrated by virginity and celibacy, poverty and obedience caused a good deal of unease. People are rightly sensitive
to the suggestion that one state of life is automatically higher
than another. It would, to say the least of it, be arrogant of me to
say to my married relative, "I am in a higher state than you."
And still there is something important in the church's teaching,
at Trent and elsewhere, that virginity is a higher state. The
wording of the teaching is highly conditioned historically. It has
given rise to a lot of misunderstanding in a way that has led
many church teachers to avoid not merely the wording but the
teaching it was intended to express. Indeed, I suspect that many
church teachers are embarrassed by both wording and teaching
and they wish that they would simply go away. But the teaching
is an expression of a central gospel teaching. For this reason, it
needs to be resituated, reinterpreted, reworded. Christian celibacy

cannot be separated from Christian poverty and Christian obedience. The celibate, poor and obedient example of Jesus Christ gives that way of life a unique and privileged place among the ways of following him. It is also a reminder that chastity, poverty and obedience are, in various ways, to be expressed in the life of every baptized person. This does not in any way imply that those in one form of discipleship are automatically better and holier than those in another. In the following of Christ, there is no place for any "holier than thou" attitude. There is no place for a see-saw in which I go up and you go down.

If I decide to live a virginal life for the sake of the kingdom of heaven, it is not because I am not the marrying type. That would be an entirely inadequate motive. Worse again if my decision were motivated by a poor view of married life. The most wholesome commitment to virginity is made by the person who says, "I would love to marry but I will happily make the sacrifice out of love for the Lord who loved the church, his bride, and gave himself up for her" (Eph 5:25). Virginity is a form of loving martyrdom. It is a strong expression of the teaching of Jesus that nobody has greater love than those who lay down their lives for their friends (John 15:13). Whatever way one interprets the saying of Jesus about those who make themselves eunuchs for the sake of the kingdom (Matt 19:12), there can be no denying that it suggests martyrdom in the area of human sexuality. It is radical in the sense that it touches gospel roots and human roots. At a time of much controversy about clerical celibacy, one would hope that the draw and attraction of the celibate sacrifice will be clearly seen to be a draw toward love, not a draw away from love. In the recent researches into the complex history of clerical celibacy, there is a realization that, rather than being simply a matter of church law, the emergence of celibate priesthood is best situated in the radical invitation of Jesus to put the call of the kingdom of God before all family ties. But in the renewal of priesthood today there is no place for complacency or contentment in the status quo in anything that concerns the topic of celibacy. There is need of much soul-searching. Celibacy needs new fires, new apologists, new prophets, new exemplars, new fanning into a flame. We are beginning to see more clearly that celibacy is only for those to whom it is given (cf. Matt 19:11). We need better discernment as to whom it is given and to how, once given, it can be better nurtured.

The Why and the Wherefore

There is no denying that in recent times there has been a weakening in confidence in what the celibate way of life has to offer. Only the highest motivation can keep the flame of celibacy burning. This motivation is sharpened the more we are aware that the Christian, simultaneously, has a dual citizenship, one of the earthly city that is not lasting and the other of the resurrection city that lasts. Cardinal Danneels of Belgium somehow manages to come to the heart of the matter. Celibacy, he says, is an issue of love and love cannot be explained or reasoned. The only motivation of celibacy, he continues, is being faithful to the total imitation of Christ. Just as, in the famous words of a novel on the rose, the why and the wherefore of the rose is the rose, the why and the wherefore of celibate love for Christ is celibate love for Christ. I am and remain celibate because I love to keep following the celibate Christ. This, the Cardinal admits, points to a difficult and daunting agenda, because celibacy requires many supports. It needs, for example, to take advantage of the collective wisdom of such people as psychologists and psychiatrists. It needs the supports of community. A celibate person who says, "I do not need community," is expressing a contradiction of what it means to belong to the body of Christ in which virginity is only one charism. It is interesting that, at the European Synod in 1999, the Cardinal called for a stronger witness to our belief in the resurrection of the body. One way he saw of achieving this was through the consecrated virginity of men and women who look beyond the corruptibility of the body to what is incorruptible.

Bringing Fire

There are strong connections between the charism of virginal love and the fire that Jesus came to bring to the earth (Luke 12:49).The fire was the fire of judgment but it was transformed into a fire of love when Jesus lovingly underwent the cross. When Hans Urs von Balthasar asked, "Dare we hope that all will be saved?" he did not state that all will be saved but he expressed a deep hope that, in the working out of the providence of the God of love, all will finally reach salvation. But he insisted that, while we cherish that hope, the whole universe is under the judgment of the God of love. In wondering how God's judgment will take effect, each of us has to make the free and crucial decision as to how we will relate to the great fire that Jesus came to bring to the earth.

Around the Campfire

The Australian aboriginal people have a number of beautiful images to express what it is to belong. One of these is the invitation to come near to the campfire. It is a striking image of the continual invitation to Christians to keep warming themselves at the fire of divine love that is Father, Son and Spirit. The sparks of life that are given to us at baptism are always in need of being fanned into a full flame. It has been said of St. John of the Cross that he was declared a doctor of the church more for his poetry than for his prose. Two of his great poems, "The Living Flame of Love" and "On a Dark Night," are both a key to all his writing and a summary of that to which he is inviting us. The flame of God's love is always active, always bringing light, love and meaning into all the areas of darkness in every human life. All followers of Christ become consecrated temples at baptism. Some get a new consecration by ordination, some in religious life. Some are single by choice, some by circumstances, and not all single people would wish to be called celibate. To all is given the call to let the fire of God's love burn and to keep starting new fires that will enrich the house of God, which is the church, for the sake of the whole human family as it prepares for the final examination which will be on love alone.

CHAPTER 9

Have a Heart

There's a lovely line in the Bible which indicates that when you and I look at each other we see only as far as the face, but that the look of God goes right into our hearts (1 Sam 16:7). The nearest I ever got to seeing into a human heart was when I was helping as a chaplain in a hospital in London. One morning, the matron asked me if I would like to be present at an operation. I was surprised. I was more surprised when she told me that it was to be a heart operation, by the most famous heart surgeon in England. I told her I did not like the sight of blood but that I might manage to watch for about ten minutes. In fact, I ended up being so fascinated that I stayed for the entire operation. I assure you that the heart didn't look nearly as pretty as it does on Valentine cards. I saw a precious but rather unattractive muscle surrounded by all kinds of veins and arteries. But I was very proud to be like God, looking into a human heart.

The trouble is that God sees far beyond the muscles, the arteries, and the veins. God sees right into

the thoughts that are going on in our hearts,

the plans we are making in our hearts,

the memories that are stored in our hearts, and

the meeting points of all of these.

The most perfect heart that ever existed was the heart of Jesus Christ.

• As followers of Jesus Christ, we have a special love for that heart.

• Whatever our theological sophistication, there are times when we are moved to pray before the picture or the statue of the Sacred Heart.

• We recognize it as a heart in which thoughts and memories coalesce into love.

And still it is a fact that Jesus spoke the hardest words ever spoken about the human heart. He said (Mark 7:21) that out of the human heart come all kinds of evil intentions:

fornication
stealing
murder
adultery
avarice
malice
deceiving others
being indecent
being jealous
slandering others
being proud
behaving in foolish ways.

And he said that all these make a person unclean, dirty.

I had often wondered if Jesus was exaggerating when he said such hard things about what goes on in our hearts. For many years, I thought he was. But I changed my mind when I spent a few years helping as a chaplain in a prison. My assignment was to visit the Catholic prisoners one day a week. As I came to know them, I found they were all good men, decent men. None of them made any secret at all about why they were in prison. What they told me was in no way confidential. They shared it openly with both fellow-prisoners and staff:

Some said they were there for stealing.
Some said murder.
Some said fraud and deceit about signing documents.
Some said sexual activity with people who were unwilling.
Some said malicious harm to another person's character.

When we talked further, they often said openly that they had acted out of pride, or jealousy, or a desire to make quick money. For reasons like this, they deceived other people and did foolish things which they later regretted. After a short number of weeks, I had heard the full list of all the bad things that Our Lord described as happening in the human heart. Then I knew that he was not exaggerating. And all these evil things are not confined to prisoners. The same kinds of things are happening in human hearts every day, everywhere. And did you notice that nearly all the sins listed by Jesus concern not just ourselves but the ways we deal with other people? That is why a regular examination of conscience is seen as an integral part of true Christian living. But the news is good: God keeps forgiving us with the prodigality of the prodigal father.

When God Looks In

When God the Father looks into your heart and mine, what does he see? We know what he saw when he looked into the heart of Jesus Christ while he lived on our earth.

- He saw a heart that was the perfect icon of his own heart.
- He saw a heart full of love. He was able to say, "This is my beloved Son in whom I am well pleased" (Matt 3:17).
- He saw a heart full of forgiveness for those who had hurt and offended him.
- He saw a gentle and humble heart, so much so that Jesus was able to say "Learn of me, for I am gentle and humble of heart" (Matt 11:29).

When God the Father looks into your heart and mine, does he see hearts like the heart of his beloved Son? The challenge to us as we examine our consciences is to see whether we recognize in our lives any of the thoughts, any of the plans, any of the memories that make the heart unclean and that make us damaged icons.

During the First World War, the devout Irish priest, Fr. Willie Doyle, SJ, was working with the forces in Flanders. One night, as he walked along the beach, he felt very close to God and to God's love. He prayed to Our Lord and said, "Lord, pour into my cold heart something of the infinite love that is in your heart." As the Lord answered his prayer, he experienced a flow of love coming into his heart. This flow is being continually offered to all of us through the Holy Spirit whom the Father gives to us (Rom 5:5). Only the love that God keeps pouring into our hearts can drive out the unclean things that are going on in our hearts. This is the meaning of the sacrament of reconciliation and forgiveness. In it we experience the need of a new heart and a new spirit. When it is well celebrated, we look out for whatever is weighing down our hearts. In an invitation to be ready for his coming, Jesus named three ways in which the heart can be weighed down (Luke 21:34). They are dissipation, drunkenness and the worries of life. All the classic examinations of conscience provide variations on these and related pressures on the heart. When we examine our consciences in the lead-up to the sacrament, we try to see what is weighing us down and diminishing us as human beings now. By any standards, this is an urgent and important task.

A Sacrament in Disarray

In spite of its centrality in a church which, by its foundation charter, is committed to the continual work of loosing people from various kinds of bondage and of forgiving whatever sins weigh down the human heart, the sacrament of reconciliation, which is the sacrament of a change of heart, is in disarray. Before things come right again, we have a lot to learn. This is understandable, since the very word *disciple* suggests one who is constantly learning. Good disciples ask themselves questions and they allow themselves to be asked a number of questions. The key question this time is, "Who is it that forgives?" The answer is that it is God alone. But God wishes us to be bearers and agents of the forgiveness that is divine.

The second question is, "When, how and where does God forgive?" The answer is that God forgives whenever, however and wherever we turn godward with a sincere and repentant heart. We do not have to wait for God's forgiveness until we go to the sacrament of reconciliation. But in the sacrament well celebrated we realize that our most secret sin has somehow damaged the whole body of Christ that is the church community. We go to be reconciled to the community through the ministry of the official representative of the community. The repentance in our hearts when we had earlier returned to God is deepened by the sacrament of reconciliation. The sacrament is made more powerful by the quality of repentance in the hearts of all those confessing. Forgiveness is experienced as a repentant heart speaks to a listening heart and a suitable medicinal penance is proposed. This is the ideal. Apparently, it hasn't been working out well in practice. The crucial question is "Why?" As we try to answer it, we can get many lights from history.

One Forgiveness: Many Forms

Many Catholics have inherited a mentality according to which God's forgiveness is virtually identified with what happens in the sacrament of reconciliation. The reality is that the gift of God's forgiveness and pardon comes to us in forms without number. We experience God's forgiveness when we ourselves

forgive an offending sister or brother from our hearts or when
the word of forgiveness is asked of us by a sister or brother who
has offended us. We experience God's forgiveness in the follow-
up to such moments of grace and we try to make amends and
seek the best forms our relationship can take in the future. We
keep opening ourselves to God's continual forgiveness if we try
to accept the crosses that are built into human living and human
dying and to link them with the living and dying of our Savior.
We open ourselves to the same forgiveness if we keep trying to
open our ears and our eyes to what God is saying to us in the
many ways that God's word comes to us in our daily lives. We
keep opening ourselves to God's forgiveness if we practice the
spiritual and corporal works of mercy. The continual practice of
these presents a beautiful ideal for Christian living. But it must
be admitted that the practice of them often presents penitential
aspects. They can be costly and even painful, but the cost and
the pain are well invested. This is one of the profound messages
of the optional prayer after the words of absolution in the sacrament that we call by the various names of penance, confession
and reconciliation. In this prayer, whatever good we do or evil
we endure is seen as contributing to the forgiveness of sins, an
increase in grace, and the reward of eternal life. More important,
the contrition that starts in our hearts and that is expressed in
our words is seen as linked with the passion of Jesus Christ, and
with the merits of Mary ever virgin and of all the saints.

The forgiveness of God comes to us in many non-sacramental
forms. It also comes to us in more than one sacramental form. As
we say explicitly in the Creed, we confess baptism for the forgiveness of sins. The connection between baptism and the forgiveness of sins is particularly clear in the baptism of an adult.
The adult who turns towards Christ in faith goes down into the
baptismal waters and comes up washed fully clean of all of his
or her sins. But both the person baptized as an infant and the
person baptized as an adult will go through life's journey sinning. Every time they receive the Eucharist, they receive a sacrament of forgiveness. They will confess their sins and they will
hear that Almighty God is being asked to have mercy on them,
forgive them their sins and bring them to everlasting life. As the
Mass progresses and as the once-for-all sacrifice of Christ becomes sacramentally present, they will be reminded that the cup
from which they drink contains the blood shed for them and for

the many, for the forgiveness of sins. The celebration of the Eucharist is the high point of the Christian life. All the energies of the church flow from it and all the church's energies are referred back to it. The other six sacraments share in that energy. All of them are colored by God's forgiveness.

A Special Sacrament of Forgiveness
So where does the sacrament of reconciliation fit into all of this? Is it just one of the countless ways in which God gives us forgiveness and pardon? Is there any cause for real concern in the fact that there is such a falling off in the reception of the sacrament today? In trying to answer questions like these, it is good to keep revisiting the great moments in the story of the sacrament of reconciliation. There can be no doubting the fact that the forgiving of sins was central to the earthly ministry of Jesus. It is also clear that he wished his church to be a community in which sin is recognized and forgiven, a community in which people are continually loosed from whatever bondage comes from life's hurts or from the temporary bindings which the church herself would decide on, in order to make people aware of their sins and of their implications.

There are good reasons to believe that, though we have scanty evidence of how sins were publicly forgiven in the early church, there was a sharp awareness of what we would now call the many non-sacramental ways in which sins were forgiven. The third and fourth centuries saw the introduction of a public penitential system to provide for the forgiveness of the more public sins. Later centuries saw the introduction, largely through the influence of the Celtic church, of private confession, repeated as often as the penitent wished. At first, this was resisted officially but it was to provide the pattern for the sacrament of confession that was to be taken for granted and unquestioned up to recent times. But the questioning has come and it is likely to be with us for a long time yet. Let's hope and pray that it will lead to a church with a heart renewed, even if this will require a heart-searching and a heart-surgery at every level.

Three Rites
It could be said that in the 1950s the practice of private, devotional, oft-repeated confession was at its high point. It was promoted and encouraged by Pope Pius XII who did much to prepare the

way for the Second Vatican Council. And still the Council was to call for a renewal of the way in which the sacrament is celebrated. A result of the call was that we now have not one but three rites of penance. The first rite envisages a celebration of the sacrament which is in direct continuity with what obtained before the Council. The second rite envisages a celebration that places much emphasis on the presence and activity of the local Christian community, in which each individual has both been damaged by the sins of the rest of the community and has contributed to the sin of the whole community. Even with this strong community emphasis, it is made clear that each penitent will place his or her sins before the ordained leader of the community. The third rite, or what is called General Confession and Absolution, does not include an individual personal confession of sin. Though there have been many calls for the use of this third rite, church authorities keep insisting that it is for rare and exceptional situations.

A Time of Opportunity

With all the renewing of rites, with all the emphasis on the community aspects of both sinning and being reconciled, with all the emphasis on the calling on the Holy Spirit, it remains evident that all is not well with the sacrament of reconciliation. One thing is clear. As baptized people, we are all called to be makers of the new ways in which the sacrament will be celebrated in the future. To help us make our contribution, a few reminders may be in order.

First, we are called to be attentive to history. Ways of celebrating the sacrament have changed before. The changes sometimes involved a struggle. We are certainly at the time of a new change. As makers of this change, we should not be content to wait for further official instructions.

Second, the way we celebrate the sacrament publicly will be effective to the extent that we recognize the presence of the forgiving God at all the other moments of our lives.

The recent multiple injuries, hurts and scandals in the church cry out for public reconciliation pronounced by the ordained leader who is himself a sinner. The public reconciliation is both the beginning of a process and a high point in a process. It is not an empty, formal ritual of the kind about which the Lord had hard things to say. It is not a guilt-trip. It calls for an atmosphere of intercession and of a heartfelt yearning for healing. It calls for much labor, many pains and many tears on the part of the entire community, not least on the part of the ordained leader.

Third, just as the sacrament and the many other expressions of God's forgiveness need each other, the three new rites need each other. In the celebration of each rite, there is space, even need, for elements from the other two rites. Each is effective to the extent that we are helped toward a real experience of God's forgiveness. The creative and imaginative use of the rites is a way of learning that, though God keeps forgiving in a prodigal way, sin does its damage to both individual and community. This calls urgently for a continual lancing of the many festering hurts that plague the body of Christ today. We always knew that sin damages the community, but what seemed like an academic teaching has become a painfully obvious fact. Drawing on the riches of all three rites and linking them with the lived experience of the local community cannot but purify and purge the body that continually needs the divine physician.

Last and most important, changes in ritual and in ways of celebrating are effective to the extent that they lead to and express a touching of hearts and a changing of hearts, since the place of sin is in the heart and the place of forgiveness is in the heart. This brings us back to what the divine physician, who sees into every human heart, diagnoses as happening in the heart. The good news continues to be that the work of the divine physician goes on and it is he who most dearly wishes to give us a new heart and a new spirit.

As for the First Time

Shortly before he died in 1989, I went to confession to Fr. Robert Nash, SJ, a man who in the course of his long priestly life helped reconcile many people to God. It happened that I was passing by the Jesuit church in Gardiner Street, Dublin, and I felt the urge to pray where the Venerable Matt Talbot often prayed, went to early Mass, received spiritual direction and had his sins forgiven. When I went inside, I saw the light on over Fr. Nash's confessional and I went hurriedly in. It was clear from his words of wisdom that he had picked up my lack of preparation and the half-heartedness of the way I confessed. At the end he said, "For your penance would you say the Angelus this evening and try to say the words as if you had heard the wonderful news for the first time."

Ever since that day, I have often thanked God for such a striking expression of what it is to make one's home in God's word, especially in the reconciling word. The heart of the holy man whose footsteps I set out to retrace was strongly touched by God's grace and he was converted fully to the Lord. To adapt the words of the *Imitation of Christ*, he may not have been able to define compunction but he continually experienced it. I am sure that, every time he confessed his sins and received forgiveness, he spoke and heard the sacramental words as if he were speaking and hearing the good news for the first time. His well-known acts of mortification were, in the spirit of the old Celtic penitentials, like the taking of a medicine that cures.

May the prayers and example of Matt Talbot and of the countless men and women who changed their ways and became as little children (cf. Matt 18:3) help the whole church today to discern what urgent steps we might need to take to journey back into the heart of God. May they help us to see that, though God's forgiveness is a free gift, it is not cheap grace. May they help us to see that it must be freely received into hearts in which a lot of blockages may call for new and radical forms of surgery. May they help us to replace our token penances with penances that are real.

CHAPTER 10

Salvation Revisited

Over fifty years ago, I made a decision about the future shape of my life. I was going to join the Vincentians. I had first heard of the Vincentians nine years earlier when two of them preached a mission in our parish. One was the young, vigorous Fr. Christy; the other was the aging, frail Fr. Bob. In 1945, the Vincentians came to our parish again. This time it was Fr. Johnny who, ahead of his time, told the people about the mother-love of God, and Fr. John, whose bursts of zeal and eloquence were like a fallout from the big bang with which our universe began. And Vincentians like Fr. Paddy and Fr. Tommy were our confessors and retreat directors at the diocesan seminary.

That was my little micro-world. But 1945 saw more important happenings in the bigger world. The *Cork Examiner* and the local radio, both graphically mediated for us by our priest-teachers, told us of the horror of the events of 13–14 February, when Dresden became a charnel-house for 35,000 people made in the image and likeness of God. We remembered enough to compare and contrast with what had happened in Coventry in 1940. When D-Day came in May, even the youngest of us had tasted enough of the war to be able to cry "Thanks be to God!'

By September, I was knocking at the door of the Vincentian novitiate. Before the year officially began on the birthday of Our Lady, September 8, the prospective seminarists, seed-people, had three days of initiation in the form of a retreat. It was directed by the ebullient Fr. Tom, an elderly priest who had guided hundreds of candidates on their way to priesthood. Early on, I decided that he wasn't too scary on topics like sin and its consequences. But he advised us that, in the interests of our eternal salvation, a general confession would be in order. After a day of sizing him up, I decided to take the plunge and tell him all. He was kindness itself and I was amazed that nothing I told him seemed to cause him any surprise. For some years, my last prayer each day had been, "O my God, I know I must die; I do not know when, how or where. But, if I die in the state of mortal sin, my soul will be lost forever. O good Jesus, have mercy on me." I said it with extra fervor that night, but I felt so renewed in grace that I thought it highly unlikely that I could ever die in such a state of loss.

In the course of my first year in seed-land, I learned that CM was short for Congregation of the Mission. I came to realize that the mission in question was the continuation of the movement of mission inaugurated by St. Vincent de Paul when he founded his community of priests and laymen, and that the seeds of this movement were his own experience of hearing the general confession of a man who had become convinced that, had it not been for the coming of St. Vincent into his life, he would have been doomed to eternal loss. In the seminary, we were taught to see the mission of Vincentians as the continuation of the mission of Christ who was missioned by his Father to bring good news to the poor. Our sense of mission was nurtured by conferences, retreats, and various forms of study of the Vincentian tradition. From the start, there was a good deal of emphasis on the five characteristic Vincentian virtues. The first four made a lot of sense to me. I must confess that I found the fifth, zeal for souls, to be far too nebulous as an ideal. I did realize that one day I might hear the confessions of many people who would be very near to the gates of hell. The ideal was helped for a while by the comment of my father when I showed him the community cemetery. "What a lot of souls they must have saved," he said. I'm sure it must have reminded him of his own life's work of saving his hay and saving his crops. But the ideal did not make much of an impact on my daily life in the seminary. Even at ordination time, I cannot say that I was burning with zeal for souls. Though I had my secret preferences, I was ready to go where obedience would lead me.

Truths Necessary

And yet, with the passing of half a century, I can say that I have never been so convinced of the urgent need of preaching the good news of salvation as I am now. In my efforts to put my conviction into words, I have been very much helped by re-reading St. Vincent's conference to his priests and lay men on December 6, 1658, less than two years before his death. In a sense, it was his last will and testament. He read and commented on the opening words of the rule he had given them. He explained the call to gospel perfection. He talked of the lofty call to evangelize the poor. Before going on to highlight the importance of instructing priests and seminarians and to justify the diverse ministries to the poor and the call to missions abroad that had already found a place in the Congregation, he reached what, for me, is the real climax. He stated as something they should well know that there is no salvation for people who do not know the Christian truths necessary to be believed. In this, he said he was following the teaching of St. Augustine, St. Thomas, and others. According to this teaching, a person who does not know what Father, Son and Holy Spirit means, and who knows nothing of "the incarnation and other mysteries" cannot be saved. St. Vincent admitted that some theologians found this teaching too strict, but it is clear that he was out of sympathy with their views, and he reminded his listeners to follow the principle that, in a doubt like this, it is wise to follow the safer opinion. He backed up his exhortation with the assurance that there is nothing in the world that ranks higher than teaching the ignorant the truths necessary for their salvation. He then gave the credit not to himself but to his "Savior, Lord and God" for founding a community for this purpose.

As I re-read this part of the conference, I realized that my own preaching of the gospel hasn't been coming out of such clearly defined parameters. Indeed, I envied St. Vincent his certitudes. He was very clear on what he meant by salvation. It meant the beatific vision of God, for all eternity, in heaven. He was also clear on what he meant by damnation. It meant being condemned for all eternity to all the pain of sense and the pain of loss that comprise hell. In his certitudes, he was heir to a long tradition of colorful preaching that was not afraid to play on people's fears and bring them on conducted tours of hell. It was a preaching laced with apocalyptic imagery from the scriptures, as well as with imagery from poets like Dante, artists like Michelangelo, and the rich, popular story-making that was the common possession of medieval European Christendom. St. Vincent was also heir to all the church teaching that has recently been so well charted for us by Fr. Francis Sullivan in *Salvation Outside the Church?* At the center of this teaching was the conviction that outside the Catholic Church there is no salvation. In telling the story of how this conviction was shaped, Francis

Sullivan highlights the teaching of medieval popes and councils, most notably in the bleak statement of the Council of Florence, in the Decree for the Jacobites, in 1442. The Decree left no place for the salvation of even the best intentioned, the most almsgiving and the most martyrdom-loving of pagans, Jews, heretics and schismatics. Francis Sullivan outlines the influence of some church fathers prior to St. Augustine, and the stark teaching of St. Augustine himself and of his followers. He deals with the questions that arose after the discovery of the New World which shattered the smug assumption that the world was practically co-extensive with Christendom. It was in this setting that theologians began to distinguish clearly between culpable and inculpable unbelief, between explicit and implicit faith in Christ, and between what is necessary for first justification and for final salvation. These distinctions, and new variations on and combinations of them, were developed by Jesuit theologians who drew on the missionary experience of some of their brethren. But any milder teaching on the possibility of salvation for unbelievers had to contend with the more rigorous interpretation of the Council of Florence. It also had to contend with the new phenomenon of John Calvin's doctrine on predestination and the Jansenist variations on the theme that Christ died only for those predestined to be saved.

By the time St. Vincent came on the scene, theology had become heir to all the questions about salvation that had surfaced in the two hundred years that followed the Council of Florence. There were questions about the salvation of the unevangelized and questions about the salvation of the evangelized. In spite of the nuancing which various schools of theology had been giving the expression, the official teaching that outside the Catholic Church there is "no salvation" remained strongly in force. We know of St. Vincent's stance against Jansenism and the arbitrary divine selectivity that it implied. He must have known of the personal agony that his hero St. Francis de Sales endured in his younger years when the topic of predestination was so much in the air. But, even with his own deep convictions about the boundless mercy of God, we can assume that he shared the view of the majority of theologians of his time that most of the human race, whether the gospel has been preached to them or not, are doomed to eternal perdition. And yet he was clear that God's boundless mercy saw to it that no human being is excluded from the divine will to save. How precisely he blended this conviction with his other conviction that all those saved must have some knowledge of the mysteries of the Trinity and the incarnation, it is hard or impossible to work out. As in other areas of his understanding of the mystery of the church, his contribution was not one of speculative theology but one of providing a motivation for the teaching and preaching of the gospel which, following the language of Trent, he saw as the breaking of the bread that saves.

New Horizons
In the three centuries that separated the time of St. Vincent from the last half-century, there was no major development in the church's understanding of salvation and damnation. Only a little over half a century ago, Bishop Poskitt of Leeds used to say that he was clear that all his non-Catholic ancestors and relatives were lost. One could say that the first dawning of a new era in our understanding of both salvation and damnation came with the publication of Pius XII's encyclical on the Mystical Body, in 1943. In itself, there was nothing revolutionary in the encyclical. It taught that only the Roman Catholic Church is the Mystical Body; only Roman Catholics are really members; one can be inculpably outside the membership of the Body; those outside the Body can be related to it "by a certain unconscious desire and wish." The encyclical left many questions unanswered, including some questions which it had itself implicitly raised. Its message about the salvation of non-Catholics became clearer in the furor that surrounded the movement initiated by Fr. Leonard Feeney, SJ. Simply put, his message was that, to be saved, you must live and die in the Roman Catholic Church. In his expounding of that message, he left no room for any shades of gray. The message of the letter of the Holy Office, in 1949, was that, yes indeed, there are shades of gray. The letter named some of these shades and it cited the encyclical on the Mystical Body as its principal authority.

While the teaching of Pius XII provided some glimpse of the shape of things to come, the real Copernican revolution about salvation topics came with the Second Vatican Council. The charter of this revolution could be said to have been the description of the church as the universal sacrament of salvation (e.g., in *Constitution on the Church*, par. 48), the statement that the one church of Christ "subsists in" the Catholic Church (*Constitution on the Church*, par. 8) and the very far-reaching statements in pars. 14, 15, 16. In these, Catholics are described not as the only people who are really members of the church but as those who are "fully incorporated into the church"; catechumens are, by desire, joined to the church; Catholics are joined in many ways to other Christians; those who have not yet received the gospel are related to the church in various ways. The links, the joinings and the relationships in question are spelled out in the *Decree on Ecumenism* which recognized different levels of communion and spoke of other "churches and ecclesial communities" (ch. 3), and in the *Declaration on the Relation of the Church to Non-Christian Religions,* which placed other world religions in a saving perspective in which Catholics had never before seen them. This perspective has continued to widen since the days of the Council. It is within it that Karl Rahner wrote about the "anonymous Christian." Perhaps the best known critique of his position is that provided by Hans Urs von Balthasar, who gives us much of his own positive thinking about salvation in *Dare We Hope that All Will Be Saved?* It is at the end of his assessment of what theologians and popes have been saying about salvation since the Council that Francis Sullivan explicitly states his own conviction that there is nothing in Christian revelation which obliges us to believe that any human person has been or will be condemned to hell, and that, on the contrary, there are good reasons for hoping that all will be saved. He goes on to speak of the "atrocious formulation" which the Council of Florence gave to the doctrine of the necessity of the church for salvation. He describes "no salvation outside the church" as "only one way, and a very imperfect way at that" in which Christians have expressed their belief that God has given the church a necessary part to play in the divine plan to save the world.

A Far Cry

All this seems a far cry from the perspective of St. Vincent in 1658, and from the time when most theologians were convinced that the majority of the human race would end up in eternal perdition. Questions about the salvation of both the evangelized and the unevangelized have been put in a very new setting. The emphasis today is on the effective will to save all by the God who is love. Many theologians wonder whether the God of infinite love could allow anybody to be punished for all eternity. They wonder how one could talk about the complete and ultimate victory of Christ if even a small section of the human race, or indeed even one member of it, could end up in eternal perdition. Even allowing for the crucial importance of human decisions, and their consequences, they wonder whether anybody, believer or unbeliever, can do evil in a way that is definitive. They feel supported by the probings into the workings of the human mind that are taking place in so many disciplines today. They are convinced that, even if eternal loss is a possibility for anybody, it is an unlikely possibility. Their optimism with regard to universal salvation could be said to arise out of their understanding of the nature of God and the nature of human decision-making.

In the meantime, the traditional language about hell is alive and well in the *Catechism of the Catholic Church*. But the catechism is careful not to attempt to tell us who or how many, if any, will be finally lost. Where does all this leave today's priest of the mission? Is there any longer a place for any real fire in his preaching? Even if he has already made the commandment of love the underpinning of all his preaching, is there still a real place in it for hell and damnation? However one answers the details of these questions, I am convinced that there is more need than ever for preaching the reality of all the eternal truths. Even with the new optimism, the mystery of evil remains. The old imagery about the last things speaks as eloquently and as truly as ever. What is called for is a new starting point in our preaching about salvation.

The Ongoing Mystery of Evil

The new optimism about salvation should not close our eyes to the mystery of evil at work in the world. If anything, this mystery has received a whole new poignancy in the last fifty years and in the events that immediately preceded them. The abuse of the poor and of the weak continues unabated. Though our Christian religion is the only one in which God is defined as love, bad things continue to happen to a good universe and to good people as well as bad people. There have been times in recent history, as well as in earlier history, when the God of loving providence seemed to stand idly by in the face of human disaster. The development of doctrine about salvation that has taken place in the last half century provides us with an optimism that should be anything but naïve. In the past, we may have been too facile in our answers as to why the providence of God allows the good to suffer and the wicked to prosper, but we have not yet arrived at an answer that satisfies. It is salutary to remember that the Spirit of the God who is love gave us the New Testament which has many strong things to say about judgment. We know, of course, that Christians believe in a judge whose goodness knows no limits and who shared our human existence and whose will to forgive goes infinitely beyond even seventy times seven times. We also know that, in a way infinitely beyond our understanding, even one little sparrow does not fall to the ground apart from the Father (Matt 10:29). And yet, though we are confident that, in the words of Julian of Norwich's *Showings of Divine Love,* the Lord "shall make everything well," we remain in the dark about many salvation questions. More than ever, we know what it is to identify with the Lord who said "No one knows" (Matt 24:36) and who, instead of answering the question "Will only a few be saved?" said "Strive to enter through the narrow door..." (Luke 13:24).

The Old Symbols Still Speak

In our hope that, somehow, all will eventually be saved, our preaching would be emptied of much of its seriousness and urgency if we were to abandon the scriptural imagery of hell and much of the imagery that has surrounded it in the course of history. I would not now be as sure as our dogma teacher in the early 1950s was that there is "real, corporeal fire" in hell. And, though it may be true that St. Alphonsus learned some of his imagery of judgment and hell as he listened to a Vincentian preacher in Naples, it might be wise for his community and ours to change the uses to which we put that imagery. But both Fr. Michael and the Naples preacher had something important to bequeath to all of us. So had the retreat preacher in James Joyce's *Portrait of the Artist as a Young Man.* The basic symbols of fire, outer darkness, separation, and the undying worm have immediate impact in every culture. We may have learned a lot about human psychology and the diversity of literary forms in which the words of salvation have been transmitted to us, but self-delusion and self-destruction, and the family-destruction and the society-destruction that can flow from them, remain painful realities in our world of monstrous addictions. The people whose eyes become opened to the real process of self-destruction at work in their own lives are quick to acknowledge their personal experience of a death that seems to know no ending. From what they have themselves experienced, they do not see the traditional hell-symbols as an exaggeration. Rather than speculate on how many might end up in hell, they can say to us, "Hell is something that has been happening to me; it is happening to me; it could continue to happen to me." This is true whether we talk of "suffering the loss of your own soul" or "forfeiting your life" (Matt 16:26). The destruction does not stop with individuals or with families. We have experienced infernos like Dresden and Rwanda. In each, we got a glimpse of the seemingly endless consequences of bad human choices and bad human decisions. The preacher of the good news does not have to invent any new infernos. In a spirit of faith and hope and love, he helps people to recognize God's hand saving them in the ones that already exist.

It is the same hand of God that helps us through all life's purgatories. While we might have problems today about the likelihood of an eternal hell, the continuing purgatorial nature of human existence makes more and more sense. For long, Catholics were defensive about the doctrine of purgatory. But that doctrine can be a wonderful context for seeing all of life's purgations and purifications. The active and passive purgations of which St. John of the Cross wrote are not just for a small category of holy people. They describe the experience of all of us in our continuing need for decontamination. In the Catholic understanding, the purification that can continue after life is the first loving glow of the beatific vision, bringing light into our pockets of darkness. Or one could envisage it as the divine artist putting the finishing touches to the damaged face that was made in his own image, in a way that finally undoes the ravages and cracks that the years have added to the canvas. Maybe the various infernos in human history would be better named as the purgatories of the human family on their journey. In his unchanged decision to make humans out of earth's dust, God sees the need to keep purifying us of our continuing tendencies to revert to what is sub-human and pre-human in the working out of the implications of original sin. The fire of God's love is not a different fire from the fire of purgatory and the fire of hell. However we name the purifications of the human family, they are all expressions of the agony that Christ's body and all that it is drawing to itself must endure till the end of the world, for the salvation of the whole human family and of the whole world. It is significant that visions of hell and of purgatory have a recurring place in the experience of saints and of visionaries. They are all part of an urgent invitation to wholeness rather than a message of ultimate doom. They should not be dismissed lightly as the remains of a more primitive worldview.

A New Starting Point

There is need for a new starting point in our talking about salvation. My own starting point is to envisage the Lord of love who by his paschal mystery is our one Savior, appealing to each of us: "Come, help me to build a new world." This is one way of summarizing one of the clearest messages of the *Constitution on the Church in the Modern World*. The Constitution sees our work as "a prolongation of the work of the Creator" (par. 34). As a consequence, we can be assured that

> when we have spread on earth
> the fruits of our nature and our enterprise—
> human dignity, sisterly and brotherly communion, and
>   freedom—
> ... we will find them once again,
> cleansed this time from the stain of sin,
> illuminated and transfigured. (par. 39)

Since the rise of the new ecumenism, Catholics have been shy about speaking of human activity as an expression of real partnership with God. At the time of the Reformation, there was so much emphasis on human merit and good works that Catholics could easily be accused of thinking that they could somehow add to or improve on the work of our one Savior. The Reformers' emphasis on "Christ alone," "faith alone," and "grace alone" provided a salutary corrective. But we can now see more clearly that both Catholics and Protestants inherited a common tradition in which Christians saw themselves as fellow-workers with God. Christians are called to be partners in a "wonderful exchange" in which we come to share in the divinity of Christ who shared in our humanity. They should be at ease both with Our Lord's statement that "apart from me you can do nothing" (John 15:5) and with his loving assurance that "the one who believes in me ... will do greater works than these" (John 14:12). In my seminary days we asked, "If humans had not sinned, would the Son of God have become incarnate?" We were told then that, though a few theologians like Scotus and a few saints like St. Francis de Sales had thought yes, the majority view, led by Aquinas, was "No sin, no incarnation." In the worldview that people like Teilhard de Chardin have helped to image for us, there would appear to be a certain inevitability about incarnation, as God's ever-creative action moves from alpha point to omega point. In this incarnational worldview, no work of God is yet completed. Though the once-for-all saving action of Jesus Christ has taken place, its effects must seep into every human being and into the whole of creation, until the end of time. A result is that what the innocent abroad said on seeing the Grand Canyon is true of everything in creation: "It should be beautiful when it's finished!" The incarnation is a call to all of us to a partnership in finishing God's work. God made the first creation without the help of a partner. But God wishes to involve all of us as partners in shaping the new creation. The gardener who, on being praised by the priest and told that it is wonderful what God and man can do when they work together, replied, "You should have seen the place when God was on his own," spoke a word of incarnational wisdom.

Jesus came to inaugurate the new creation. He preached the imminent coming of the kingdom of God. He described the kind of attitudes and relationships that God wanted in the kingdom. In his own ministry and miracles, people both heard and saw the coming of the kingdom: "The blind receive their sight...the poor have the good news brought to them" (Matt 11:4, 5). It is clear that he wished his disciples to continue and help to complete this work. His decision to involve all of us has many profound implications:

First, even though it is God and God alone who can make the kingdom come, we are all invited to be cooperators with God in a way that does full justice to both God's sovereignty and human freedom.

Second, we have to find continually new ways of imaging heaven. It will not be just seeing God in a kind of monochrome way. Heaven will be a whole set of renewed relationships with each other and with a transformed universe, all pervaded by the glory of the God who is love, in a way that is the full flowering of everything Jesus said about the kingdom. It will be a *nunc stans,* a standing now, but it will also be that continued ecstasy which is the standing outside of time and of our self-centered interests, in a way that will make us fully and consciously present to the God of love, to ourselves, and to the whole renewed creation.

Third, every decision, every prayer, every action that each of us will have performed on this earth will be part of the new creation. Heaven will be a richer place as a result of each of our efforts. Each of us will recognize our own part in the making of heaven and others will recognize it too. Far from being a reason for self-glorification, the recognition of our own parts will be a reason for saying to the God of love "How great thou art." Fr. John K., who taught us philosophy, used to tell of the Persian potentate who said he would reward the visiting orchestra by giving each member an ornament of gold the size and shape of the instrument he was playing. The pessimist who was the piccolo player complained afterwards, "There was I with my little piccolo!" In heaven, he will see that his contribution cannot be measured in gold. In the same setting, the widow's mite will be part of the eternal treasury. The cup of cold water will be part of the torrents of delight.

Fourth, perhaps the most helpful images of salvation are provided by the gospel parables and stories that speak of seed sown, trees growing and bearing fruit, harvests ripening, good measure, pressed down, running over. Christianity is in many senses a seminal religion, in which every little good deed is a little seed. As Jesus himself taught us, there is no more lovely image of salvation than the language of the good farmer who spends his life saving. He may not know that the basic Greek word for saving means "to make healthy," but his daily program of work is one of making healthy, preserving from destruction, saving.

Fifth, our cooperation with the God of love is in the shaping of a civilization of love. As scientists give us a glimpse of the trajectory of our universe from big bang to final breakdown, we may feel "a stranger and afraid, in a world I never made" (A. E. Housman). But, as we experience the Lord of love, he reassures us and says, "I made it, flaws and all; I entered it anew in the incarnation, life, death, resurrection, and promise of return of my Son; please be his partners in the making of a new heaven and a new earth and in draining the world of the evil and sin which have entered it." This draining can take many forms. It can involve our urgent daily calls to peace-making and justice-making, as agents of the Lord who came in the prophetic tradition and brought good news to the oppressed poor. It can involve the daily work of reconciliation, of the kind so beautifully symbolized not so long ago in the shared building of a golden orb over the restored Frauenkirche in Dresden. In heaven, each of us will be able to say, "I am not a stranger; I am not afraid; I am in the new world which I helped to make." This very world which we are daily helping to make is the one that the Lord will transform at his second coming.

Sixth, though the Lord who saves invites all of the human family, believers and unbelievers, into the making of the new creation, those who constitute his believing church are the "universal sacrament of salvation." These are three words that contain a whole program for the church and that need continual unpacking. They remind us that the church must be always in the business of saving—saving every person and every thing, and thereby being continually the sign and sacrament of Christ the one Savior. As we share in the saving activity of the one Savior, both the parable of the talents and the parable of the eleventh hour workers have a continual message for us. As we keep trying to harmonize the two parables, we realize more keenly that "from everyone to whom much has been given, much will be required" (Luke 12:48), that salvation is both God's gift and our endeavors in response to it. This would be a good setting for a renewed theology of merit.

Finally, St. Irenaeus has left us a great program for Christians by telling us that the glory of God is a human being fully alive and that to be fully alive is to see God. The question for the Christian is not how many of the human race will finally see God, but how many human beings are fully alive now. Each of us is called to be an agent of God in making each other fully alive and keeping each other fully alive. It is not enough for me to aim, in a self-centered way, at "getting to heaven at all costs." Each of us has a precious part to play in the making of heaven, for others as well as for ourselves. If heaven is beatific vision, the visibility there will be improved as a result of the good that each of us will have done on earth. This good we do as members of the "whole body, joined and knit together..." (Eph 4:16). To be an inactive member of the body is the one tragedy for the Christian. To help motivate people to be fully alive is the work of all evangelizers. It is a work that needs a lot of new fire.

In Focus

St. Vincent de Paul shared the limitations of his contemporaries in his understanding of many of the details of salvation. But his overall vision of the source and purpose of salvation was profoundly in focus. He could not even begin to speak of salvation except in the context of the Trinity and the incarnation. Recent explorings of the mystery of Father, Son, and Spirit and of the mystery of God incarnate indicate that without them nothing else in our religion makes sense. The Trinity is the mystery of persons in relationships of knowing and loving, in ways that are infinitely creative and fruitful. The incarnation draws us into that mystery in ways that we could not have dreamt of. As today's preacher motivates people to be partners in the paschal mystery, there is a continual need for confessing the sins that keep us and others from seeing God. There is a place for good preaching of both personal responsibility and of God's continuing judgment. There is a place for my way and your way. In the preaching of the good news of salvation, there is a place for many ways of telling people that it is time for them to wake from sleep: the mother language of Fr. Johnny, the blaze of Fr. John, the youthful vigor of Fr. Christy, the autumn gentleness of Fr. Bob. As each of us comes to recognize what should be our distinctive contribution to the final showing of divine love, we will learn to say "Not to us, O Lord, not to us but to your name give glory" (Ps 115:1). We move from a cry of fear of being lost to a cry of joy that we are asked to be carriers of God's glory.

CHAPTER 11

Church of a Sacrificing God

When I was a boy at school, we had a teacher who was in love with the English language. This love took many forms. He would stop suddenly in the middle of class and ask us what was the most beautiful word we had heard in the course of the previous week. He gave each of us time to answer, and nobody was ever wrong. More difficult were the days when he asked us what was the most disturbing word that had come our way over the week. At this stage of my life, I cannot remember any of the words that featured on either our beautiful lists or on our disturbing lists. In the meantime, I learned many new words. A lot of them are gospel words. In the light of the lessons I have learned in the school of life, what words would feature high on my two lists now?

On the beautiful list, the word *gift* would rank very high, as would the very many related words that express giving and receiving. Up until a short time ago, the words that expressed sacrifice and sacrificing would have been high on my disturbing list. This is very strange indeed, since the two sets of words are very closely related. A few years ago, I had, in fact, reason to do quite a lot of homework on the meaning of sacrifice. I came to the conclusion that a sacrifice is, above all else, a gift to God, the source and resourcer of all gifts. And still, I continued to regard the language of sacrifice as chilling and disturbing. Did this come from the bleak and negative atmosphere that had surrounded the word since my childhood days? Or had I been totally converted to the values of our consumerist culture, in an age that Frances Young, the lecturer in Birmingham who has brought much light to the meaning of sacrifice, calls the age of self-sufficiency?

God Started It
And then I had my eureka moment, the moment in which I said "This makes sense!" I picked up a new book called *The Power of*

Sacrifice. It is by the Scottish theologian Ian Bradley, a man in the Reformation tradition who draws often on the Catholic tradition. He turned much of my thinking upside down, inside out. For years, I had taken it for granted that sacrifice is what we feel the urge to do as we look toward the all-holy God. As I read and re-read the new book, I became convinced that sacrifice is primarily what God desires to do when God looks lovingly toward us. In the book, I was introduced to God the sacrificer. I soon found myself redefining all my sacrificial words. I looked again at the somber language of propitiation and expiation. I got a new understanding of the exemplary nature of the sacrifice of Christ. As I did so, I became less and less happy with any suggestion of an angry God who needs to be appeased and placated. But I also realized that many vestiges of that language are alive and well. I got a whole new appreciation of Julian of Norwich's *Showings of Divine Love,* in which, though she is not afraid to describe God in terms of human feelings, she is quite clear that the God of love cannot be really angry. I came to interpret the language of expiation not as our fussy attempts to be at peace with God but, rather, as our loving attempt to respond to a loving God who always takes the initiative in the work of reconciling us. In trying to understand the exemplary nature of Christ's sacrifice, I recalled that Christ is the exemplary cause of the whole of creation. Since he is God's own image, all things were created "through him and for him" (Col 1:15, 16). The incarnate Christ somehow carried out in time what the Father had been doing from the beginning of creation, and indeed, from all eternity. He had received an example from his Father. He, in turn, set us an example that we should do as he did (John 13:15). The example of both Father and Son provides the example and pattern for all human behavior.

The book gave me new help to look for the key to the meaning of sacrifice, not so much in the controversial words of the Reformation, though these were biblical words, but rather in the elementary but infinitely rich language of gift and giver, a language which is at the heart of the Christian good news. In all instances, the initiative of giving comes from God. Very often, this is, on God's part, a costly giving. God's costly giving motivates us to give back at any cost and to be further enriched at the source from which all gifts come. It is in this heart-to-heart giving between us and God that genuine sacrifice resides. It is here that Ian Bradley invites us to tread ever so lightly and reverently as we ask whether it makes sense to talk of God as one who personally experiences pain. His own conviction is that yes, it does make sense. For him, speaking of God in this way throws light on many of life's dark questions. I believe that, though he leaves many questions unanswered, he remains securely within the bounds of Christian orthodoxy. His language about a sacrificing God is, in the very best sense, provocative.

• He talks of the God who, by creating, decided to be somehow dependent on creatures.

• He finds some aspects of the sacrificing God reflected in the inner workings of the created universe.

• He talks of the divine self-giving that is costly.

• He talks of the God who, in order to share fully in our condition, freely shares some of the limitations of humans and of other creatures.

• He talks of the God who keeps descending into the world of his creatures so that we might ascend into the world of the creator.

• He seems to be in sympathy with the controversial writings of Jürgen Moltmann who has written about *The Crucified God*, though he prefers to speak of death in God rather than of the pain of God. In general, he seems more at home in the language of Moltmann than in the language of Edward Schillebeeckx, who prefers to speak of God entering compassionately into all our pain and dying without personally experiencing either pain or dying.

• He keeps introducing us to the language of the life that comes through death and that flows from the inner nature of God and is the basis for all self-giving love, all self-emptying, all Christian sacrificing, all Christian service.

Giving and Giving Away
All this is very heady language indeed and one cannot but wonder whether we are left with a big amiable God who is ultimately powerless to help us. One may also wonder whether this is the new face of an old heretical movement. The movement in question was called "Patri-passianism." In essence, it maintained that just as the Son of God suffered and died, the Father too is, in some sense, a suffering and dying God. The author of the new book is keenly aware that he leaves himself open to be charged

with a new form of the old movement. But the charge does not stop him from searching reverently for a new yet orthodox language to deal with a question that bothers many people today and bothered people like St. Augustine in years past: "Either God cannot prevent evil or he doesn't wish to; if he cannot he is not all powerful; if he does not wish to he is not all good." Ian Bradley is clearly unhappy at the thought of a God who stands idly by and refuses to lift a finger to help those who are suffering. He finds something off-putting about a God who is totally impassible. He is searching for a language that will image God as freely suspending aspects of the divine omnipotence in order to enter more fully into the depths of our human pain and death. He is unhappy about those who dismiss a lot of the finest biblical language about the feelings of God as being merely "anthropomorphic." He revisits much of the language of the Bible and of Christian theology in order to describe the God who, on every level, keeps giving and keeps giving away. If God the Son emptied himself, became obedient, and became like us in all things except sin (Heb 4:15), perhaps he was giving flesh to what had somehow been going on in God the Father all the time. The surest way we can find out what God the Father is really like is to look at the face and actions of God's Word made flesh.

God's giving and giving-away are at the heart of all God's sacrificing. There is a wonderful richness in the biblical language about giving. The very same word is used:

- to describe God so loving the world as to give his only Son (John 3:16);
- to describe the fact that God did not spare the beloved Son, but gave him up for us all (Rom 8:32);
- to describe the fact that, at the Last Supper, Jesus gave his body and blood (Matt 26:26, 27), in anticipation of the giving and outpouring that were to be his sacrifice on Calvary;
- to describe the action by which Paul gave over to the Corinthians the message of salvation which he himself had been given by the Lord (1 Cor 11:23); and
- to describe the action by which Judas gave Jesus over to his enemies in an act of betrayal (Matt 26:48).

Some of these givings are strange bedfellows indeed. It would be hard, for example, to see anything in common between the betrayal by Judas and the handing-over which is at the center of the Last Supper. But even the best of human giving can go sadly wrong. This is surely what sinning is about. Only the giving that is motivated by selfless love ensures that sacrifice is true.

Trinity, Creation, Incarnation
Each of the great source-mysteries of our religion is a mystery of giving:

The generous self-giving of God is at the heart of the mystery of the Trinity itself; this is the great mystery of the loving self-giving of divine persons to divine persons.

The same self-giving is at the heart of the mystery of creation. As we keep revisiting the great symbols of creation that have nourished the imaginations of Jews and Christians over the centuries, we get some light from the creation myths of other religions. Some of these suggest that the creative activity of God involved giving away something of the divine. This mythological language is always in need of correction and refinement, but it provides some pointers to the sacrifice that was involved in God's original work of creation.

This all links up very well with the contemporary emphasis on the Pauline teaching on *kenosis,* about the great act of humiliation by which the Son of God "emptied himself" (Phil 2:7). It would appear that the divine self-emptying did not begin with the incarnation. It had been going on from the beginning. It was expressed in God's initial decision to create. God's self-giving and self-emptying have continued ever since. The world as we know it seems to have begun in the "big bang." It was not an ostentatious bang. There was no created ear to hear it. The coming into existence of our world was the work of the self-effacing God. God's quiet self-giving has been at work throughout each of the ages of the evolving world, as ice age led to stone age and stone age led to iron age, and in all the other ages and sub-ages with which these have been linked. Most of all, it was at work in the emergence of life and the eventual coming of the first human beings.

The Christmas after I read Ian Bradley's book, I was given a copy of the most recent *Guinness Book of Records.* As usual, I found it to be a fascinating book. This time I started with the section that helped me to trace my family tree. I found that, if one were to use the model of the year's calendar as we know it, my ancestors, the first hominids, appeared at 3:35 P.M. on the 31st of

December. My Irish ancestors came at 10:50 P.M. on the same day. I was both fascinated and bewildered as I traced my cousins through the primates and the hominids. I was happy to shake hands, or at least shake eyelids, with the first *homo erectus,* who appeared less than two million years ago. At the end of my reading, I was convinced that the first prize in a book containing such a galaxy of records must go to God the creator. I gave it to the creator God under two headings of imagination and patience. Only human beings are made in the image and likeness of God. Only a self-giving and self-sacrificing God could make us in such a lowly way. Only such a God could wait for billions of years before the earth was ready to produce the first human beings. Only such a God could involve creatures as co-creators. The God revealed in the story of creation is indeed the God of self-giving, the God of self-sacrifice, the self-effacing God, the self-emptying God, the hidden God whose purposeful hand could easily go unnoticed as we study the story of the developing universe.

As I reflected on the story of the human family over the last million or so years, I realized very sharply that it is a story of many falls. But, I was not preoccupied with the event that we normally call the Fall. I re-read the very powerful pages in Julian of Norwich's *Showings*. With breathtaking imagery, she sees the whole history of creation as a series of "falls." For her, the most important falls are not our fallings into sin; rather, the great fall is the falling of God's creative power and love into every pocket of creation, leading to the incarnation which, in the words of Julian's poet-contemporary, was "as dew in April that falls on the grass."

The incarnation was the great act of God's sacrificial self-emptying. The coming of God in human flesh was not noticed by the rest of the human family. Later, the saving of the whole human family in the dying of Jesus was scarcely distinguishable from the deaths of ordinary criminals. The resurrection of Jesus took place when people were asleep. There was no human witness to vouch for the manner of his rising from the tomb. Only a self-emptying, self-sacrificing God could design the salvation of the human race and of the whole of creation in that way.

A Light on Many Questions

A search for the God of sacrifice brings light into some of the darkest questions that keep troubling even the most devout of believers:

It throws light on the many shocking faces of the problem of evil. It helps us when we are tempted to think of God as standing idly by in times of innocent suffering. It helps us to attempt our own answers to the agonizing cries, "Why oh why?" "Where were you, Lord?"

The search for the God of sacrifice helps to make sense of all the active and passive purgations which are so much part of life's journey. The whole of the saving work of Jesus during his earthly life is a story of action and passion. His passion was as salvific as his action. He would take no more saving initiatives after the night on which he was handed over (cf. John 13:30). He had finished the work that his Father had given him to do (John 17:4). Indeed, there are those who say that the gospel was originally a passion story that was later provided with an introduction describing the actions of Jesus that led to his passion. However you look at it, the passion story is an account of what Jesus freely underwent in order to save his people from their sins. What he underwent could have been allowed only by a God who was used to the idea of sacrifice and who refused to make a miraculous intervention to save the beloved Son from what sinful human beings did to him. By all human calculation, it was a strange way of saving the world, but it was the way acceptable to a sacrificing God. The passion of Jesus was to become the model for all the passive purifications which, centuries later, St. John of the Cross was to describe so powerfully in his attempts to outline the journey of all of us to God. In a sense, John of the Cross gives more prominence to these passive purifications than he gives to the active purifications which we initiate and which God initiates. All the purifications, all the purgations, are the working out in us of the spirit of sacrifice which is so dear to the heart of God.

There is a close connection between active and passive purgation and the gospel teaching on endurance. Jesus assures us that it is by enduring that we will take full possession of our lives (cf. Matt 10:22). One recalls that a popular Irish song has a lover saying, "What cannot be cured, love, must be endured, love."

There is, of course, no special Christian virtue in mere endurance. But a wholesome spirit of endurance can help activate in us a whole world of love and compassion that might otherwise lie dormant. This is the theme of a religious book that continues to be popular. Its author is an English Catholic, Mary Craig. It has a simple title: *Blessings*. It is the personal story of a mother of four children. One of them was badly deformed from birth. Before the author's fourth child was born, she had many dark forebodings. They proved to be right. This child, too, was born with severe deformities. The good news is that, as the child grew up, he drew out of Mary, her husband, the other children, and their relatives and neighbors reserves of kindness and compassion they never thought they possessed. In this unfolding of undreamt-of resources, Mary came to recognize the call to holiness. She came to identify with the sentiments of the French novelist Leon Bloy, who was convinced that "there is only one tragedy: not to become a saint." In all of this, I believe that we are touching on the real depths of the meaning of sacrifice. There was a lot of wisdom in the advice of an older Christian generation which taught us to deal with life's setbacks by "offering them up"!

The spirit of sacrifice is the key to the Christian understanding of waiting. Henri Nouwen once wrote a book which he called *The Path of Waiting*. He images God as the one who was never known to be in a hurry. God was ready to wait until the evolving world was ready for the first human beings. In all the divine work of saving, from Abraham to the present day, God has been ready to wait for the free response of human beings, in the promotion of the divine plan of salvation. The great figures of salvation, in turn, were ready to wait for God. This was often a waiting that was costly and bewildering. It was, indeed, a sacrificial waiting. It was a waiting in hope.

Our sacrificing God is the patron of all true donors. A phenomenon of our age is the willingness of people to be donors. There seems to be no end to the number of ways in which people are willing to be life-giving donors. While we lament the disappearance of God from so many areas of public consciousness, we should welcome the divine presence in this movement which is so characteristically divine, so sacrificial. It keeps reminding us of Christ the donor whose gift to us is both costly and priceless. It helps us redefine sacrifice in terms of the loving will to keep on giving at any cost.

It is in the ambience of active and passive purification, of Christian endurance, of Christian waiting, of the will to be donors, that our lives become a living and pleasing sacrifice to God and that our ritual sacrifices continue to take on new meaning. This is why we pray at every Eucharist that our sacrifice may be acceptable. It is significant that the word *sacrifice* literally means making holy, making sacred. It is by entering into the sacrifice of God that we enter into and share the holiness of God. This is indeed our divinization. It is our sharing "in the divinity of Christ, who humbled himself to share in our humanity" (Preparation of the Gifts at the Eucharist).

We have been hearing a lot recently about the advance of secular attitudes and an eclipse of the sense of the holy. However one assesses this, it is becoming very clear that to live the Christian life as a lay person today, to live the call of ordained ministry, to live the "religious life," demands many new and old forms of Christian sacrifice. We have had many calls for renewal on every level of the church. Many of our efforts at renewal have been ineffective. This has brought all of us our share of disillusionment and disappointment. Perhaps the only renewal that will endure will be our renewal in the spirit of Christian sacrifice. In the middle of the last century, a great Christian educationalist, Abbot, later Bishop, B. C. Butler told millions of surprised television viewers that the only purpose of Christian education is to teach people to die. It was a disturbing message, but one difficult to refute. It is good to remember that the only death that saved the human race was the sacrificial death of the one who said, "I am the Way, the Truth, and the Life" (John 14:6).

Sacrifice that Is True
It would be easy to caricature the Christian understanding of sacrifice. It is not an invitation to lie down under unjust and oppressive systems. It is not a statement that Christians should not be involved in human liberation and in the work of justice and peace. It is not a suggestion that Christians should be passive and supine in any oppressive regime. Rather, it is a call to let the events of life, especially the painful ones, draw out of us resources that would be otherwise forever dormant and keep us from becoming the saints that our sacrificing God dearly wishes us to be.

CHAPTER 12

A Church Always Interceding

When I was twelve years old, my mother became suddenly ill. The doctor was very sure that she should be taken to the hospital immediately. I was old enough to realize that the situation was serious. I was mature enough in the faith to decide that this was a time for special prayer. As the word spread, the neighbors began to promise their prayers too. I was determined to storm heaven. I somehow was convinced that my mother's recovery, of which I became more and more confident as my prayers multiplied, would be a feather in my intercessory cap. I said all the prayers that I remembered my mother saying when we prayed the rosary. I made all kinds of promises to God and I entered into many bargainings. I even carved my promises into the bark of an old tree behind our house.

On the third day, a neighbor knocked gently at the door. She had come to break the news. My mother had died. It would be easy for me now to describe how I think I felt for the rest of that day. But it might be a description of how I felt at various stages in the intervening years rather than a true record of what went on then. All I am sure of is that I felt that somebody had let somebody down. I wondered whether I had let my mother down and, in the process, let down the whole family. Had my prayer been only on the surface? I even dared to wonder whether the God to whom we all had been praying so earnestly had somehow let the family down. I did try to banish such unworthy thoughts, but they kept recurring. Indeed, they have recurred off and on in the intervening years. It is one of the reasons why I tend to envy people who say that God always answers their prayers. I listen with amazement when people tell of the times when St. Anthony helped them out by finding what was lost. I am edified when people from devout Marian groups tell of the wonders that Mary does in their own lives and in the lives of those for whom they pray. I am disarmed by the look of complete assurance on the faces of people in some prayer groups. I know instinctively when I am in the presence of the praying *anawim,* the little ones for whom the kingdom of heaven is assured. And still I must honestly say that, in all my Christian and priestly lifetime, I have rarely found myself saying spontaneously, "This is indeed an answer to prayer."

All this in spite of my friendship with and admiration for people like Sr. Briege McKenna. I have read and re-read her *Miracles Do Happen.* I have never doubted the truth of anything she says in the book. But it makes me wonder why I myself have never, but never, been part of any event like the ones she describes. To a recent enquirer who asked me directly "Does she really heal people?" my spontaneous reply was a rather mischievous "She hasn't healed me yet!" This led me to a more reflective statement that I believe God has gifted her in a way that should alert us all to the fact that we are called to be healers to each other in life's many hurts and that we ourselves should be God's answer to the prayers we make for each other.

Mention of Sr. Briege reminds me of Lourdes. I have been there often. Each visit was a time of grace. Both there and at home I have been moved by the stories of many people who, at a time of serious illness or of other shakings of human foundations, have received new strength and new answers to prayer at the healing waters of the grotto. But I have never myself witnessed anything that people would call a cure. I have never been part of the prayer story of anybody who received an extraordinary healing or answering of prayer in Lourdes or through the intercession of those who were there. This is true also of the whole range of prayers of intercession that are part of my story as a priest. On countless occasions I have been asked to pray or say Mass for somebody in special need. I have always said yes and I have carefully carried out the yes, in faith. Yet, while many have thanked me for both the prayers and the Masses and for the blessings that they attribute to them, I keep envying those who have first-hand experience of miracles or prayers obviously answered.

A Communion of Interceders

And still, I have never before been more convinced of the need for and the power of the prayer of petition, and of the prayer of intercession which is one expression of it. Never before have I been more aware of the power of the prayer seed that keeps growing in the night as well as in the day (cf. Mark 4:26ff). In line with the whole church's awareness of herself as a great communion, I am coming more and more to envisage us all as a communion in intercession. I am coming to appreciate the great truth that, though the sacrifice of Jesus has taken place once-for-all, he lives forever to intercede with his Father for us. His sacrifice now takes the form of continual intercession. This is one of the profound messages of the Letter to the Hebrews (7:25). It is a teaching that has many implications for all of us, his body. The unnamed author is telling us that the once-for-all sacrifice of Jesus continues in an uninterrupted way in the holy of holies of heaven. In his days on earth, his sacrifice rose up from the altar of his body (10:5). His whole body, in earth and in heaven, is now drawn into this continuing sacrifice, this continuing intercession. This is why his mother Mary has, from early Christian times, been recognized as an interceder. The early pictorial representations of the woman at prayer, the *orante*, could be looked on as any individual praying person, as the praying church, as Mary interceding. The three meanings fuse into one. Early on, Mary came to be recognized as the great interceder who prays for each of us now and at the hour of our death. The stormy church days around the year 200 tossed up the beautiful "We fly to your patronage...Do not despise our prayers and our petitions..."

Out of a growing appreciation of this great network of mediation grew up all the church's rogation days, all the litanies of the saints, all the novenas, all the prayers of intercession and bidding prayers in the Prayer of the Church and in the celebration of the great sacrament of the Lord's sacrifice. Through this continual succession of prayers of intercession, the Lord keeps pouring gifts on his beloved, not only while they are awake but while they sleep (cf. Ps 127:2). Indeed, the much made request to Mary to pray for us who have recourse to her had its origin in the experience of a young novice who was led to pray while others in her community were asleep. Nothing makes more faith-sense than the intercession of Mary and the saints and that we should seek it and seek it directly. I, for one, am not at ease in going to Mary and the saints by any kind of side path. I much prefer to say "Pray for us" than to say "May they pray for us" or "Lord, may your Mother pray for us." Any talk about comprecation can complicate what should be the spontaneous urge of the believer. The saints, and especially the queen of all saints, are the ones who take the Lord seriously when he says that we ought always to pray and not to lose heart (Luke 18:1), that our prayers are always answered (Luke 11:10), that we should remain in the vine (John 15:4). When people brought to the Lord the sick, the blind, the lame, the maimed, power went out from him and he healed not a select few but all (Luke 6:19). The saints keep bringing us to the Lord in all our brokenness, but they also teach us to go directly to the Lord. Either way, he prays for each of us before his Father as he once prayed for Peter when his faith could have failed (Luke 22:32). He calls by name and by need everyone who comes to him or is brought to him.

Five Qualities
The five qualities of Christian prayer—simplicity, filial trust, joy, humility, the certainty of being loved—which are described so beautifully in the *Catechism of the Catholic Church*, apply most fittingly to the prayer of Jesus himself. A recent book (*Holy Daring*, by John Udris, 1997) shows very effectively how these same qualities were exemplified in the prayer of St. Thérèse. They can also be recognized in the prayer of the many men and women of faith whom we keep meeting in pastoral ministry. One thinks of some zealous members of the Legion of Mary who, with disarming love and fidelity, describe ways in which they keep experiencing the workings of Mary's intercession. One thinks of elderly religious who talk of friends they have made in the communion of saints and who keep sustaining them through the exilic experience that is the lot of so many religious communities today. The examples could be multiplied. The privilege of meeting such men and women of faith who are at home with the God who keeps answering prayer is a continual invitation to many kinds of conversion. It is an invitation to a conversion of mind, of heart, of faith, of one's moral perspectives, of feelings, of attitudes. It also helps us to keep refining our images of God, of God's will, of our learning to recognize the way God answers prayer.

Our Changing Images of God
I still believe in the God who is the unmoved mover and the uncaused cause. But my understanding of God in these terms is

becoming more and more subsumed into my continuing discovery of the "Abba, Father" who has made each of his children in his own image and likeness and who lovingly accompanies each one of us at every stage of our being shaped further into the likeness. The God who is Father of Our Lord Jesus Christ does not let the world and humans fend for themselves. He is the God who likes to start new processes, not the God of closed systems. Though he holds the whole world in his hands, he leaves himself somehow helpless before our free choices, which he respects and encourages. In that sense, he is the God of sacrifice who does not keep rushing in to show that he is in control. Just as the Son emptied himself (Phil 2:7) at every stage of his saving mission, the Father emptied himself by remaining hidden as the great creative plan unfolded.

The sacrifice of his Son was the act of divine emptying that saved the world. In this emptying, our Savior revealed himself as the wounded healer. One recalls the doctor who said that Lady Macbeth needed the divine more than she needed the physician. The truth is that, in the full Christian perspective, she needed the divine physician who has healed us all by his wounds. It was by entering into the holy of holies of heaven with his own blood that he offered the sacrifice that saves us. Is it any wonder that Good Friday became the great intercession day? It is the day on which we celebrate the "loud cry and tears" (Heb 5:7) in which Jesus asked to be saved from death. From one perspective, his cry and his tears had no effect, but it is precisely in them that Jesus was most effectively heard by his Father. In this lies the secret power of all prayer of intercession. The sacrament of the sacrificial intercession of Jesus continues whenever the Eucharist is celebrated. In every Eucharist, we are in living contact with the sacrifice of Christ as Jesus continues now to intercede for us before his Father (Heb 7:25; cf. Rom 8:34). In every Eucharist, we learn through the sacrificing and interceding Christ, as well as with him and in him, in the unity of the Holy Spirit, to keep giving all honor and glory to the God whom Jesus teaches us to address as "Abba, Father." We learn to appreciate the fact that the full life of Father, Son and Spirit is always going on in our own inner depths where they love to make their home and where the Son keeps interceding. His interceding is continually accompanied by the groans and sighs of the interceding Spirit (Rom 8:26, 27).

Our Changing Images of God's Will

As we deepen our prayer of intercession, we get a new under-standing of the closely related topic of the will of God. Many of us were brought up with the idea that every detail of God's will for each of us has been fixed and determined from all eternity. In that perspective, the prayer of petition could present a problem. It could be understood as a kind of attempt to change God's mind. That is why it was all important to add "if it's God's holy will." In the same perspective, the prayer of the poor man in *Fiddler on the Roof* was very real: "Would it change some great eternal plan...?" In line with the same mentality, praying for fine weather could present a problem; it could mean asking God for a change of plan. I recall being told a few years ago by Pádraig, a mature student who had just embarked on a theology course, that his young daughter was ill in the hospital. When I said, "I'll pray for her," he looked somewhat skeptical. It was clear that the God to whom he thought he had recently been in-troduced in theology was too sophisticated for that kind of prayer of petition. His spontaneous reaction prompted me to re-assess my own understanding of what goes on in the mind of God, in my own mind, and in the mind of the petitioner when I promise to pray for the many people who come seeking prayers to support them or their dear ones in various forms of need. It also prompted me to reassess the role of our guardian angels. It helped me to see more clearly that though Christian education should indeed help us to live and to die, God's will for us is not a predetermined plan, that it is an open process that leaves full space and room for all our free decisions, that it is somehow al-ways in the making. It even convinced me that we are co-makers of the will of God for us. It made me appreciate that each of us is in a full-time partnership with God and with each other. It made me realize that when Jesus brought the blood of his sacri-fice into the holy of holies of heaven, the ceiling between earth and heaven was lowered and we all became part of a great earth-heaven network.

This realization was helped as I reflected on how far human communication has come in my lifetime. We have come to take for granted the wonders of the fax, voice-mail, the Internet ...what next? All this provides intimations of the communica-tion that leads us beyond our planet and our cosmos and that teaches us of the heaven that lies about us in our infancy and at every stage of life's journey, enabling us to view the invisible, touch the untouchable, know the unknowable (cf. Francis Thompson, "In no Strange Land"). The marvels of modern communication keep giving us inklings of the fact that we are in a partnership with God and with everything and everybody in God's creation. In the communication system of this vast network there are many kinds of transmission and many transmitters. We will never finish discovering them. We keep getting new intimations of what it is to be divinized, to be partakers in the divinity of Christ who humbled himself to share in our humanity. When we intercede, we are linking up with a great transmission system. We discover not only that without the Lord we can do nothing, but also that he has, in a sense, willed to do nothing without us. In the Christ who dwells in us and divinizes us we have the answer to all prayer of petition. In one sense, every grace is mediated for us through the paschal mystery of Jesus Christ. In another sense, we need no broker; the trinitarian God is at home in us.

Images of an Answering God

As we go deeper into the world of interceding, we find new ways of imaging the ways God answers our prayers. In answering our prayers, God does not change any plans. God changes us. God makes it dawn on us that answering our requests in the way and at the time we make them might damage us rather than help us grow. One recalls Archbishop Bloom's delightful story about the boy who begged God to give him his grandpa's gift of taking out all his teeth and putting them on a plate, going to bed, rising, and replacing the teeth without effort; when his prayer was answered fifty years later, he begged God to take back the gift. I think of the religious community that stormed heaven and earth for vocations to continue their teaching apostolate. No vocations came. Today they are an aging community. The many lay people in whom they have awakened a deep sense of vocation are an answer to their prayer. They recognize the many new people who have come intimately into their community lives as an answer to prayer. They themselves have become great teachers of how to live and how to die.

At the time of her long terminal illness, many must have prayed for the recovery of St. Thérèse. If their prayers had been heard in the ways they had wished, we may never have gotten the gift of a new doctor of the church. In the ways Thérèse dealt with her illness, she showed us some of the connections between suffering, loving and interceding. It is not quite correct to say that God never answers our prayers in the ways that we would wish. Sometimes God answers them quite dramatically and instantaneously as an assurance that all our prayers are heard all the time and that Jesus really meant it when he said "Ask, and it will be given you...everyone who asks receives" (Luke 11:9, 10). Most times, most of us have to wait, in faith and hope, for his way of enabling us to receive, to find, to have the door opened. In the process, he changes and expands our desires. He helps us to move from a one-dimension life to a life of many dimensions. This is one of the lessons we learn from great teachers of prayer like St. Catherine of Siena. She has taught us not so much to ask for individual favors as to grow richer in our desires, so much so that she has been called the doctor of desire. She teaches us to journey from asking for the little things to asking and receiving the greater things. This is what happened to the Confederate soldier who tells us:

I asked for health, that I might do greater things;
I was given infirmity, that I might do better things.
I asked for riches, that I might be happy;
I was given poverty, that I might be wise.
I asked for power, that I might have praise of people;
I was given weakness, that I might feel the need of God.
I asked for all things, that I might enjoy life;
I was given life, that I might enjoy all things.
I got nothing I asked for, but everything I hoped for.
My unspoken prayers were answered.
I am among humans richly blessed.

In the Heart of the Church
St. Thérèse spent a long time searching for words that would describe the depths of her vocation as a follower of Jesus Christ and as a Carmelite sister. Eventually she said, simply and profoundly, that her call was to be love in the heart of the church. There is a sense in which this is the vocation of every Christian, of every religious, of every priest. It is also the vocation of every Christian family, every Christian community, every parish. Every Christian lover is called to be an interceder. The call to be love in the heart of the church is a call to be an interceder in the heart of the church. As a priest, I am called to be an agent of

making the word of God come fully alive in the community in which I am a leader. My relationship to the word is a call to love and a call to intercede. How often have I been approached by people with the request, "Say a prayer, Father, that..." Even by saying a heartfelt yes there and then, I start a movement of intercession that travels like a current through the whole communion of saints and becomes part of the intercession of Jesus before the Father. Our prayer of petition is heard to the extent that we, sometimes painfully, learn to put on fully the mind that Christ showed during his life on earth and that continues in his ongoing intercession. It is heard to the extent to which we identify with what he is thinking, what he is desiring, what his priorities are, and what he is asking his Father.

As I keep reflecting on this continual traffic of Jacob's ladder, I still find myself asking "Who has known the mind of God?" (Rom 11:34). I still find myself asking "Why, oh why?" I still await an answer to the question as to why bad things happen to good people. I still wait for a recognizable answer to many prayers of petition which I have made or of which I have been a part. But I am beginning to think that God did hear my prayer when I cut those words into the tree in 1941. I thank God for the illnesses from which I recovered in the meantime and for those from which I did not recover in the ways I had hoped. In all of them, many prayers were answered. My eyes have been opened to the daily wonders that God is working in our midst, wonders that are as great as the gospel miracles. I look forward more and more to the annual month of Intercession for Priests, led by Sr. Briege and Fr. Kevin. It is a joyful reminder of what all of us are called to be and to do, all the time. I was delighted recently when Pádraig came back to me and said, "My daughter has recovered fully, thank God; and thanks for your prayers." As he came to know the God of theology, he had found anew the God of his childhood prayers, the God in whose house there are many dwelling places (John 14:2) and in whose will there is space for us all. He is, I think, beginning to see that the answer to prayer does not always come in the form of a quick restoration to health. He is learning, I think, that our prayers are answered when we enter more deeply into the mystery of the living, dying and rising of Jesus, and experience the loving kindness of the heart of our God.

CHAPTER 13

Making Our Home in the Lord's Word

A short while ago, a distinguished monk of the Order of St. Benedict gave a public lecture on the monastic ideal. He traced the ideal as it has been expressed and lived throughout the Christian centuries, and he tinted his account with illustrations from his own story. He asked himself out loud whether he regarded his monastery as his home. His answer was "Yes and no," more "no" than "yes." My first reaction was to wonder whether I had before my eyes a real-life gyrovague, a wandering monk, one of the species on which St. Benedict did not look kindly. But, as I listened further, I heard great words of wisdom. Our speaker told us that, in deciding to become a monk, he had left home. Home is a place of siblings, of a father, of a mother. It is the place where one uniquely experiences that kind of family love which, as C. S. Lewis told us, has a coloring all of its own, a coloring that is not identical with any of the other three great loves, friendship, eros and charity, or with any combination of the three. A monastic community in which the abbot presents himself or is seen as a father to a family is bound to run into difficulties. A monastery calefactory room where efforts are continually being made to create the atmosphere of home will also run into difficulties. A vowed community of celibate adults is certainly a unique expression of the assurance of Jesus that those who leave houses or brothers or sisters or father or mother or children for his sake will receive a hundredfold (Matt 19:29), but words would need a lot of nuancing if we were to describe them simply as a family at home.

Houses and Mansions

Our speaker led us on to the exciting and thought-provoking conclusion that his home as a monk is in the word of God. This is how, over the years, he has come to understand the invitation of Jesus to "make my word your home" (John 8:31). When I searched my Bible afterwards, I realized that this invitation describes where a true disciple should "continue." When we take it in conjunction with the other such invitations that have their source in the Lord, we are indeed right in interpreting it in terms of home-making. In the fourth gospel and in the other Johannine writings, the invitations describe the place where true disciples should "remain," should "abide," should "make their abode." Those who believe are invited to make their home

in the Lord's word (1 John 3:15),
in his truth (2 John 1:2),
in his anointing (1 John 2:27),
in his light (1 John 2:10),
in his teaching (2 John 9), and
in his love (John 3:17).

In this way, they are contrasted with unbelievers who make their home in darkness (John 12:46) and in death (1 John 3:14). Believers are enabled to do this work of home-making because it is the desire of the Lord and of his Father to come and make their home with those who are loving disciples (John 14:23). In fact, the Lord is all the time standing at the disciple's door and knocking; as soon as the disciple recognizes the unique voice and opens the door, the Lord comes in and gladly shares a meal (Rev 3:20). This is why the going away of the Lord from his disciples is to be seen in the context of the assurance that "in my Father's house there are many dwelling places." In them, the Lord keeps preparing a place for his disciples (John 14:2). These dwelling places are the "mansions" that have provided a basis for the exalted but intimate teaching of people like St. Teresa of Avila. This teaching is as much about our present experience as it is about our hope of future glory. Is it any wonder that words like *space* and *place* are finding their way back into our spirituality these days?

The monk's question and his answer have implications for every believer in Jesus Christ. To the question "Have you a home on this earth?" the Christian answer is "Yes and no." We say "There is no place like home." There is something special about "the green, green grass of home." We speak of places that are a "home away from home." Even the lights of my home city can be what the poet called "home, sweet home to me." Over the years, the staff at All Hallows College, Dublin, have been dealing with many men whose mission has brought them a long way from home. This was particularly true in the days when "coming home" was an event that, for some of them, took place about every ten years. The implications of this were so shattering that a small number simply decided never to come home. Those who did decide to come sometimes paid us the compliment of saying that All Hallows was home to them. Is it any wonder that the College folk-memory has many stories about home-coming and home-leaving? It is in this setting that Fr. William Purcell, after whom one of the College's buildings has been renamed, wrote an evocative Christmas meditation. One of its most attractive paragraphs begins with, "Christmas is the feast of home."

For the Christian traveler on life's journey there is no simple answer to the question "Where is your home?" The full truth is that "there is no permanent city for us here; we are looking for the one that is yet to be" (Heb 13:14). We all have something in common with Benedict's wandering monks. To draw on the scholastic language that still rings bells with us, *home* is an analogous word, and the primary analogate is the homeland of heaven.

Many Homes; One Home
It was with a view to expanding our understanding of the meaning of home that God's Word became flesh. Nobody has expressed the lovely implications of this as well as did G. K. Chesterton when he described the Christmas stable as the place where God was homeless and all of us are at home. It was in the same wide perspective that he was able to write of the man who decided to travel a very long distance in order to have the thrill of returning and seeing his home for the first time. I have a feeling too that this was part of the reason why the late Christopher Casson so loved a poem by an unknown fourth century Chinese author. It is entitled "Sailing Homeward." As the poet sails in to the place of his home, he gets a whole new perspective on the cliffs, the lake, the sands, the woods, the streams, the trees. All of them are now healing "the pain of a traveler's heart" and, in a lovely blending of images, moving his brush "to write a new song." Not so long ago, I myself had the experience of discovering for the first time the house where I was born and the farm on which I lived for many years. Twelve years back they had been sold to a good neighbor. More than once I found myself saying "I never realized how lovely this place was." More recently still,

I met a lady who had been making a number of attempts to sell her house. Having looked at a number of houses that were up for sale, she seriously considered staying put, in the surprise discovery that her own house was somehow more attractive than any of the others. Is it any wonder that the word *house* is at the hidden Greek root of such words as *economical* and *ecological* and such key church words as *ecumenical, parochial* and *diocesan*? It would appear that, on all levels, the Christian shares in the paradoxes of Jesus who, unlike the foxes who have holes and the birds who have nests, had nowhere to lay his head (Matt 8:20), and was still able to invite people to come and stay in the place where he had his dwelling, the place he presumably called home (John 1:38, 39).

Making a Nest
One of my favorite psalms is the pilgrim song, Psalm 84. As the psalmist gets a first glimpse of the temple in the setting of God's city, he cannot resist breaking into song.

> He is overwhelmed by the loveliness of the place where God dwells;
> already his soul longs and faints with the desire to go right into God's courts.
> He notices that even the sparrow has made herself a home in the temple building and the swallow has made a nest where she can lay her young;
> how much happier, he says, are those who go right up to the altar and live in God's house, forever singing God's praises.
> Indeed, the prospect of coming to dwell in God's house helps all the pilgrims to see all the stages of the journey, including the "bitter valley" stage, in a new perspective;
> as they make their way from height to height, they come to see the God of gods in Zion.
> The happy psalmist is sure that one day in the Lord's courts is better than a thousand elsewhere;
> he would rather be a doorkeeper in the house of his God than to live in the tents of the wicked.

I love to read this beautiful psalm in conjunction with the many Johannine words about making one's abode, abiding, remaining. In particular, there is both a daring and a loving intimacy about the imagery of the sparrow and the swallow. I know that, in some contemporary writings about the psychological aspects of priestly formation and of initiation into religious life, formators are often cautioned to look out for those who are "nesting." Indeed it would appear that, many hundreds of years ago, no less a person than the prophet Isaiah was aware of the fact that there can be an unwholesome kind of nesting. He describes God in terms reminiscent of an activity strongly discouraged in my youth. God, for Isaiah, is a scatterer of birds' nests! God is represented as saying:

> I have abolished the frontiers between peoples, while I have plundered their treasures . . .
> my hand has found, as though a bird's nest, the riches of the peoples;
> like someone collecting deserted eggs, I have collected the whole world;
> while no one has fluttered a wing or opened a beak to squawk. (Isa 10:13, 14).

Here is one of the many instances in the Bible in which God is cast in a strange role. I suppose the truth is that there is a time for building nests and a time for plundering nests, and only God knows the correct time for either. I, for one, would not like to have my nest plundered by God. But I am willing to take the risk of building one. The building, though, must be done in the temple setting. I feel that Jesus, though he had no "nest" for himself (Matt 8:20) would approve of the image.

Men of the Word

At different stages in our lives, we find different ways of describing the role of a priest. For the reasons I have been indicating so far, and for many other reasons, I am more and more coming to describe ordained ministry in terms of making one's home in God's word, and of nestling in God's word. For a long time now, I have believed that a priest can be described, quite simply, as a man of the word of God. And I have believed that what is distinctive about Christian spirituality as lived by a priest lies in his relationship with the word of God. Priests shepherd God's people with God's word. This does not rule out other approaches to Christian spirituality and human spirituality generally. Neither is it intended to belittle contemporary concerns about the relationship between spirituality and human development. But it does provide a focus for all of these. At ordination, a man is authorized to proclaim the word of God,

to celebrate the word at its highest level of sacramental
intensity,

to be a good shepherd, bringing the word of God into human
hearts in every human situation.

To do this effectively, he must keep pondering the word, he
must keep savoring it, keep devouring it, keep praying it. To put
this another way, he must keep making his nest in God's word.
In a sense, his profession is to make the word of God come alive.
You are surprised and pleased when somebody says to you, in
appreciation, "You don't know me, Father, but you were describing my situation in that homily." Similarly, you are grati-
fied when, after the passing of many years, you meet a parish-
ioner from your first parish who tells you, "I will never forget
the helpful words you spoke to my son when he had the breakdown." You may have forgotten both mother and son, but they
have not forgotten; and God has not forgotten. The word of God
remains ever alive and active. It knows no past tense. Of course,
the fact that we are its special agents does not make us into
supermen. Indeed, we know too well that all pastoral ministry is
the great expression of divine power working through human
weakness. The power of God does not make our words into
oracular statements. But it is in our human and weak words that
God continues to write a new song. Maybe the good priests we
all know who are pastorally very effective but whose theoretical
understanding of the word of God is rather rudimentary are
God's way of reminding us of this.

St. Francis is said to have told his brethren that they must be
at all times preaching and that, if it were necessary, they should
do so by the use of words. In this profound program, he draws
our attention to the biblical reminder, made memorable by
Jesus in his temptations and his fast, that we do not live on material bread only but on the bread which takes the form of every
word proceeding from the mouth of God (Matt 4:4). God is continually speaking words of life. Some of God's living words
have been captured in a privileged way in the biblical words.
Ordination is a call to help people be alert to both the biblical
word and the word that God is daily speaking into all their life
situations. The vocation of the ordained is one of continually
baking and breaking God's word. I believe that the primary
priestly tragedies and scandals today are not the ones that

commonly go under these names. Rather, they are the lost opportunities of alerting people to the words that God keeps speaking.

Both the biblical words and the other words are bread that must be broken. And I can't help feeling that many of the biblical readings in our daily Masses remain unbroken bread. Not only have they remained undigested but they haven't touched people in the areas of their existence where digestion takes place. The reason, I fear, is that we who proclaim them or have them proclaimed have not always made our own home in them. Back to Christopher Casson. Both he and another great Christian, Eamon Andrews, were known to tell priests, politely but firmly, that they would not read in church unless they had been given adequate time to prepare. They had too much of a respect for the word of God to present it unbaked. They knew that the word of God calls for a special kind of reading, a special kind of *lectio*. At this crucial stage of the developing of new ministries, their example is a good reminder that the whole church is in need of a new and more effective system of baking gospel bread. The ordained person has a key role in this work of baking. But it is in no way an exclusive role. It is a collaborative one in which every man, woman and child in the community is involved.

God's Bakers

I have moved from the image of being at home to the image of baking. But the two are, of course, closely connected. There is nothing like home baking, home cooking. There are innumerable possible connections between both images and the image of the sparrow who provides a nest to nurture and feed her young in the temple setting. One of our greatest masters of words (J. B. Keane) says that it is the privilege of the writer to introduce words to each other. All ministry of the word involves introducing words to the source of all words, the Word of God. It is in the intimacy of that Word that we are daily called to be at home, to make our nest, to keep baking and breaking the bread from heaven. In that intimacy, we keep introducing words to each other. In the power of that intimacy, the word we speak or preach will never be a hand-me-down word, never a cliché.

A Text and a Prayer

To help us all be a people fed by the word, it is good to keep revisiting a text of scripture and the prayer before the proclamation
of the gospel that many of us remember from the old Missal.
Maybe we would hear them as being spoken directly to each one
of us in our ministry of making God's word come alive. The
scripture text addresses us as scribes (teachers of God's law)
who have ourselves become learners in the ways of the kingdom
and who live in a treasure-filled house:

> Every scribe
> who has become a learner in the kingdom of heaven
> is like a householder
> who brings out of his treasure what is new and what is old
> (Matt 13:52).

The prayer before the gospel was and is a salutary reminder
of the daily cleansing of heart and lips that is needed if one is to
proclaim God's word effectively:

> Cleanse my heart and my lips, O Almighty God
> who did cleanse the lips of the prophet Isaiah with a burning
>   coal.
> Grant in your gracious mercy to purify me
> so that I may worthily proclaim your holy gospel.

CHAPTER 14

Bake Before You Break

At the time when I was coming to terms with the call to make my home in God's word I took part in a liturgy on the evening of Saturday, January 24th. It was the eve of the day on which Vincentians normally celebrate the coming into existence of the Congregation of the Mission. The readings were those for the current Sunday. They were three magnificent, if rather long, readings. The first was from Nehemiah and it described a great renewal of the covenant. The second was from St. Paul on the variety of gifts. By a series of happy coincidences, the third was the mission statement of Jesus in the synagogue at Nazareth. It is a statement about fulfillment and it has been the inspiration for any mission statement that the Congregation of the Mission has ever made. All three readings were very well proclaimed. The responsorial psalm was sung very beautifully. The homilist spoke very well on the ways that the missionary dream of St. Vincent has been fulfilled over the centuries and is still being fulfilled. He decided that there was so much to say about this topic that he would not draw on the words of the readings. I did not question the wisdom of his decision or of any decision taken in the planning of the liturgy. Yet, I must confess that, at the end of the long celebration, I had some unnamed feelings of frustration and saturation.

A Question of Digestion

The next morning, I was better able to name some of those feelings. I was in Bonnybrook parish church for two Masses. From my experience of *lectio divina*, I was used to the practice of listening and listening again to the same passage from scripture, thereby learning to savor its contents. But this did not dispose me to listen a second and third time to Nehemiah, Paul, and Luke. I felt, rather, that I was in for an endurance test. I decided to ask the reader, as diplomatically as I could, to abbreviate the reading on

the gifts, in the way envisaged in the missalettes. But the newly
installed lector got there before me. She is a delightful person,
Dublin of the Dubliners. Her words came as rapid fire. "Father,"
she said, "would you mind terribly if I read the shorter version?
...And would it be out of order if I left in a few lovely lines from
the longer version?...And skipped a few from the shorter
one?...Would I be cheeky, Father, if I suggested that we often
have too much scripture read to us and that we don't get a chance
to take it in, with the result that we suffer from a kind of indigestion?" I was left in awe of the words of wisdom that fell from the
woman's lips. Indeed, I was left without words. I do remember
nodding my head approvingly. The words had come from a
woman who loves the Mass and who obviously loves the word of
God. I am sure she would be as impatient as I am with priests who
take liberties with what is fixed in the words of the Mass and who
make arbitrary changes instead of availing themselves of the rich
range of legitimate choices. What she was showing, I believe, was
a mother's instinct for what truly helps the digestion of little ones.
I hope that what I recommended to her both met that instinct and
conformed fully to the spirit of the liturgy.

The Art of the Baker

It all brought me back to my Vincentian call to "break for little
ones the bread of salvation." St. Vincent took the words from the
Council of Trent and it is obvious that he had thought and
prayed over them. It reminded me of what Jesus did with the
bread at the first Eucharist: he took, he blessed, he broke, and he
gave. It reminded me that this is what I am expected to do at
every Eucharist. It reminded me of the sacrificial breaking of the
Lord's body and the pouring out of the Lord's blood that give
meaning to and interpret every eucharistic meal. It reminded me
that a process like taking, blessing, breaking and giving must be
done with the word as well as with the bread. It reminded me
that before our bread becomes the bread of life, earth had to give
it and human hands had to make it. It reminded me of the lovely
words of the *Didache* about the grains of wheat being gathered
from the four corners of the earth. It reminded me of the great
parable of Jesus about the sower who went out to sow his seed
(Matt 13:3). It reminded me of the oatmeal and the bag of wheat
that came yearly to our family from the mill, in my young days,
and that provided us with many a substantial breakfast and

supper throughout the winter months. Before we got the oatmeal and wheatmeal, my father had to plough, to harrow, to
sow, to reap, to thresh, to put in bags, to bring to the mill, to wait
for the joyful postcard that said "Dear sir, your oatmeal and
wheatmeal are now ready." Ready indeed for the excitement of
the baking of the first cake. I remember my father frequently reminding us that, in his younger days, when all the work was
more manual, the women outshone the men when it came to
binding the corn. He would have been the first to admit that
when it came to the baking and cooking there were even fewer
contests. In the renewal of our eucharistic celebrations, I suggest
that the best of recent feminist concerns are a kind invitation
from providence to introduce more truly feminine baking
touches to the table of the word and the table of the Eucharist.

Before the bread of the Eucharist is broken, it has to be baked.
This brings us right into the depths of the mystery of our being
called to be co-creators with God, the only creator. The woman
who smiled when Pope St. Gregory the Great gave her the body
of Christ got it beautifully right when she explained afterwards,
"I'm so proud of it; I baked it myself." One of the countless reasons why we have to thank God daily for our mothers is connected with the baking of bread. They were living expressions of the
text of scripture about the yeast that a woman mixes with a
bushel of flour until the whole batch of dough rises (Matt 13:33).
The text has helped the relationship of Jesus with his mother to
come alive for me. In the same context, I recall Sr. Irene, a
Daughter of Charity who herself excels in the culinary arts,
telling me that a good cook should caress the food. This is in
some way connected with the love of all of us for home-baking,
and my own pride when my first cousin Julia got fame for a
while by her association with "Julia's hotbread." The stress today
on using real fresh bread in the Eucharist is more than a passing
fashion. It touches deeply on the mystery of what St. Paul experienced when he saw the implications of the whole eucharistic
community partaking together from the "one loaf" (1 Cor 10:17).

All that concerns the good baking of the bread of the Eucharist
has its implications for the good "baking" of the bread of the
word. It is good to remember that when Jesus said, "I am the
bread of life" (John 6), he was referring as much to the bread of
his word as he was to the bread of the Eucharist. He himself had
lived on the words from the mouth of his Father when he had no

earthly bread during his forty days in the desert. All of us are wearied rather than refreshed by receiving news that is stale, and we can be damaged rather than nourished by bread that is stale. God never intended his word from heaven and his bread from heaven to be anything other than fresh and refreshing. Much as we may have loved the Latin liturgy that nurtured us until the Second Vatican Council, we cannot but recognize its limitations. We may even find ourselves rejoicing that we are now living in more enlightened times. But are we? There are new and less obvious forms of spiritual indigestion. All good ministry of the word involves continual good baking, tasting, breaking, and digesting. The four are inseparable from each other; they are a good checklist for any ministry of the word.

All the Senses
We have heard much about the importance of involving all the senses in a full celebration of the word of God. In my recent reading, I have become more and more convinced that the word of God well prepared and well celebrated should be a delight to taste. I have been reading what people like St. Bernard and Guigo II had to say about the honey that comes to us when we taste, ruminate on and contemplate the word of God. I have re-read the late Jock Dalrymple's advice on letting a word from scripture dissolve like a lozenge on the tongue. I have read more of what Basil Pennington has to say about the place of the "love word" in centering prayer. I have continued to translate *Recta sapere* as "to have a taste for what is right." In the same context, I appreciate the significance of the literature we call "sapiential." These new appreciations of the place of the sense of taste have led me to rediscover its close relation with the sense of smell. I have read of Archbishop McQuaid's advice to the entertainer Jack Cruise not to add to his small night adoration group in Merrion Square in case that group might "lose its fragrance"— shades of God's promise through Hosea that the chosen people will be "fragrant like the cedars of Lebanon" (Hos 14:6). And I have come to learn that what St. Francis de Sales had to say about bringing the fragrance of prayer with us throughout the day is not quaint advice from another culture; it is being said less colorfully by those who stress the importance of bringing a "word of life," a love-word, away from every Bible prayer group. All of this helps me to see the importance of presenting the word of God as freshly baked bread.

Two Convictions

With the new urgency that comes with the passing of the years, the months, the weeks, the days, I am growing deeper in two convictions, one of which is founded on the other. The first is that the vocation of priests is to live by the word of God: to know it, to love it, to dream it, to ponder it, to "bake" it, to taste it, to ruminate on it, to preach it, to celebrate it at sacramental intensity, to bring it into every area of people's lives. The second is that Cardinal Yves Congar was very right when he said that there would be a faster de-Christianization in a place where the sacraments were frequently celebrated but the word of God poorly preached than in a place where the word of God was effectively preached and the sacraments celebrated in a very limited way. Dare I say that it is in this perspective that we could best assess the findings of recent surveys about religious practice in Ireland and of similar surveys elsewhere? Is there a question of new forms of spiritual indigestion and a gradual dulling of the sense of taste by food that can best be described as insipid? Is it an urgent reminder to us preachers that if taste is to be re-sharpened and restored we need ourselves to bake and taste the gospel bread before we break it?

Our task is to touch the God-space in the hearts of our listeners and to create a prayerful atmosphere in which they can recognize their hunger for and need of the nourishing word that we proclaim. In the course of a recent train journey, I sat close to two upwardly mobile professional young Irishmen. They were involved in a deep conversation. It concerned the death, a short time before, of the mother of one of them. It was clear that their religious world had been and is Catholic. The bereaved young man talked of his reasons for bitterness with God and with the church. It was far from my thoughts to condemn either those involved in their religious education or whatever priest presided at the Requiem Mass for the young man's mother, but it was clear that I was listening to two young men who felt they had not been fed. I couldn't help thinking of our growing opportunities to have the humble courage to ask people, 'What things did you talk about on the way?' (Luke 24:17) and to keep bringing light from the word of God into their lives. Perhaps if I had a truly evangelical fire, I would talk about obligation rather than missed opportunities.

Is the emphasis on the many dimensions of the word of God a capitulation to one form of Protestantism? Is it promoting a

Catholic-type fundamentalism that would leave us with nothing more than the questionable riches of hot-gospel Bible-belts? The best answer I can give is to invite you to keep reading what is arguably the most important document of the Second Vatican Council, the one on Divine Revelation, significantly called *The Word of God*. If you read it carefully and prayerfully, you will have no inclination to jettison anything you have ever truly cherished in our Catholic tradition, but you certainly will appreciate more deeply Our Lord's teaching that "the seed is the word of God" (Luke 8:11), that "every word that proceeds from the mouth of God" (Matt 4:4) is intended to be in the richest sense seminal. But the word of God does not always come to us ready-made. The seed that is sown in the ground has a long journey ahead of it before it becomes food. If the written word of God is to be truly nourishment for God's people, it must be made into a living word both by God and by us. We are never more co-workers with God than when we invite people to taste his word and to relish it.

For a long time now, we have, I think, come to recognize the need to explain and nuance the classic teaching that the sacraments produce their effects *ex opere operato*. We have come to see that the teaching in no way dispenses with the need of continual new work on the part of both minister and recipient. I wonder if we are equally nuanced in our understanding of the effectiveness of the word of God which is an essential ingredient of every sacrament. I sometimes feel that our reading of the word of God smacks of the automatic, indeed the magical, the druidic, a caricature of "say but the word..." It would be wonderful if we were always seen as people whose profession it is to shape and mold words in order to make them live carriers of the food of God's word.

Artists in the Word

When I talk of shaping and molding "till the whole batch of dough rises," I am reminded of the example of two Vincentian colleagues, both rejoicing in the name of Johnston. On a morning after a dark and dreary winter, Fr. Seán once came to the oratory to lead us at prayer. The sun, which had been hiding for months, was shining gloriously. "Lads," said Seán, "we'll dispense with words this morning." It was an inspired decision. It was good at least on this occasion. Without any words, Seán was helping us to watch a new day "making known the message" (Ps 19:2). In his heyday, Fr. James preached the word of God with great power. But there were times when he was carried away by an occasion and he would avail himself of every opening in the liturgy to insert some words of wisdom. His close collaborator, Fr. Charlie, had a mischievous way of chiding him for this. He would say, "James, I liked your fourth homily most of all."

To be an artist in making the dough of the word to rise has nothing to do with either being histrionic or with wordiness. Indeed, I am convinced that it calls for fewer rather than more words. Many of us have already become word-weary; we want fewer words, more word. The great artist in preparing and presenting the word was none other than the Word made flesh. In his inaugural sermon, he wasn't content just to speak words. He attended carefully to the setting. He stood up; the book was handed to him; he unrolled the scroll; he found the place; he read; he rolled up the scroll; he gave it back to the attendant; he sat down; all eyes were fixed on him; only then did he say that the scripture was here and now being fulfilled (Luke 4:16-21). He certainly activated people's taste buds, even if they were soon to experience a taste-swing and the sweet taste was to turn into wormwood. Jesus had shown the same power over words and the word when he rejected the advances of Satan and told him, simply but magisterially, to go away (Matt 4:10).

This art of "baking" the word can be recognized in many great men and women who have influenced the world by molding evangelical words that lead to deeds. One recognizes it in rules of great founders like Benedict, Francis, Clare, all of whose rules of life comprise largely a series of words of scripture on which they had for long been ruminating. One recognizes it in the conferences of such people as St. Vincent de Paul, Abbot Marmion, and Fr. William Purcell. One recognizes it in the Confessions of people like Augustine and Patrick. One recognizes it in the life of St. Thérèse who, though her access to the books of the Bible was very limited, learned to taste and relish the word. All of these people of the word remind us of the son in the gospel who learned to ask his father for bread and who received nothing less than bread (Matt 7:9, 10). As a result, they themselves would give nothing less than well-baked bread to God's hungry people.

The Prayer of the Church
All good community prayer and good liturgy require time to

savor the word of God in its freshness, to sip it, to drink from it. This is what happens in the growing number of communities that, in praying the Prayer of the Church, have such practices as pausing after each psalm to taste together from lines that somehow touched the hearts of individual participants. All this requires the kind of preparation that I have been describing as baking.

The psalms comprise a very large part of the daily prayer of people committed to Christian community living. As we pray them, we praise God in all the moods that people experience, individually and in groups. We do this in the context of the history and experience of a particular people. It was the history and experience of a people for whom everything in Jerusalem, the great king's city, was very special, very evocative. It was the history of a people who had a keen appreciation of the fact that the whole earth had been made by the hands of the same Lord who brought his people through the Exodus experience and who brought them home from exile. All of these intersect with our own story. And yet they are not our story.

An Irish community with a republican tradition is very much at home in the singing of republican songs. The story of Fr. Murphy of Boulavogue is somehow part of their memory, and the song that carries his name does not really have to be explained to them. It is not so when we recite or sing the psalms. It is not surprising that many say, with honesty, "Try as I may, I get nothing out of the psalms." To the words of the psalms they could apply the words of Cardinal Newman about the words of the Mass: "Quickly they go," or the words of one of the psalms themselves: "They are soon gone and we fly away" (Ps 90:10). We need much help on the way. A short, discreet word of introduction, suitable words that link each psalm and each reading with what went before and what follows after, moments of silence carefully chosen, psalm prayers from the standard books or spontaneously composed, bidding prayers that draw on the actual words of the psalms or readings—these are but a few of the ways that the scriptural words in psalm or reading can be made to come alive and give nourishment. A community morning prayer, both in religious communities or in the growing number of parish churches in which a cross-section of the baptized gather to praise God, can, if celebrated in this way, provide a powerful nourishment for personal prayer, just as personal prayer can enrich the quality of the praying of the community.

Three Helpful Trends
The search for better ways of baking and breaking the word and of continually making it into fresh bread has helped me to evaluate three trends which recently have been having considerable influence:

The first trend concerns our re-learning to savor the Prayer of the Church. It is a suggestion that Basil Pennington has made more than once. He suggests that, if a priest is having difficulty in making the liturgy of the hours really prayer, he could try this: estimate how much time it should take you to pray each particular hour well; if a word, phrase, sentence or passage comes alive for you, stay with it; if by the end you have only prayed a sentence or two or half the words that are given, but you have really prayed, don't worry, because the rest of the words will be there for another time; your commitment to spending full time shows the seriousness of your purpose. There is much in this that ruffles the understanding of the Prayer of the Church in which I have been shaped and in which I continue to believe. But we are dealing here, I think, with re-finding a taste for the word of God, which is always in danger of being blunted and which, let's face it, does become blunted for many priests in a way that makes them wonder what are they really doing when they open the church's book of prayer.

The second trend concerns the implications of Walter Brueggemann's oft-reported conviction that Christians are at present in a state of a new exile. One is reminded of Michel de Verteuil's two kinds of story-reading: the one that is alienating and the one that is home-coming (*Your Word Is a Lamp for My Steps*, pp. 13ff). The exile theme helps us to cope with many aspects of alienation and of our being far from home. Entering into the exile message can color the ways we read, meditate and pray the word of God. The exile experience was of a people whose tears had become their food by night, by day (Ps 42:3). But it was also a people's experience of the God who, wherever we are, wants us to be fed with a food better than tears. This is the God whom Julian of Norwich experienced as "homely."

The third trend is the search for entries into the world of Celtic spirituality. The Book of Kells and kindred books could only have come from people who were forever tasting and ruminating on the word of the God whom they also kept finding outside of books in God's creation which they saw, tasted, touched, heard and smelled.

Fed by the Living Word

St. Thérèse is an admirable teacher of how to be fed by the word of God. In one sense, she was starved of the scriptural word of God—there was not even a copy of the Old Testament in her convent library. But this did not stop her from attentive listening to the biblical word in the limited forms in which it did come to her. From her prayerful listening to two texts from Isaiah and one from Proverbs, much of the foundation was laid for her little way. She is on record as saying that, while moving from spiritual book to spiritual book sometimes gave her a headache, one word from the scriptures was enough to make her mind and heart take flight. A single word, she said, uncovered infinite horizons for her soul. Only a woman who had made her home in God's word could have personalized the contents of John, chapter 17, in the way reflected in the final exercise book of her autobiography, shortly before her death. She had indeed made her home in Jesus Christ and his words had made their home in her (cf. John 15:7). She had done her own baking.

The word of God is the thread of Ariadne that stitches together all our praying, all our desiring, all our hungering for the God who gives us the makings of the daily bread that prepares us for all our tomorrows. It is worth baking well and breaking well.

CHAPTER 15

From Lecture to *Lectio*

At the beginning of my two years of Vincentian novitiate, our group was introduced to the program for the year ahead. The timetable made provision for every hour of the day, every day of the week. The meaning of some of the items was obvious. Some items needed explanation. Some seemed not to have need of explanation, but they did. One of these was for an exercise called "lecture." A half an hour was allotted for it every day. When the time came for the first lecture period, we expected that the group would go into a class hall to be addressed by our director or another member of the staff. We discovered that, in fact, each of us was expected to do the lecture on his own, in silence, at his desk. Later it became clear that *lecture* was a French word for reading, a rather special kind of reading. It was one of those words passed on to us by St. Vincent de Paul or by some of his interpreters over the centuries. Another such word described our status during the first two years of formation. We were not called novices; we were seminarists. Our section of the formation house was not called the novitiate; it was the seminaire, literally the "seed place." It is good to recall this at a time when the word of God is receiving so much prominence in church thinking and we are finding new shades of meaning in the Lord's teaching that the seed is the word of God (cf. Luke 8:11). Each of the passing years makes me appreciate more fully the oft-quoted words of one of our superiors general to a group of seminarists: *toujours seminaristes,* be always seminarists.

Lecture and Prayer

Though our director was soon to teach us that our daily lecture was to be done slowly and reflectively and that we should absorb the contents into our hearts, I cannot remember seeing any connections between the daily lecture and our hour's prayer in common every morning. As a help for that hour, there was a standard meditation book. We were encouraged to go to bed each night in a spirit of recollection, a word that suggests a gathering of fragmented pieces. The next morning, our hour began with some non-biblical prayers and ended with the Litany of the Holy Name. At regular intervals, a point from the meditation book was read aloud.

In the prayer itself, we were encouraged to find help from a nine-step outline which drew a lot from St. Vincent's method, which itself drew on the methods of people like Louis of Granada and St. Francis de Sales. It was made clear to us from the start that the outline was intended to be a help and that we were not expected to follow it slavishly. The first two steps consisted of placing ourselves in the presence of God and invoking the assistance of the saints. To use the terminology to which I was introduced much later in life, we were encouraged to be kataphatic, not apophatic. We were to use our imaginations in ways that would help us to enter into and become part of some gospel event. The last of the nine steps was the making of petitions. Halfway through the nine steps came what were called affections. Somehow we were made to feel that here we were near the heart of what praying is about. The affections were preceded by reflections and followed by resolutions. Though we used meditation points from a meditation book, none of the steps was actually called by the name of meditation. Neither was the whole hour of prayer called meditation. There was no step called "contemplation," though even then we were told, in other contexts, that St. Vincent saw contemplation as being within the reach of all; he told the young Daughters of Charity that they could all become St. Teresas. The spirit of the morning hour was carried over into a further half hour of praying together that was actually called "meditation." Its official name was "afternoon meditation." Neither morning prayer nor afternoon meditation included anything from what we now call the Prayer of the Church. Our public introduction to that was Sunday Vespers and sung Compline on the Sundays of Advent and Lent.

Repetition and Colloques; Conferences and Chapters
A link between lecture time and praying time was the practice of various forms of what was called "repetition"; at least that is how I see the connections now, years after our seminaire days.

In the daily seminaire reading of the New Testament we were expected to memorize three verses. This was seen as so important that we were then to go to another seminarist and repeat the words aloud with him. Every Sunday morning, our hour together ended in what was called "repetition of prayer." One seminarist or student was called on to describe what had gone on in his praying time. The superior or director finished by baring his own soul in the same way.

Another precious word in our vocabulary was a more domesticated French word, *colloque*. Each week, the group was given a topic to read and report on. One of us was deputed to lead a sharing of thoughts and reflections on the topic. This was followed by a short contribution from each of the rest of the group. As well as this regular colloque, there was also a weekly psalm-colloque which followed a similar pattern. By way of preparation, we were asked to read and read about one of the psalms.

Related to the colloques, we had two other practices the names of which have strong monastic resonances—conferences and chapter. Every Monday, our director gave us a high quality talk which, for reasons I cannot yet fathom, was called a conference. The topic was not related to any other exercise of the week. It put the director's distinctive mark on what books on ascetical theology had to say about the following of Christ. There was no sharing before or after. On Friday evening there was a different kind of conference. A seminarist or a student gave his reflections on a topic named beforehand. This was followed by a longer reflection by one of the priests. The Friday morning chapter, unlike the daily monastic assembly of the same name, was a gathering at which each of us publicly named and admitted our faults.

Communication and Retreats
The monthly meeting with the director was called "communication." It was a good experience. The director usually spoke encouraging words. He was wise enough not to ask us to give an account of everything that had transpired in the maze of exercises since the last time, but it was the nearest thing we had to providing a unified vision of these. Beforehand, you had given the director a written account of how you saw your progress or lack of it over the month. Nowadays, I would say it was our introduction to journaling.

Toward the Days of Renewal

I have been describing the forms of prayer and related activities that shaped my introduction to formation in a community that was careful not to describe itself as religious, though it had much in common with various religious orders. My later years as a student and my early years as a priest continued to include quite a number of the seminaire practices. Through all the years, weekly confession and daily Mass took place in an atmosphere of faith and devotion, but I cannot remember any ways in which either was directly connected with any of these practices. For this work of connecting, we had to wait until the days of the Second Vatican Council. The perspectives of the Council, the publication of many fine documents on consecrated life, the renewal of constitutions and the absorption of these into daily community practice, make some past observances seem more like historical curiosities than expressions of a living and vibrant spirituality. For much of this change I thank God. I am thankful especially for a good deal of simplification and for the disappearance of practices that had become so formalized and ritualized that they sometimes resulted in our seeing the trees and missing the wood. They became part of a program that had become overcrowded and that thereby blurred the vision. And still, it is more and more dawning on me that there was a wonderful idea behind not some but each of the old exercises. That is why I believe they are well worth revisiting. The reality is that my seminaire days coincided with a time of fragmentation of a great spiritual vision. The individual pieces were soon to cry out for reintegration into a new picture. It brings to mind the theory that St. Paul's teaching on the new man was influenced by the myth according to which the man in the heavens fell accidentally to earth and the work of the Savior was to reassemble all the fragmented pieces.

Welcome Lectio Divina

Among the many living movements in the church today, the practice of *lectio divina* seems to me to be the most striking agent of this work of reassembling, this getting into focus, this gathering together of fragments, this re-collecting. As I read the theory of *lectio* and take part in its practice, I find echoes of seminaire practices that I had long since consigned to the museum of memory. They were *lectio* in fragments. And just as I once found

myself stumbling over the French word *lecture,* I now find myself stumbling over the Latin word *lectio.* More intriguingly, it
has dawned on me that the two are the same word refusing to be
translated adequately. You do justice to neither word by simply
translating it as "reading." Both words are about reading with
the heart, reading with the imagination, reading with the whole
person. This divine reading, sacred reading, prayed reading, is
fed by the kinds of exercises that made up our seminaire program. Both the new prominence of *lectio* and the rediscovery of
the old practices find their best context in the Second Vatican
Council's gift to us in the *Constitution on Divine Revelation.* Our
many seminaire prayers included one at the putting on of the
cassock. It began "Clothe me, Lord, with the new man." It is the
prayer I find myself saying most often nowadays as I begin the
time of *lectio.* The daily clothing in the seamless garment of the
word of God is as basic as the daily putting on of the clothes
without which I wouldn't venture out of my room.

Monastic?

As I reflect on the movement from lecture to *lectio,* I find that far
from believing that our patterns of praying are too monastic, I
believe that they are not monastic enough, which does not mean
that the apostolic community or parish should, in its praying
patterns or timetable, just copy the monastery. The monastic
ideal combines the call to be alone and the call to be with the
group. The monastery way of blending the two calls is a kind of
paradigm for what is to be realized in the very differing situations in which praying people find themselves.

A second conviction is that, no matter what our work en-
gagements are, each person committed to consecrated life or to
public church ministry needs some time each day in some combination of reading, reflection and prayer. This, it would appear,
is what St. Francis de Sales was convinced of when he said that
each Christian should pray daily for half an hour, the exception
being the busy person who should do so for an hour.
Interestingly, he was not confining his words to those in consecrated life or in public church ministry.

A third conviction is that each seminarian, priest, religious,
and committed lay person, would benefit enormously from an
hour of *lectio divina* with a group, at least once a week. Well
prayed, such an hour has a way of coloring and enriching the

ways we celebrate the Eucharist and the Prayer of the Church, as well as how we pray in private.

Tasting and Seeing
For both lecture and *lectio,* there never has been a greater teacher than Guigo II, the twelfth-century prior of the Grand Char-treuse. It was he who best described *lectio* in terms of the food that we eat. He described reading as the putting of the food whole into the mouth, meditation as chewing it and breaking it up, prayer as abstracting its flavor, contemplation as the same flavor continuing to gladden and refresh us. This is a wonderful perspective in which to keep looking afresh at the daily heaven-ly manna of word and sacrament. I thank God for the introduc-tion to lecture in my seminaire days. It was in the same days that we sang *"Jesu dulcis memoria"* and some related motets at Benediction. We sang of the delightful taste that comes from the name of Jesus and the joy that comes from experiencing his presence and his love. In more recent years we have been given many new ways of experiencing this taste, this presence, this joy, this love. Many of them have come in the new forms of lecture and *lectio.* The church's daily Office of Readings used creatively can keep opening us out to great spiritual treasures, old and new. Besides, a new understanding of grace is helping us to find spiritual nourishment in some of the most unexpected areas of secular literature.

Good reading leads to meditation; meditation leads to the prayer of the heart; the prayer of the heart leads to contempla-tion. It is good for us to let the spirit of contemplation linger on beyond the fixed praying times. Some of the new forms of wor-ship of the Eucharist outside Mass are an ideal setting for this prolonged contemplation. In our eye contact with the manna from heaven, we let time go by doing what St. Frances de Sales described in terms of experiencing the fragrance of the fresh flower and what many moderns describe in terms of staying with a word of life. In this setting, the Lord invites us to be car-riers of the fragrance of his word. *Lectio* helps us to respond with delight to this fragrance.

A Simple Way
The most accepted and the most attractive way of approaching prayer in the *lectio* way is in terms of four stages, in an atmos-

phere of recollection and in a readiness to take away a "word of life" that will help shape our daily attitudes and behavior.

You *read* alone or in a group the word of God and you re-read it; you hear the word as addressed to you now.

You *meditate* on it in a way that stirs up memory and imagination.

You *talk* to the Lord in a spirit of thanksgiving, repentance and petition.

You *contemplate* by resting peacefully in God's word.

Each of the classic ways of praying gives special prominence to one of these four, but it cannot live without the other three. Good *lectio* respects each of the nine praying stages of my seminaire days. It places them all in the perspective of God's living word.

CHAPTER 16

The Consecrations of Christians

In the course of the church's history, it has sometimes happened that words that describe the vocation of all the baptized tended to become associated exclusively or primarily with the ordained or with those in religious life. A good example is the language of consecration in the seventeenth chapter of the gospel according to St. John. For the past few centuries, the chapter has often been described as the "priestly prayer" of Christ. Seen in this perspective, it is not surprising that it formed the warp and woof of many a retreat and prayer vigil for those receiving holy orders. The understanding was that the prayer was originally a great prayer of blessing on the twelve special disciples of Jesus and on their successors in ordained ministry. In other settings, the same language of consecration is sometimes presented as if it were the monopoly of those in religious life. With their renewed appreciation of the sacrament of baptism, today's readers can more quickly see that that prayer embraces all the disciples of Jesus, all those countless followers who would continue the work and mission of Jesus after the time of his glorification by his Father, all those who would continue his mission.

If the language of consecration is truly reclaimed for all the baptized, the consecration of the ordained and the consecration of religious can be more clearly seen as two expressions of the great baptismal consecration that all the disciples of Jesus have in common. It was in this perspective that Pope John Paul II gave the title *Vita Consecrata*, "Consecrated Life," to his postsynodal document (1996).

A Priestly Prayer

Whether we are talking about the call of all the baptized, the call of the ordained, or the call of religious, it is still useful to speak of John 17 as the priestly prayer of Jesus, not primarily on account of its beneficiaries but on account of the priestly dispositions with which Jesus himself approached the completion of his work on earth as he returned to his Father. It is the prayer of one being lifted up from the earth (cf. John 12:32). His priestly dispositions are expressed especially in the words variously translated "consecration" and "sanctification." The Father had sent Jesus into the world (John 17:18) in a sending that sanctified him (cf. John 10:36). Jesus, in turn, sanctified himself for the sake of the disciples whom he was sending into the world, and for all who would believe through their word (John 17:18-20). He asked his Father to sanctify them in the truth, which was nothing less than God's own word (v. 17).

The language of sanctifying and of consecration is highly evocative of the language of worship, of sacrifice, of priesthood, of holiness. The God worshiped by Israel was always experienced as the uniquely holy God. True sacrifice was seen as a gift offered to that God, in a search for communion with the one who alone deserved the name of the Holy One. By their consecration, priests were enabled to offer sacrifice to that Holy One. The world dreamt of and promised by the prophets was a world in which people would be truly holy by a sharing in God's own holiness, in the offering of sacrifice out of the temple of the human heart, with priestly dispositions that would bring them into touch with the holiness of God. The author of the Letter to the Hebrews saw this dream and promise fulfilled in Jesus Christ who was the perfect meeting-place between worship, sacrifice, priesthood, and holiness. The priestly body of Christ was the perfect altar of sacrifice on which God was worshiped in the perfect temple.

Persons, Places and Things Apart
Over the centuries, holiness had been associated with persons, places, and things that were somehow apart, somehow separated from the normal day-to-day areas of communication between human beings. There was an aura of separateness and holiness about the ancient sanctuaries and shrines, about the tabernacle, the ark, and the temple. These places and things apart were especially evocative of the holiness of God.

The same aura surrounded the people most intimately associated with the holy places and things. All were somehow points of contact with the God who alone was holy, the God who dwelt in a world apart, unaffected by any of the limitations of creatures.

The exact nature of God's inner holiness could only be guessed at, but somehow it was understood to be the source of and criterion for all standards of moral and ethical holiness in human beings. All the great biblical theophanies were seen as manifestations of the name and the holiness of God. Any act of consecration of persons or of things placed them in a special relationship with that holiness.

Consecration and the Temple
It was in the temple that the holiness of God came to be manifested in a specially privileged way. Hence the importance of the consecration and dedication of the original temple, which was seen as the dwelling place of the glory and holiness of God. It is significant that, in later biblical times, a special feast of the dedication of the temple came to be celebrated annually, for eight days. This annual feast of Dedication was really a celebration of rededication. It was established because the altar of the temple had been desecrated, de-consecrated (2 Macc 1:1–10:8). Judas Maccabaeus had the altar rededicated (1 Macc 4:36-59).

The annual feasting, which came to celebrate the memory not just of the Maccabaean rededication but of the original dedication of the two great temples, became a time of sacrificing, a time of rejoicing, a time of lighting of many lamps. All the ancient dedications of altars and all the ancient moments of light shining in darkness were remembered. The whole eight days of rededication were a time of feasting and gift-giving, of dedication and consecration. It was in the setting of such a celebration that, in answer to questions about the grounds to his claims to be messiah and good shepherd, Jesus said that his Father had sanctified him and sent him into the world (John 10:36). Because he was in the Father and the Father was in him (v. 38), he was able to speak living words and perform life-giving deeds. Both the words and deeds had their source in the Father who had sent him on a consecrated mission into the world (vv. 37, 38). Because he was sanctified and consecrated by the Father, the success of his messianic and pastoral mission was assured.

There were some connections between the feast of the Dedication and the annual harvest-feast of Tabernacles. This festival included the renewal of the covenant and the celebration of the reconstruction of the temple after the exile. It was in the atmosphere of festive light and festive water that characterized the last day of this festival that Jesus, himself the light of the world, invited all those who were thirsty to come to him and he promised that out of every true believer's heart would flow rivers of living water, the waters that come from the Spirit which believers in him were to receive (John 7:37-39).

New Temple; New Dedications; New Tabernacles
In his reinterpretation of the meaning of the temple feasts of Dedication and Tabernacles, Jesus gave a whole new meaning to all the words that expressed worship, sacrifice, priesthood, and holiness. He disclosed that the holiness of God is the loving inner life between Father, Son, and Spirit, a life that we have come to call trinitarian. The perfection of God as revealed by Jesus Christ is not a remote abstraction; it is an intimate knowing and loving that unites persons. For the disciple of Jesus, being "perfect" like the heavenly Father means being admitted to a sharing in the Father's own way of knowing and loving, and in the Father's unique way of being compassionate (Matt 5:48; Luke 6:36).

The result is that every place where the disciple of Jesus stands is "holy ground" (cf. Exod 3:5). For the disciple of Jesus, sacrifice must be offered not in or near a temple of stone and wood but in and out of the human heart from which flow the rivers of living water which the Holy Spirit provides. The human heart, united to the heart of Christ, is the place that truly deserves the name of "privileged altar." From it arises the priestly and sacrificial action that gives glory to God. Because the Word became flesh and tabernacled among us (cf. John 1:14), every day is the feast of Dedication and Tabernacles for the disciples of the Word made flesh. All the disciples can truly be called the saints, because they are the temples in which dwells the all-holy God.

The Consecration of the Baptized
Is it any wonder, then, that *consecration* and *dedication* have become special words in the Christian vocabulary? These old religious words were given endless riches of new meaning by the one whom the Father sanctified and sent into the world (John 10:36). For all Christians, lay, ordained and religious, the sacraments of baptism and confirmation, and all that derives from them, are especially deserving of the language of consecration. These are distinctively Christian ways of designating people as "holy to the Lord" (cf. Luke 2:23). All other ways are secondary.

It is no surprise that the word that has been most used to describe the moment when bread and wine become the body and blood of Christ, as food and drink for the consecrated baptized and confirmed, is the moment of consecration. In a variety of movements of devotion in recent centuries, baptized people in all walks of life have been encouraged to consecrate themselves to the heart of Jesus and the heart of his mother who was uniquely blessed in being uniquely pure of heart. We use the language of consecration in connection with a number of the church's sacramentals. We use the language of consecration and dedication liberally in connection with the blessing of churches and altars. The anniversaries of the dedication of churches are celebrated in different places with varying degrees of solemnity. Behind these practices is the conviction that the church building deserves a special consecration as the gathering place of the living temples and living altars that constitute the whole community of the baptized.

The Consecration of the Ordained

It is in this context that we must keep re-situating the two areas of church life in which the language of consecration has had a special prominence. One is in the various stages of the conferring of the sacrament of holy orders. The language of consecration and sanctification has always been strong in the Judaeo-Christian tradition of worship. Already in Exodus we find detailed prescriptions for the "glorious adornment" of the sons of Aaron (Exod 28:40). Gloriously adorned, they were to be anointed, ordained, and consecrated, so that they would serve God as priests (v. 41; cf. 40:13). In the same spirit, there was a consecration of Aaron and his vestments and of his sons and their vestments (Lev 8: 30).

In the ages when Christian ordinations drew heavily on the traditions of Aaron and Moses, much attention was given to the kind of ritual detail associated with the consecrations envisaged in Exodus and Leviticus. Even when emphasis on that kind of detail waned, the language of consecration, sanctification, and dedication remained strong in ordination rites. The basic image of the Christian temple, the living stones of which are being continually built up by priestly ministry, always remained prominent in these rites. This continues to be true of the ordination rites of bishops, priests, and deacons that have come into existence since the Second Vatican Council. It is true that in recent years we have been speaking of the ordination of a bishop rather than the consecration of a bishop. But this development is not the result of an effort to phase out the language of consecration. Rather it is the result of a theological and doctrinal development whereby diaconate, presbyterate, and episcopate are more clearly seen as three related manifestations of the one sacrament of holy orders, in its task of being continually at the service of all the baptized who are living altars, living temples, living stones.

The Consecration of Religious

The second area in which the language of consecration has a prominent, indeed a central place, is in the church's understanding of religious life. From the consecration of virgins, which became a public feature of church life in the fourth century, until the reemergence of a similar rite in our own day, one could say that there have been no more evocative words to describe religious life than "consecration" and the cluster of words that surround it. This is good to the extent that it helps us to see religious life as a particular flowering of the consecrated life of baptism. It is confusing if it fails to keep making that baptismal connection.

From three other sources, there has recently been some hesitation and even confusion about the language of consecration as applied to religious life. The first source of hesitation is the historical investigation of the word. In its origin, it suggests separation, being set apart. In an age when people are suspicious of dualisms and dichotomies, and in which there have been many attempts to redefine the secular and the sacred, and in a church which sees herself as sacrament of the world, religious are suspicious today of any language that suggests separation or removal from the world. But, if they keep probing into the meaning of Christ's own consecration, they will find that their suspicion is based on insecure foundations. All the stages of the paschal mystery of Jesus Christ have radically redefined the holy, the sacred, the secular. Each of the stages was the bearer of continual life to the world which God loved so much, at such a great cost (John 3:16). For those baptized into Christ, consecration can never be a "sacralization" if sacralization means being removed and set apart from the world. All new consecration must always be seen as part of the sanctification and transformation of the human heart, the dwelling place of the God who is holy, in the theater of the whole created universe where the drama of the kingdom of God is being continually performed and made manifest. The only separation that is mandatory for the disciples of Jesus is separation from sin and that worldliness which is the enemy of the kingdom. Religious life should be a continual invitation to share in God's own love for the beautiful world which God made and for the sinner-saints who inhabit it.

A second source of hesitation is the language of consecration that finds its place in the Code of Canon Law and related texts.

The Code speaks, in book two, about institutes of consecrated life and societies of apostolic life. Consecration is envisaged as expressed through the profession of the evangelical counsels; the person thus consecrated is described as dedicated to God, who is supremely loved, by a new and special title; this dedication is seen as an expression, by vows or other sacred bonds, of the perfection of charity. The societies of apostolic life are described as being like the institutes of consecrated life; their members do not take religious vows; the members of some of the societies undertake the living of the evangelical counsels, through a bond defined in their constitutions.

This combination of canonical and theological language has its own cohesion and its own value. But, for those not used to thinking and speaking this way, it can come across as a begrudging concession that leaves the members of societies of apostolic life wondering whether they should really call themselves consecrated people. In the light of the rich language of consecration and sanctification which forms the texture of Jesus' words at the temple feasts of Dedication and Tabernacles, and in the light of the riches which the church has kept discovering and rediscovering in these words throughout the ages, there should be no doubt about the answer to their wondering. The person consecrated in religious life and the member of a society of apostolic life can both say, in Christ, "for their sakes I sanctify myself." He or she says this of the temple of his or her own body (cf. John 2:21), in loving relationship with the other members of the body of Christ. He or she makes this act of new consecration in a way that reflects his or her own present experience of God and of people, in terms of a particular religious charism and tradition, at a time of a particular need in the church and the world. Each of these circumstances provides its own very personal outpouring in the sacrifice going up from the altar of a human heart already consecrated in baptism. The religious lives a life of consecrated celibacy and of the kind of gospel poverty and obedience that support it in its direct relationship with the Lord. He or she is called a "religious" because his or her primary profession in life is defined in terms of the virtue of religion. In the meantime, the person who has received the sacrament of marriage lives out his or her baptismal consecration in intimate bodily union with another member of the body of Christ; the person who is single, by choice or by circumstances, is called to the living of the baptismal consecration in the way that arises out of his or her personal situation, now. For both the single baptized and the married baptized, the members of the "institute of consecrated life" and the members of the "society of apostolic life" should provide a constant sign of the consecration to which all the baptized are called.

The third source of hesitation is the fear that emphasis on consecration might rule out or play down an emphasis on mission. It is ironic that such a doubt should even exist. In the words of Jesus at the feast of Dedication, as presented in St. John's gospel, the very purpose of consecration is mission. The Father had sanctified Jesus and sent him into the world (John 10:36). In justifying his claim to be called messiah and shepherd, he appealed not to texts of scripture but to the works which he did in his Father's name (vv. 37, 38). In this perspective, the ongoing consecration of all those in religious life is a continual call and invitation to a life of apostolic mission, a call and invitation which keep inserting them into the consecration and apostolic mission of Jesus himself.

Renewal of Consecration

The language of consecration is an excellent setting for understanding the call of all the prophetic, priestly and kingly people who are baptized into Jesus Christ the new temple. The baptismal consecration has to be continually renewed. Those baptized into Christ can learn much from the Jewish people who found joy in rededicating the desecrated temple, and in renewing the celebration annually, in the Hannukah, which was a festival of joy, light, and gift-giving.

The body of the Christian consecrated at baptism to become God's temple is subject to many desecrations along life's journey. There is room for much reconstruction after life's many deconstructions. Dedication (and rededication) is not a once-for-all event. It is a continual process that calls for a continual renewal of baptism, especially in the celebration of the church's liturgical seasons. Every celebration of a sacrament, every expression of the church's faith and devotion, in para-liturgies and sacramentals, is an opportunity for the renewal of the covenant and of baptismal consecration. Every new stirring of evangelization is an opportunity for the re-evangelization and rebirth of those once born of water and the Holy Spirit.

In the tradition and practice of every religious community, there are many built-in opportunities for re-consecration and rededication. These include annual retreats and other retreats, the renewal of vows, the celebration of community feasts. Each of these is a kind of festival of dedication and rededication. Each can be a kind of community Hannukah, a feast-time of sacrifice, of joy, of light, of gift-giving.

All of this applies too to those consecrated in the sacrament of holy orders. It is significant that nowadays we see the "character" of this sacrament less and less as a stamp imprinted once-for-all and more and more as a lifelong process set in motion by ordination into a special covenant relationship with Jesus Christ and his people. This calls for a continual program of living the qualities of the God of the covenant, the God whose love is strong and who is true forever. This program of strong love and of continuing truth calls for the continual renewal of the consecration and dedication once made at ordination. The search for suitable renewal programs and support groups for the ordained is a striking expression of this need for rededication. The Chrism Mass on Holy Thursday at which the presbyterate join their bishop in the sacrament of unity and oils are provided again for the many anointings of the people of God is an eloquent expression of the re-consecration not of the ordained only but of the entire baptized and priestly people.

A People Sanctified

In the perspective of the New Covenant, the baptized comprise a people "sanctified in Christ Jesus, called to be saints" (1 Cor 1:2). In their hearts, they are called to "sanctify Christ as Lord" (1 Pet 3:15). They are a people washed, sanctified, and justified (cf. 1 Cor 6:11). They are called to be "holy because God is holy" (1 Pet

1:16). They live by a message that builds them up and that gives them an inheritance among all who are sanctified (Acts 20:32). All this is possible because they belong to a church which is the bride made holy by the washing of water and by the word (Eph 5:26). Though the bridegroom has been taken away (Matt 9:15), he is still the one whom the Father has sanctified and sent on a mission into the world and who went back to the Father praying that all who were given to him would be sanctified in the truth as they were sent on mission into the world. His work of sanctifying will continue until it is absorbed into the celebration of the great marriage feast in the final tabernacle of God with the human family (cf. Rev 21:1-3).

CHAPTER 17

Can These Consecrated Bones Live?

As far back as any of us can remember, there has been a close connection between the eucharistic words of consecration and the heart of the mystery of our faith. For long, the words "mystery of faith" were intertwined with the words of consecration themselves. In the Mass as we now celebrate it, the mystery of faith is proclaimed immediately after the words of consecration. The simplest and most succinct of the four expressions of the mystery is
Christ has died;
Christ is risen;
Christ will come again.

It is significant that the most recent official church statement on the ways of life that highlight the "evangelical counsels" begins with the words "consecrated life." It has something to say to all who belong to any institute of consecrated life or any "society of apostolic life." All of these institutes and societies are seen as expressions of the basic Christian baptismal consecration. They are consecrations within a consecration. All of them are alive and life-giving to the extent to which the lives of their members proclaim the full mystery of faith.

There are parts of the world, large parts, in which consecrated religious life is flourishing, but in most of our "first world," with such notable exceptions as parts of post-Communist Europe, the aspect of the mystery of faith which is now being most experienced by those in the consecrated life is the fact that Christ has died. To be in consecrated life today is to have an acute experience of dying. Nearly every community of consecrated life into which I have any form of entry can say, "Yes, indeed, we are dying." Each of them can say that they belong to a community of death. The dying we are all now experiencing is of a kind undreamt of when I took my vows. It is of a kind undreamt of when the bishops of the world were formulating their teaching on religious life at the Second Vatican Council and when, under the inspiration of Pope Paul VI, we began to get such rich religious fare as *Evangelica Testificatio*, "Witnessing in the Gospel Way."

As I visit communities of consecrated life and become involved in their work of renewal, I am forever experiencing a wealth of faith and hope and love. But I am also becoming acutely aware of "bare ruined choirs" and of the "silence of unlabored fields" that up to quite recently were full of apostolic laborers. When I meet a novice or a small group of novices, I cannot help wondering whether their future apostolic labors will consist of administering geriatric care in their own communities which may be already dwelling in the shadow of death. Those of us who have been influenced by the spirituality of the "French School" and who found much of it restated by Columba Marmion were often reminded that we must live through and experience the whole range of the states of Christ, including his dying state. All of this is now coming to us with a new poignancy.

But dying is not the same as dying out. It is doubtful whether any community of consecrated life is ever right in saying, "We are dying out." In terms of the mystery of faith, every dying should be a birthing. Every dying we are now experiencing is an invitation to give new life. Now, more than ever, the Lord is telling us that he is coming once again that we may "have life and have it more abundantly" (John 10:10). In these days of dying, I am daily finding new meaning in the words of the *Anima Christi:* "At the hour of my death, call me." I find myself changing the words to "In this hour of our death, call us and bid us come to you." To what is the Lord calling us at this hour of our death?

A Call to Seeing More Clearly

The purpose of all our consecrated communities is the promoting of the kingdom of God. Jesus saw himself as the "Son of Man" bringing good news about God's reign. His sole concern was to bring about the kind of society in which the dream of his Abba, Father, would become a daily reality. For me, there are two great texts that capture the atmosphere of the kingdom of God in a special way and that are an agenda for all people who have a passion for the promotion of the kingdom of God:

• The first is the answer of Jesus to the questioners who came from John. It is not an academic answer. It is a description of what people could actually see and hear, now that the kingdom of God was becoming a reality: blind people were recovering their sight; lame people were walking; lepers were being made clean; deaf people were hearing; the dead were being raised to life; the poor were getting good news (Matt 11:4, 5). The doctor was healing people of all kinds of illnesses (cf. Mark 2:17).

• The second is the startling response of Jesus to those who told him that his mother and his brothers were outside asking for him. He asked "Who is my mother? Who are my brothers?" Looking round at those who were sitting in the circle about him, he said, "Here are my mother and my brothers. Whoever does the will of God is my brother, my sister, my mother" (Mark 3:31-35).

The prime time of all the community meetings of every consecrated community of brothers or sisters of the Lord should be spent not in administrative details, necessary though these are, but in a common visioning and dreaming of how we can help call each other to make the kingdom of God a reality now. Maybe it is time to recover a community devotion to St. Joseph who dreamt dreams and had the faith and courage to ensure that the dreams were realized.

A Call to Radical Discipleship

In contemporary writing on models of the church, a much-favored model is that of "community of disciples." To be a disciple means to be ever willing to learn. To be radical means to keep continually in touch with the roots. Religious consecration is a continual call to being disciples and being radical. What kind of teacher is the Jesus from whom we should be continually ready to learn? Back to what roots is he drawing us?

The picture that emerges in much of contemporary writing about Jesus is of a man who subjected himself to the limitations of being human and who became a nobody so that everybody could be truly somebody. Here, indeed, is the one who "though he was rich, yet for your sake he became poor, so that by his poverty you might become rich" (2 Cor 8:9). Here indeed is a continual program for every circle of radical disciples. This is the context for a preferential option for the poor that can never be optional. Here is why *Vita Consecrata* gives us many reminders that there can be no radical discipleship unless we keep our eyes fixed on our radical teacher.

A Call to Be Truly Virginal, Poor, Obedient
The classic if not the oldest expression of consecrated religious life is in terms of virginity, poverty and obedience. It is difficult to say anything new about any of these three facets of radical discipleship. The ground has been covered, systematically and beautifully, at many stages of Christian history, not least—indeed perhaps most of all—in the years that have followed the Second Vatican Council. It is good, though, to keep searching for images, new and old, that capture the spirit of the three.

• Virginity must keep finding its place in the relationship of love between Christ and his church for whom he "gave himself up" so that she should be "without stain or wrinkle" (Eph 5:25-27). Christian virginity is a form of marriage. This way of speaking has its critics, but it is encouraged in *Vita Consecrata* and it has strong foundations in the Judaeo-Christian tradition. Even the virgin who is a hermit and is wed to the Lord is also wedded to a community. On every level of human need, he or she needs the supports that a community can provide. We are rediscovering these days that Jesus is the proto-martyr. He is also the proto-virgin. In his radical way of being both martyr and virgin, he came to cast fire on the earth (Luke 12:49). It is to this fire-caster that the church is wedded. It is in fire-casting that virginity keeps finding its meaning.

• Religious poverty is a call to be rich and to enrich others. For me, one of the most powerful images of religious poverty is the color purple. We are wrong in presenting purple as the color for mourning. This way of speaking leads to a confused catechesis for the purple of Lent and Advent. In the biblical world, purple is the precious color, the color of the wealthy. The most famous rich man in the gospel was dressed in purple (Luke 16:19). In his passion, Jesus was robed in the purple of kings (John 19:2). Lydia, the seller of purple goods, was obviously a woman of wealth (Acts 16:14, 15). It is for reasons such as these that I like to see purple as the color for religious poverty. We are painfully aware today of the apparent contradictions in the lives of those vowed to poverty. The contradictions between what we are and what we say we are can be so glaring that we can't see them. These contradictions are sometimes expressed in our spacious properties and in prodigality in forms of transport, to mention just two areas. Too often, there is a justification for the half-joking, half-in-earnest quip from our lay friends: "You take a vow of poverty and we keep it." We can be light years away from the "simple and austere way of life" to which *Vita Consecrata* invites us. Be that as it may, I do fear that the most harmful caricature of religious poverty in some religious communities today comes in the form of poverty of conversation, a poverty of culture. People have a right to be enriched by their dealings with vowed and consecrated people. The opposite is sometimes the reality. That this should be so is sad, especially when we consider that the vowed person has all the riches of God at his or her disposal. The prospective candidate for a community of consecration should be assured of an affirmative answer to the question "Will I be happy? Will I be rich?"

• It is sometimes said that there is little explicit scriptural basis for the vow of obedience. The contention is correct only if we are looking for texts that justify our obeying the decisions of religious superiors. But every call of the kingdom of God is, in fact, a call to be obedient. Doing the will of his Father was the sole concern of Jesus. The vow of obedience names various power points that locate for us the expression of the will of the same Father. This is why I like to see the vow of obedience as a vow of sacrifice and why I am coming to see sacrifice primarily as a return gift to the God who is the giver of all gifts.

A Call to Depend

Disciples depend on their teacher. They also depend on their fellow disciples. If there ever was a time when religious communities could somehow go it alone, that time is well past. The survival and growth of one community has implications for the survival and growth of every other community. Every director of vocations has a portfolio that involves the welfare of all men and women who live the consecrated life. Those of us who are members of societies of apostolic life are very conscious of our dependence on the prayers of members of contemplative communities. We tend to ask for these prayers in times of various forms of crisis. In these days of many dyings, all communities are in a state of crisis. One expression of this crisis is that contemplative communities are as dependent on their active counterparts as we have always recognized ourselves to be on the contemplatives. At a time when young people especially are suffering from a kind of religious amnesia, contemplatives are very much dependent on the kind of catechesis and preaching that makes sense of lives lived far from the madding crowd. All communities are responsible for the healthy life of all the called, at all the stages of all of their calls.

This mutual dependence is finding one expression in the blossoming of new forms of community and of indications that those in the traditional forms of religious life do not have a monopoly on the evangelical counsels. One thinks of Catherine Doherty of Madonna House, Jean Vanier of L'Arche, Andrea Riccardi of St. Egidio. We are hearing of the emergence of mixed institutes which comprise men and women, married people and celibates, Catholics and other Christians. Maybe these are glimpses of the setting in which some communities of consecrated life will flourish in the future. Certainly they are alerting us to the fact that, in any geographical area, all the baptized are called to be truly brothers and sisters to all the rest of the baptized. The well-being of religious life is a responsibility of lay people, just as the promotion of the lay vocation is a responsibility of religious.

Recently, in a large urban parish, it transpired that there were ten different vowed communities. Most of the lay churchgoers were unaware of even the existence of any of the ten. It also appeared clear that each of the ten groups lived as if the other nine didn't exist. It all expressed a poverty of understanding of what it is to be the body of Christ. Recent efforts of vowed communities to develop various forms of associate membership have many healthy implications here. It is in this context too that it is best to see recent discussions about temporary commitment. I think the expression, though, is a misnomer. Every community, contemplative or active, should have a place and space for those who, once in a lifetime, or several times in a lifetime, wish to share their life and apostolate. For this reason, perhaps, we should be slow to speak of people who "leave" a community.

There is a close connection between our call to mutual dependence and our call to collaborative ministry. In promoting this style of ministry, we learn that we all depend both on God and on each other. And we discover that there is a very real sense in which God wishes to be dependent on us.

A Call to Be Re-founded
In some recent writing on the consecrated life, the language of "re-founding" has been finding a place. The very language of re-founding raises problems. It presents particular problems when

it is suggested that the church itself is in need of re-founding. For some, the expression suggests arrogance, even blasphemy. Has not the church been founded once-for-all? Have not our communities of consecrated life been founded once-for-all? There is a sense in which the answer must be a resounding yes. But there is also a sense in which both church and community of consecrated life must be re-founded daily. The call to be converted comes to us daily. For this very reason, the call to re-found comes to us daily. Each day, we are called to place our lives, individually and collectively, back on the original foundations. Any admission that the church always needs to be re-formed is an admission that it always needs to be re-founded. In our communities of consecration, who are called to be the re-founders? Is it the younger members? Those appointed leaders for the time being? A small group of men or women who have special gifts of vision? Some one person who is discerned by the community as being noticeably in touch with the founding charism? To each question, the answer is yes. But every one of us is called to a task of re-foundation. When St. Francis was told by the figure on the cross in San Damiano to repair the church because it was falling into ruins, he thought for a while that the words referred to the church edifice. Later he interpreted the words in a more metaphorical way. Both interpretations were right, but the figurative interpretation proved to be the richer and the more lasting one. Francis came to learn that he was being asked not just to improve a building, to re-found his own Christian life and to found a new community. He was also being asked to re-found the church itself. Ever since, his brethren have had the vocation to re-found both the Franciscan Order and the whole church.

Each member of each community of consecrated life is, in the literal sense of the word, called to innovate. By a creative approach to the work or ministry in which we are involved, we are called to make all things new. This call is not confined to any age-group. Most religious communities today are, in fact, aging and graying. This is no reason for an apologia. The median age in the society that surrounds us is getting higher and higher. Maybe part of the mission of religious is to help people, by word and example, to age gracefully and to die gracefully. For the same reason, maybe we should not be too defensive when a prospective novice wonders whether much of his or her ministry will be care of the aged. We have recently been seeing wonderful examples of the work being done by elderly religious who belong to a community that is alive. We have also seen beautiful examples of new religious provinces coming into existence in cultures where the church is young, as a result of the missionary labors of aging religious whose parent province is in the throes of dying. There is a well-known story about a depressed community of Christian monks whose whole life was transformed when a holy rabbi told them that the messiah was in their midst. The story has much to tell us about the call of each of us to refound. The conviction that each of us has received this call distinguishes a community that is dying by fully living the mystery of faith from a community that is simply dying out.

A Call to Hear God Calling

Those called to the "consecrated life" have no exclusive claim to any of the words that describe Christian consecration. There is a need today that all the baptized reclaim their call to consecration. Only in the baptismal setting can those consecrated by what the Second Vatican Council called "vows or other sacred ties of a similar nature" (*Constitution on the Church,* par. 44) get a clearer vision of their distinctive call, and of their distinctive way of calling.

We have always recognized that all vocations involve the action of God, the action of the called person, and the action of the calling community. We have gotten used to one pattern of the blending of these three ingredients. Maybe our new way of praying for vocations should take the form of begging God that our community may have and give life more abundantly. Perhaps a stronger place should be given to the call by the community. Perhaps there are times when it should simply take the form of "Join us!" St. Augustine is said to have told some people who were worrying about predestination, "If you are not predestined, see to it that you are predestined!" Perhaps this could be a basis for a vocations program that says, "If they are not called, see to it that they are called."

Every community of consecrated life is a charismatic community. It came into existence when God gave a new gift, a new charism to the church. Every charismatic community must live charismatically. This means that it must live in a way that is visibly full of the faith, the hope, the love, the joy that comes from finding and re-finding the pearl of great price (Matt 13:46). This is what St. Vincent de Paul had in mind when he told his missioners to live together as dear friends. For the same reason, the charismatic community must be a prophetic community, with all the marks that have characterized good prophets throughout the ages. To be charismatic and prophetic, each community needs daily conversion. In making possible this daily conversion, the members depend on each other. The conversion will be expressed in the way they speak together, the way they keep silence together, the way they pray together, the way they hear and do the word of God together.

Religious are not the only people called to be religious. Religion is about ties. True religion improves the quality of our ties with God, with other people, with the communion of saints, with the whole human family, with the whole of creation. Nowadays, it is fashionable for some people to say, "I am not religious but I am spiritual!" Very often, this is a spurious distinction. One call of those in religious life is to help people make ties and connections between their spiritual searchings and the religious celebrations that, far from being empty rituals, should ensure the worship of God "in spirit and in truth" (John 4:24).

Living, Dying and Rising

If a particular community of consecrated life is to die, it must die giving birth. Even with all the dying that is happening at present, we are surrounded by signs of assurance that Christ has indeed risen. There is a lot of significance, I believe, in the fact that the film with a religious theme which has been most influential in recent times is called *Dead Man Walking*. It is the story of a man who was dead long before he died. But he was helped to become partially alive through the ministrations of a woman who was searching for ways of expressing the charism of her gospel community and of giving life through the same gospel. In the duel between death and life in which all those involved in the consecrated life are involved today, we are being called anew to be bearers of gospel life. We are being called to immerse our consecration in the consecration which is at the heart of our daily Eucharist.

CHAPTER 18

Called and Calling

"Let us pray for an increase in vocations to the priesthood and to the religious life; Lord hear us, Lord graciously hear us." It would be hard for any of us to count the number of times we have heard this bidding prayer. We are always sure to hear it on vocations Sunday. We are almost sure to hear it in communities of religious, especially where there is a preponderance of elderly religious. Indeed it is likely to come up in any Eucharist where space is given for petitions *ad libitum*. The petition keeps getting a greater poignancy as more and more seminaries and religious houses are becoming "bare ruined choirs." In becoming aware of the implications of what has been happening, we have been going through a wide range of thoughts and moods. Some of us, in our darker moments, might be wondering whether God is tired of us and has decided to stop listening to our petitions. We may even have had moments when we thought he had simply stopped calling in this part of the world; or maybe that he is getting more select in those whom he is calling. We may even have been wondering about the authenticity of the large numbers of calls in the past.

Through all our thoughts and moods, the salutary reminder of St. James has never been far away: "When you pray and don't get it, it is because you have not prayed properly" (Jas 4:37). But we may, with all respect and some impatience, have said, "You're right, brother James, but please tell us what is the proper way!" Some of us with longer memories might take consolation in recalling the millions of Hail Marys that used to be said for the conversion of Russia. They went on and on and on for decades, apparently unanswered. Eventually we gave up saying the Hail Marys altogether. And then we woke up one morning and found that the Iron Curtain was no more. We saw this as at least a step toward the conversion of Russia. This may be one of the Lord's ways of teaching us that he does always hear our prayers but that he refuses to be programed as to when, how or where. And maybe it is that he has decided to take the kingdom away from our part of the world for a while and give it to the fruit-producing people in what we condescendingly describe as the "third world" (cf. Matt 21:43).

Touching the Depths

However we approach it, the topic of vocations has touched many depths in all of us. In recent years, we all have, in various ways, been through the vocation equivalents of Elizabeth Kübler-Ross's five stages of death and dying.

• Many of us have indulged in denial. We have argued that vocation numbers in the past were inflated; or we have said that the present situation is only a temporary setback, that things will be back on an even keel in a few years.

• We have experienced our share of anger. This has taken various forms. Some of us have taken part in demonizing the media, the criticizing of dioceses and religious communities for poor-quality catechesis, inept vocations programs and the unimaginative choices of vocation directors.

• We have had our moments of subtle bargaining. While we haven't directly tried to manipulate the Lord, we made quick moves in the deployment of personnel away from ministries that did not appear to reflect directly the charism of our community or what should be the pastoral priorities of a diocese, in an unspoken expectation that this would automatically turn the vocation tide. Sometimes our redeployment of personnel may have appeared as a new "vocations deal" with the Lord.

• In varying degrees, we all have had our days or months of depression in which we could see no sign of the presence and action of the finger of God's right hand.

• Hopefully, by now, we all are on some level of acceptance. We have largely stopped pointing fingers of blame. We are coming to see that the consecrated life of the future will be far from being a carbon copy of what we have known.

In our exploring the stages of death and dying as they apply to the vocation process, we have in some way become aware of the five great forms that radical discipleship has taken since Jesus walked this earth.

• The first was the unique way of those who were called directly by Jesus to be disciples and apostles and who left all to bring the good news beyond the land of Jesus.

- The second was the way of the hermits who left the familiar moorings of conventional social life to be with Christ in the desert.
- The third was the way of the cenobites in a common life that combined the hermits' values and the experience of brotherly and sisterly communion.
- The fourth was the way of the mendicants who followed the one who had nowhere to lay his head and who knew what it was to be weary from life's journeyings.
- The fifth is the way of the apostolic, missionary, health services, and educational groupings which has seen a multiplicity of forms in the last several centuries.

In our response to the question "What next?" opinion seems divided between those who emphasize that something entirely new is called for and those who say that we are called to live all five of the classic ways of discipleship, in new and creative blendings. In this perspective, the ancient hermits' *fuga mundi*, the flight from the world, far from being a historical eccentricity that could be seen more as an embarrassment than a source of inspiration, will in fact be an essential ingredient of the radical discipleship of the future. The recent interest in the new "desert" foundation in the diocese of Killala, and the growing number of consecrated virgins would seem to indicate that we are seeing something that is more than curiosity about an unusual way of life. It is significant, too, that Walter Brueggemann, the man who in our time has most successfully distilled the message of the ancient prophets, keeps emphasizing that taking the Judaeo-Christian tradition seriously today requires following an alternative lifestyle. This alternative lifestyle calls for many new forms of desert. It is far from being the monopoly of cloister and presbytery. No wonder the church is looking for candidates for sainthood among people like Dorothy Day whose life in the marketplace embodied so much of what the gospel stands for.

Step by Step
All of this is helping us to appreciate the meaning of the gospel imagery that describes our call to "follow" Christ. It is an invitation to walk all the steps of the journey which Christ himself walked, or rather the steps that correspond to them today. There is a popular hymn that says, "Our Lord the path of suffering trod." He has also trodden every step of the path of all the basic

experiences that could be called human, "tempted in every way that we are" (Heb 4:15). He has taken every step in the daily blending of joy and sorrow, of triumph and failure, of acceptance and rejections that are human living.

In our following in the same steps, there can be no shortcuts, no missing of a step. It is in the light of this daily call to tread all life's steps after the manner of Jesus Christ that we must evaluate some of the views about vocation that have come to be articulated in recent times. One such view suggests that God is daily calling large numbers to priesthood and other forms of radical discipleship but that these calls are no longer to be identified with a call to celibate priesthood or to vows of poverty, chastity and obedience in the forms in which we have known them. This view sounds plausible enough, but it raises at least as many questions as it might solve. It would be a strange church in which God would cease to call large numbers to virginity for the sake of the kingdom. Where can his call be better identifiable than in new blendings of the traditional expressions of gospel virginity, poverty and obedience? And where could the charism of virginity be more fittingly expressed than in the presidency of the Eucharist? In the same context we must evaluate suggestions that the Christian communities of the future will be little remnant groups, little cells of Christian presence who are part of ordinary society but not apart from it, or, to use another image, little oases in the deserts of secular culture and unbelief. We certainly will always be called to be a little flock, but the quality of gospel littleness cannot be measured by diminishing numbers only, and the apparent inevitability of diminishing numbers does not justify any inertia on our part.

In all the soul-searching about vocation today, there is one constant: all vocation is from God: "You did not choose me but I chose you" (John 15:16). What is true of the priestly call is true of every Christian calling: "One does not presume to take this honor, but takes it only when called by God" (Heb 5:4). We can never afford to forget the profound truth that every call is God's call. And yet, that is only half the truth. The other equally important half is that every call comes through the Christian community and the whole community must keep calling everybody who has been once called. It is also true that, though there is a diversity of vocations, each of us, in a very real sense, is called to live everybody else's vocation. These aspects of vocational truth have recently been showing signs of dawning on Christ's faithful, on the whole community of disciples, and they have many implications.

The Community Calls Us

Many of us were, I believe, brought up in a rather static understanding of vocation. Vocation was somehow like Adam's apple; you either have it or you don't have it. We did admit that you could lose your vocation, but it was somehow like losing an object, a commodity. In recent years, for a variety of reasons, we have all become accustomed to a more dynamic language, a language of process and becoming. This has influenced our understanding of vocation. In the perspective of process, we see vocation rather as a seed sown, a seed that is subject to all the vicissitudes of growth and setbacks that are the lot of seeds. To use older language for a moment, vocation is a God-given gift in the form of a potency that needs to be continually activated by human cooperation.

Though all initiatives and beginnings come from God, we are, on every level, God's cooperators. This truth has very strong biblical foundations, though it received severe setbacks at the time of the Reformation controversies and in some attitudes that have prevailed since then. It is true that since the Reformation times we continued to discuss the relationship between God's sovereignty and human freedom, but this was done in a rather academic way and in rather abstract language. Recent ecumenical dialogue finds little difficulty in seeing that we are indeed God's collaborators and that God's activity and human activity are mutually related and mutually interconnected. This interconnecting and this interdependence are strikingly illustrated in the program of the Rite of Christian Initiation of Adults (RCIA), which has been flourishing so much in recent years. The language of the Rite gives much prominence to the aspects of "election" that are the visible face of vocation. Election is seen as coming from God but it is also seen as coming from the support of the whole Christian community which is all fully involved in the stages before initiation, in the sacraments of initiation themselves, and for the rest of the life of those initiated. In the words of the Rite (par. 106), "acceptance made by the church is founded on the election by God."

Recent studies of the history of ordination rites in the

Western church give striking indications that, as with the election in the RCIA process, vocation to ordained ministry was, in the healthiest stages of our history, seen as coming from God and mediated and supported by the whole Christian community. At some important stages in the history of the church, the call of the community often came before the called person had any awareness of a call from God. The election by the community was, in a very real sense, the vocation. The perspectives of history show the very weak foundations for such dismissive statements as, "John had no vocation; it was a mother's vocation." John's vocation, like your vocation and mine, was his mother's vocation, his father's vocation, the vocation of every man, woman and child that made John into the person he is. This is strikingly confirmed by the search for new and diversified communities in the church today. One can hope that, in such communities, a diversity of vocations will be born, nurtured and supported. It is also confirmed by the search for new forms of inculturation. The seeds of every Christian vocation are sown in a particular cultural setting. Their growth depends very much on the extent to which they will be supported by that culture or, if necessary, by what is counter to that culture.

I Call You; You Call Me
The fact that vocation comes as much from our fellow humans as it comes from God has important implications for all of us, all the time. It has particular implications at this time of testing in the church. One cannot deny that though we have reached a certain level of acceptance, we are still experiencing new forms of collective depression in everything that concerns church life. We are experiencing many of the expressions of darkness from which we pray daily to be delivered. Our Father in heaven is the only one who can deliver us, but we are all agents of all the work of deliverance. Many people who have put their hand to the plough seem to be turning back these days. At every level of the church, we have all been meeting dispirited priests, dispirited religious, dispirited lay people. They are among the many who are called, but they need to be called again. If truth were told, we often find ourselves experiencing the same weakening of spirit. Each of us has our moments, sometimes prolonged moments, of mourning in which we need the comforting that one of the Beatitudes describes as "paracleting" (Matt 5:4). Each of us needs

to be called and called again. More than ever, each of us is called
to be a "son of encouragement" or a "daughter of encouragement" (cf. Acts 4:36). Each of us is continually being called to give
a word of paracleting to a sister or brother who is having difficulty in believing any longer in the vocation about which they once
felt so confident, or is ready to abandon it, while still remaining
sufficiently open in heart to be called again. Each day provides a
suitable *kairos* for speaking such a word of hope and light that,
under God, can touch human hearts. It may well be that the very
moment in which we feel tongue-tied is the one in which "it will
be given to us" (Matt 10:20) what to speak.

All Called to All
The teaching gifts of St. Thérèse are nowhere better expressed
than in her approaches to vocation. In her girlhood days, she
was once asked to choose from a range of gifts that were arrayed
before her eyes and the eyes of her sisters. She surprised everybody when she said, "I choose all." Later, as she spoke of her
Carmelite vocation which she so much cherished, she said that
she felt within her other vocations too: she felt the vocation of
the warrior, the priest, the apostle, the doctor, the martyr. However we interpret her oft-repeated wish to be a priest, it must always be seen in the context of her choosing all and of feeling
within her the stirrings of each of the other vocations. It must
also be seen in the setting of her conviction, expressed at the
time of her greatest spiritual insight, that her vocation was to be
love in the heart of the church. She came to realize that love included all vocations.

This vision of vocation has profound implications for the
church today. A vocation to one form of Christian life is a vocation to all its forms. I am called to be a Vincentian priest. I am
also called to be a member of St. Thérèse's community and to be
a married man. The call to one way of life is a call to openness,
transparency and accountability to all other vocations. But, because I am called to every form of Christian life, I must live one
form to the full. I will enrich the marriage vocation by the quality
of the living of my celibate vocation. As I do so, I will be slow
just to say that the celibate state is higher than the married state.
But as I try to avoid every form of smugness or arrogance and as
I search for new ways of expressing the insight behind this older
way of putting things, I will not throw out the insight itself. My

prayers for vocations will be as intense and as urgent for the promotion of the married way of life and for Carmelite sisterhood as they are for new members for my own community. There is need for new communities that will be like "rainbow coalitions" reflecting all the forms that the Christian vocation can take.

In all of this we have recently been seeing signs of new life:

• A community of Irish Carmelite sisters who have been doing much soul-searching about vocations have decided to turn one of their underutilized buildings into a quiet "hermitage" where married people, single people, priests, religious can come for quiet days of desert experience.

• A busy diocesan priest recently decided to spend his six-month sabbatical in an Irish Trappist monastery. At the end of it, the community decided to ask him to direct their annual retreat.

• A community of retired teaching sisters recently accepted the invitation of the administrator of a cathedral to form a community of prayer in the busiest part of the cathedral precincts.

• A community of sisters of apostolic life recently asked their superior general for permission to open a house of prayer. They were gently told that the house of prayer already existed! It was their community of retired sisters.

In these and similar movements of the Spirit of God, I believe that many new vocations will come to life and many old vocations will come to life again. In this contribution to a new heaven and a new earth, there will be many harrowings of many hells. There will be further descent before there is a new ascent.

CHAPTER 19

Being Really Present

In his South American diary, *Gracias*, Henri Nouwen wrote of a celebration in Lima, in 1982, of the first anniversary of the martyrdom of four American churchwomen who were raped, tortured and murdered in El Salvador. In the course of the service Fr. Jon Sobrino called out a martyrology of men and women who had been murdered in South America in the previous decade. When he had read the list of victims for each year, all the people responded with a loud *presente*. Those who, in the spirit of Jesus (John 15: 13), had given their lives for their friends were still very present in the minds and hearts of those who were remembering them. As the list of names grew, the word *presente* became louder and clearer.

The people assembled in Lima were using a word that sums up much of what Christians believe about the God who is always near to us and who enables us to be near to God and to each other. We believe in the God not of the dead but of the living (cf. Matt 22:32). Our whole Christian faith is a continual call to be present. We believe in the God who has always been present to the chosen people and who still keeps giving us signs of that presence. It is no wonder that, reflecting on his own experience of the God who said "I am who I am" (Exod 3:14, 15), Moses asked, "What other great nation has a god so near to it as the Lord is whenever we call to him?" (Deut 4:7). This intimate presence of God was of old expressed in many visible signs. Notable among such signs were:
the cloud
the fire
the tabernacle
the temple.

These four became, and have remained, powerful symbols of God's presence. In Christian spirituality, writings and devotion, there have been limitless variations on them. The temple symbol has had a particular richness of meaning. The temple was, above all, the place where God was present. As time went on, one temple building gave way to another temple building. Destruction and desecration led to reconstruction and rededication. As the final destruction of the temple building was about to take place, Jesus himself emerged as the true and lasting temple of God (cf. John 2:19-22). The body of Christ, living and dying and rising, became the great dwelling place of God, the real temple of God. In a short time, the disciples of Jesus came to recognize themselves as the body of Jesus and they saw themselves as the temple in which he continued to dwell. As members of his body, the living temple, they were sustained by his parting assurance: "And remember, I am with you always, to the end of the age" (Matt 28:20). They knew that their martyred founder was fully alive and fully present to them.

For the two millennia that have just finished, the disciples of Jesus have kept drawing new life and hope from this great assurance. As they came to grow in appreciation of his eucharistic presence, a presence that had its powerful impact on their eyes as well as on their hearts, it was understandable that they should reserve the words "real presence" for this particular expression of his nearness to them and his oneness with them. At the Second Vatican Council, the *Constitution on the Sacred Liturgy* gave us a very fine context for appreciating the eucharistic presence of Jesus Christ. It assured us that the risen Lord is "always present in his church" (par. 7).

The key word is *always*. One could say always and in all kinds of ways. The real presence of the Lord is not confined to the Eucharist. It is not confined to the church's worship, though it is especially palpable when one of the seven sacraments is being celebrated. It is in the sacraments that Christians most obviously celebrate the fact that they are the body of Christ and that Christ dwells in them as in a temple. The sacraments are high points of what is going on in all of us all the time. Christians come to celebrate the fact that they are the living stones of a temple alive. As they go away from the eucharistic celebration, they are invited to keep showing their brothers and sisters that Christ is always present in his church which is a sacrament, a visible sign of what all human beings can become. Each believer is called to be a real presence, a face, and a voice for the risen, ever-present Christ. The whole church could be described as "a people of the presence."

From Presence to Spirituality

Presence is an elementary word in all human communication. If I am truly present to you, I am not just physically near you. My nearness to you must be personal. It must express itself in a readiness to listen, to communicate, and to relate. We are quick to recognize the person who is a loving presence, or the person who is a reassuring presence, or the person who is a threatening presence, or the person who is a judgmental presence. We soon recognize the person who is fully present to us and who gives us undivided attention. Equally quickly we recognize persons who give us only half of their attention or look over their shoulder. When we feel that people may have lost our attention, we may have to ask, "Are you with me?" As a sign that we can be some-how present to our absent friends, we give them well-chosen gifts that we significantly call "presents" on days that are impor-tant in their lives.

Spirituality is concerned with the human spirit in its relation-ship with the Spirit of God. In the communication between the depths of my spirit and the depths of God's Spirit, I keep shap-ing my ways of understanding myself, other people and the rest of creation. The quality of my spirituality is tested by the quality of the ways I am present, really present. My communication with my friends and the ways I indicate my presence to them become models for my communication with God and with the whole communion of saints. To be holy means to keep extend-ing my awareness of the divine presence and to keep living in that presence, in the aura and atmosphere of the kingdom of God. A great Christian teacher who had spent his life leading countless people in the following of Jesus Christ was recently asked, on his deathbed, what his program for discipleship was. He replied simply: "Walking through life with Our Lord." If he had been pressed to elaborate further, he might well have added "and with those who are dear to him." He was putting in a dis-armingly simple way the Christian version of the profound invi-tation of the prophet Micah to "do justice, and to love kindness, and to walk humbly with your God" (6:8). In the Christian per-spective especially, the third of Micah's recommendations might be put first. It is this perspective of the nearness of the Lord that is the unifying element in the many and diverse ap-proaches to Christian spirituality.

The Christian is encouraged to recognize God present and at work in all persons and in all things that constitute God's creation. It is in this perspective that St. Ignatius taught those searching for holiness to "find God in all things." It is in the same perspective that St. Vincent told the early Daughters of Charity not to hesitate to "leave God for God." In a similar perspective, St. John of the Cross, influenced no doubt by the world of silk-weaving that was part of his family background, spoke of the God whose presence is unveiled to us in what we do every day and in what happens to us every day. The veiling image already had a fine Christian pedigree (cf. 2 Cor 3:12-18). It was to be further developed by Fr. J. P. de Caussade. Like the Carmelite Brother Laurence before him, he talked of each moment as a "sacrament" of the presence and action of God in our lives. Indeed, his whole spirituality could be described as an elaboration on this theme. He saw the events of life as so many unveilings of the action and providence of the loving God who accompanies us throughout life's journey and who invites us to respond lovingly to the divine presence.

In the perspectives of these and many other Christian teachers, the partial but continual unveiling of God's presence, is an anticipation of the final unveiling when we will see God "face to face" (1 Cor 13:12), "as he is" (1 John 3:2). The recent surge of interest in creation theology and in the ancient Celtic worldview, both of which stress the immanence of God in creation rather than the divine transcendence, can help us in this continual unveiling.

Presence and Praying

As I learn to be really present to the God who is really present to me, I learn to pray. This is the profound wisdom behind the teaching that the first step in all prayer is to "place oneself in the presence of God." In this setting, there is more than ample space for all the well-known ways of praying, as well as for new approaches to prayer and devotion. There is place for the many activities that over the centuries have come to be called "spiritual exercises." There is place for the many forms of examen of consciousness, all of which are designed to promote our awareness of God's presence in particular persons and specific situations. There is place for devotion to the saints who are the "great cloud of witnesses" (Heb 4:16). In that cloud of witnesses there is a special place for the woman whom Pope Paul VI taught us to call the "attentive virgin" (Marialis Cultus).

Maybe it is in this setting of attentiveness that spirituality and spiritual direction can best deepen their links with the art and skills of counseling, at a time when "attending" is regarded as a primary requirement for anybody who would be a counselor to a fellow pilgrim on life's journey. All questions about the when, the how, the where, the how solitary, the how communal, the how long of my prayer are best answered in the context of my desire to grow in attentiveness and in real presence. The celebration of the Eucharist calls for a special quality of attentiveness, especially on the part of the person presiding—an attentiveness to the different ways the Lord is present in the people assembled, and an attentiveness to the word that the same Lord wishes to be spoken now into the realities of their lives.

A spirituality of real presence has space for each of the four classical ways of praying. It has space for the "speculative" way with the emphasis on the mind and its many activities. It has space for the "affective" way that draws on our feelings about our daily experiences, as part of what St. Bonaventure called our journey into God. It has space for the "positive" (kataphatic) way that draws liberally on the world of images, with the help of such great teachers as St. Ignatius. It has space for the "negative" (apophatic) way in which we empty our minds of all concepts and images as we enter for a while into "the cloud of unknowing." Rather than attempt to rate these four classic ways of praying in order of merit, it is better to see them as complementing each other and even correcting each other. It is significant that St. John of the Cross, who was so much at home in imageless prayer, has provided us with some of the most powerful prayer-images. The test of each of the four forms is the extent to which it helps us to be really present.

It is in the same perspective that we can best evaluate the various approaches to spiritual direction. When I go to my *anam chara*, my soul friend, I have a right to expect that he or she will help me to be really present to the risen Lord. A session in which I am the giver of spiritual direction is effective to the extent that I help my brother or sister to grow in the same real presence.

Widening Circles
My real presence to the risen Lord helps me to be really present to myself, in a realism that works out the implications of the "know thyself" that pagan teachers first put into words and that many Christian teachers came to make their own. It helps me to

be present to and to reverence the whole of creation which is the work of God's hands and which God's Spirit is always making new and inviting us to make new. These forms of real presence are helps to my real presence to other people, especially those with whom I have daily dealings and of whom the Lord says, "Just as you did it to one of the least..." (Matt 23:40). Ideally, each form of real presence should flow over into others.

The various forms of "I am present" which we said or were said for us at key moments in our Christian journey are indications of our will to let the flow continue:

• At baptism, the equivalent of "I am present" was said for us by our sponsors. At the renewal of baptismal promises, we take ownership of what others promised for us.

• At marriage, husband and wife so promise to be present to each other that they become one body with each other, inserted into the union of Christ and his bride the church until the parting that comes at death.

• At religious profession, a man or woman commits himself or herself to a lifelong presence to a community with a particular tradition, whether it be in terms of a preferential option for the poor or of whatever charism situates the community in the body of Christ which is the church.

• At ordination to priesthood, candidates in older times said *adsum*, "I am present." More recently, they said "I am ready and willing." More recently still, they have simply been saying "Present," a word which is a whole program for the way of life that they are undertaking.

A program of real presence is a good context for ecumenism, for interfaith dialogue and for an understanding of our call to mission. The preacher of the Christian gospel in a land hitherto regarded as pagan is not the bringer of the saving God to a place where God was not present before. Recent reflection on the mystery of God's saving presence and action in all places and at all times helps us to see the task of the Christian missionary as helping to open people's eyes and hearts to recognize the God who was already present among them in a saving way and who is now inviting them to know the only true God and Jesus Christ who has been sent by the God who is true (cf. John 17:3).

When Real Presence Breaks Down
The invitation to be really present includes a call to "do justice and to love kindness," to let my awareness of the Lord's real

presence make me so really present to myself that all other expressions of my real presence are ensured. The call to being really
present is a program not for one area of Christian living only but
for the whole range of human and Christian ways of being and
doing. The second chapter of the Acts of the Apostles merits a
continual study as an example of such a successful program. A
group of St. Peter's fellow Israelites were told that God had
raised up Jesus and the result was the wonders they could now
see and hear. When they heard of this, "they were cut to the
heart and said 'What should we do?'" (Acts 2:37). They didn't
stop asking until "they had all things in common" (v. 44). This is
in strong contrast to what we find described in the eleventh
chapter of the First Letter to the Corinthians. St. Paul there presents the classic example of a breakdown between ritual and
life. He describes the story of a community in which Christ was
really present eucharistically but the people were completely
blind to his real presence in the poor with whom they rubbed
shoulders and to whom they failed to be present in a real way.
Paul had to tell them (vv. 20-27) that when they came together it
was for the worse rather than for the better. They hadn't really
come to eat the Lord's Supper. They humiliated those who had
nothing and they were thereby answerable for the body and
blood of the Lord. Here indeed is a classic example of real presence gone tragically wrong.

The members of the eucharistic community at Corinth were
in close touch with the signs of the Lord's presence but they mis-
read the signs. In the growing secularization in today's society,
the difficulty for many good people is to find signs of the Lord's
presence and to help young people especially to interpret the
new signs that are emerging. This is a difficult task at a time
when, for both the young and the old, the sociological supports
have been taken from under many accepted religious beliefs and
practices. Our society has moved from "pre-modernity" through
"modernity" to "post-modernity." The result is often a sense of
bewilderment and alienation. Perhaps in our continual attempts
to deal with this bewilderment, this alienation, we can get some
consolation from the fact that the Lord who is always really present to us must also be absent, since he dwells in inaccessible
light (1 Tim 6:16). The Lord who assures us that he is with us always has been taken up into heaven and, as we wait until he
comes again, he "must remain in heaven until the time of the

universal restoration" (Acts 3:21). The paradox of the "absent presence" of the Lord generates its own winters in our lives, in ways that make us empathize with the poet who complained, "How like a winter has my absence been from you" (Shakespeare: Sonnet 93). Our living in this state of absent presences and our searching for new ways of recognizing the Lord's presence can be done in the context of the various triads that have become commonplace in Christian language over the centuries. The approach to spirituality in terms of real presence can be helped by the triadic approach. Some of the triads merit special attention.

Purgation, Illumination, Union
Even before Christian times, some Greek philosophers used the words *purification, illumination* and *union* as a framework for understanding many aspects of human existence and experience. The words were taken up by Christian writers to express the dynamics of the Christian life in various stages of our growth in the experience of the God who is continually present and active in our lives. People like St. Teresa of Avila would seem to speak in terms of one stage succeeding another. People like St. Bonaventure preferred to see the three at work in every stage of our relationship with God. Neither Teresa nor Bonaventure would want to see us enslaved to a rigid understanding of the three. In the handbook tradition, in which much of the wisdom surrounding the three stages has been passed on to us, there has sometimes been a rather inflexible understanding of the three as following one after the other in a somewhat linear way. More recently, we have come to see the three as continually linked in our lives in what might be called a recurring, cyclic way.

All of us experience purification. The call to what John of the Cross termed "active" and "passive" purgations comes to us in various forms at various stages of our lives. In these purifications we ourselves sometimes take the initiative at the Lord's promptings. More often, we are purified by the events in our lives that are largely beyond our control. Reflecting on life's many purifications helps us to see purgatory as a possible continuation after death of a process that is already going on all through our lives.

All of us have moments of enlightenment. As Christian believers, we recognize Jesus Christ as the light of the world and as the light of our own lives. There are some moments when we have a deeper perception of our need to be illumined in our darkness. As with purification, the work of Christian illumination in our lives is both active and passive. We try to accept the Lord's invitation to let our lights shine (Matt 5:16); we leave ourselves open to be illumined by the light of Christ mediated for us in all the circumstances of life. Both forms of illumination are a story of both light and darkness, both presence and absence.

All of us experience the desire to be one. It is built into us at every level of our being. This built-in desire receives its fullest expression in the desire to enter into and share the unity that bonds together the divine persons. The initiative for what Julian of Norwich calls "one-ing" comes from God. The great prayer of Jesus was that his disciples would be one as the Father was in him and he was in the Father (John 17:21). It is not surprising that the "unitive stage" is regarded as the high point of all religious experience. It is reached, in varying degrees and at various levels, along life's pilgrimage. It is only in the full light of the beatific vision that it will be fully reached. In that full light, our presence to God, to each other, in a transformed creation, will have become fully and irrevocably real.

Faith, Hope, Love

Purification, illumination and union are authentic for the Christian to the extent that they are shot through with faith, hope and love. It is good to remember that these are called the "theological" virtues. Every act of each of them starts with God's initiative, God's reaching out to us in love. They are magnets by which God draws us into the divine presence and into the divine life. The divine persons keep coming to us, telling us who they are and assuring us that they want to make their home with us (John 14:23).

We walk life's journey by faith and not by sight (2 Cor 5:7). We cannot come to this faith ourselves; it comes on the initiative of God. We walk life's journey in the hope that is Christ himself who is in us as our hope of glory (Col 1:27). We walk life's journey in a love that makes us "rejoice with a joy that is indescribable and glorious" (1 Pet 1:8). It is on the quality of this love that our lives will be finally assessed.

In the continual networking of faith, hope and love, we have a mysterious blend of seeing and not seeing, of being present and being absent, of the now and the not yet, that are the warp and woof of the Christian journey on the way to the promised "rest" (cf. Heb 4). This rest is the hope of those whose yearnings are focused on "what no eye has seen, nor ear heard, nor the human heart conceived, what God has prepared for those who love him" (1 Cor 2:9). We know that the one who began the good work in us will bring it to completion (Phil 1:6), as we come finally and completely into the divine presence, full of thanksgiving (cf. Ps 95:2).

CHAPTER 20

Emptying and Filling

I once had to fill in an Italian immigration form. Under the heading of profession, I wrote *prete,* priest. Later the same morning I was in a Roman bus. A middle-aged lady noticed that I was somewhat hesitant in my steps. She rose graciously and said, "Sit down, Father." Then, to my surprise, she added, "You are a *sacerdote,* aren't you?" I'm sure she didn't realize that the word she used had more sacral connotations than the one I had put on the form. Sacral, sacerdotal words point to our relationship with the all-holy, invisible God. Presbyteral words, with their variations priest and *prete,* attend more to the role of the elder in a community. They have more space for human experience and what promotes human fulfillment.

In recent years, we have heard a lot about human fulfillment. The search for this fulfillment has been expressed largely in terms of advances in psychology and psychology-related sciences. There has been a good deal of emphasis on personal development. A lot has been written about what hinders and what promotes human growth. All of this provides a new perspective on the ancient Greek dictum "Know thyself." Knowing ourselves includes knowing our psychological strengths and weaknesses. We would ignore the new knowledge and new insights at our peril. The new knowing of who we are is surely in line with the plan of a Savior who came that we all may have life and have it more abundantly (John 10:10). It is in accord with the desire of the author of the letter to the Ephesians that we would be "filled with all the fullness of God" (3:19). It fits well into the lovely program that St. Paul set before the church at Philippi: "Whatever is true, whatever is honorable, whatever is just, whatever is pure, whatever is pleasing, whatever is commendable, if there is any excellence and if there is anything worthy of praise, think about these things. Keep on doing the things that you have learned..." (4:8, 9).

Fulfillment in God's Way

While we thank God for our new understanding of the workings of our body, mind and spirit, it is sometimes good to remember that what we might regard as fulfillment can sometimes, in God's eyes, be a diminishment of the human person and that what we might regard as failure can be triumph in God's eyes. This happens especially if we forget the limitations of human wisdom. The tension was well expressed in the writings of Hans Urs von Balthasar. He recognized the tension as being particularly noticeable in some understandings of ordained priesthood, but each of his concerns has implications for the whole priestly people, for all who minister in the church, for all those consecrated in religious life, for all those called to be love in the heart of the church. Balthasar saw the priesthood of Christ as pervading his whole body which is the church. He saw clearly that the quality of ordained ministry reflects the quality of the whole range of callings in the church, just as the quality of all these reflects the quality of ordained ministry. He had no difficulty in appreciating the place of psychology, sociology and the behavioral sciences in helping us to see the role of a priest today, but he believed that many recent writers on priesthood were so anxious to draw on secular language that the distinctive religious foundations were not being sufficiently laid and that there was a blurring of the language of the sacred. He talked of writers who regarded the very language of priesthood as a concession to residual paganism that Christianity must outgrow. He also talked of people who disliked any suggestion that human beings could in any way be our mediators with God, on the grounds that the human race had outgrown such a need.

In his concern about the erosion of the language of the sacred, Balthasar was anxious to re-situate all Christian living and all Christian ministry in the context of the once-for-all sacrifice of Christ our Great High Priest and in the foundational language that describes it in the scriptures and in Christian tradition. In doing this, he wished to keep plunging the whole communion of the church into the mystery of Christ and into the mystery of the Trinity. He envisaged God as both the composer and director of a great symphony. He saw what he called a great symphonic movement in the network of relationships that draw us into the relationships between Father, Son and Spirit. Each relationship, human and divine, keeps flowing into the others. No part of the symphony can be seen in isolation.

A Kenotic Trinity

Balthasar saw the total and loving self-giving of each of the divine persons as the only context for the self-emptying of Christ. Christ's self-emptying was his *kenosis*. This word is at the center of what could be called the signature-tune for Holy Week. This signature-tune is the invitation of St. Paul to "let the same mind be in you that was in Christ Jesus who...emptied himself" (Phil 2:5, 7). Jesus is God made human flesh. His style of giving himself is kenotic because the divine persons are, by their very nature, kenotic. Jesus held on to nothing for love of his Father who, out of love, holds on to nothing. In the plan of God's love, the self-giving of the Son mirrors forth what is going on all the time in the depths of the Trinity.

Because self-giving and self-emptying are the Father's agenda, the Son's agenda and the Spirit's agenda, they are to be the church's agenda too. Because the Father, Son and Spirit hold on to nothing, the church and her ministers should hold on to nothing. All of this constitutes a great drama. It is no wonder that, as well as seeing God as the composer and director of a great symphony, Balthasar also wrote of God as the author and producer of a great drama. The pouring out of love is the key to this drama. It is the key that interprets all the ways that Jesus handed himself over and allowed himself to be handed over. Because Jesus gave everything away, he was the most God-forsaken person that ever lived. For the same reason, he was the most God-pervaded person who ever lived. The cross of Christ is the key to all the God-forsakenness and all the abandonment that he experienced. By this very fact, it is also the key to all the ways that God can be very close to us in times of apparent abandonment. It is the great icon of the meeting place of all God-forsakenness and God-pervadedness, all dying and all rising from death. Jesus invites each of us to be part of this great drama of self-giving love.

Anybody involved in any form of church ministry soon learns that the cross is not a popular word in a culture that seeks fulfillment without pain and tears. This is true even when people are experiencing the pains and the absurdities of life to which the cross and the cross alone is the key. The cross calls people to empty themselves of self-interest by entering into the mind of the self-emptying Christ. It involves a continual program of active and passive purgation, at every level of one's being. What sustains and motivates a joyful carrying of the cross of Christ is the continual reading of its message in terms of the call to love, since it is on love that we will all be examined at the evening of our lives. It is precisely here that human wisdom and the wisdom of God can have different understandings of what diminishes and what fulfills us as human persons, of what constitutes triumph and what constitutes failure. Human wisdom, left to itself, has no place for a cross that is the expression of what St. Paul calls the foolishness of God (1 Cor 1:25). As believing Christians we do not seek the cross or look for it for its own sake. We accept it and the apparent absurdities to which it is the key as facts of life and we try to see how God revealed the depths of the divine wisdom in the mystery of Calvary and in the descent of Christ into hell. We try to identify with that wisdom. Balthasar wrote powerfully about the beauty of God being disclosed in the body of Christ precisely when "He had no form or majesty...nothing in his appearance that we should desire him" (Isa 53:1, 2).

Secular and Sacred
All of this is the context for seeing what Balthasar meant when he said that secular models are inadequate for an understanding of the priesthood of Christ and its continual expression in the church. What is secular is not primarily a thing, a place, an activity. It is rather a perspective from which we look at reality. It is a perspective in which we keep within the parameters of what we can know by human reason, human science, human exploring. The sacred, too, is not primarily a thing, a place, an activity. It is a perspective in which we are continually open to recognizing the presence and activity of the action of the unseen God in whatever we do and whatever happens to us. To be a Christian is to recognize that presence and activity in Jesus Christ in whom God has spoken to us in a unique way and who rose triumphantly out of death and hell and who assures us that he is with us always (Matt 28:20). Priestly ministry involves continually pointing people toward the world of the sacred that Jesus Christ came to disclose for us.

But where is the sacred? Is the ordained priest a man of the sacred because he is someone associated with going from sacristy to sanctuary and back? Is his work to be described in terms of the sacred because he handles sacred vessels and vestments and other sacred objects and is in a special way associated with places that are called sacred? Certainly, many popular understandings of priesthood, including some that have been encouraged by the French school of spirituality, might support that way of thinking. If we look at the world of the sacred in terms of a place, a building, a temple made by human hands, we will tend to regard all these as settings in which we are in touch with the sacred. In that perspective, the holy of holies in Jerusalem was the most sacred of places. But if we search for the realm of the sacred in terms of the temple not made by human hands, the body of the risen Christ in which we worship the Father, in spirit and truth (cf. John 4:24), we see things in a very different way. The search is worth pursuing and eventually it leads us into the most important of all depths, the depths of the heart.

The Depths of the Heart
Christians find the sacred in the heart, in the perspective of what God has told us about the heart. We find the sacred especially in the depths of the heart of the God of loving kindness whom nobody has ever seen (John 1:18) but who was made visible in the heart and body of God's incarnate Son and in the hearts and bodies of those who are members of that Son's body. Priestly ministry helps link human hearts with each other and with the Father's heart, through the heart of his Son which we significantly call the Sacred Heart. It is effective and credible to the extent to which it facilitates the flow of living water from the heart and side of Christ who is the new and living temple (cf. John 2:21). Buildings, places, things and activities are sacred to the extent that they help us to be men and women of heart. The only sacrifice that saved the world was the liturgy of the human heart of Jesus which reached right into the sanctuary of the heart of his Father. This meeting of hearts made it possible for every human heart to be an altar from which true sacrifice goes up to God.

Whatever way we understand the priesthood of the whole of the baptized and of the ministerial priesthood which serves it, the perspective must always be the free flow of trinitarian love, in the Jacob's ladder of God's continual descent to us and our continual ascent to God, as heart speaks to heart. It is the perspective in which trinitarian love becomes accessible and visible. Ordained ministry is a special call to keep people continually in touch with the loving and open heart of God. Just as the cross is the icon of God's presence when he seemed most absent, the priest is a living icon assuring us that the presence continues. In his ministry of word and sacrament and in his pastoral activity, he keeps disclosing the presence, the face, the heart, the true *persona* of Christ. His ministry is an enabling ministry, a ministry of giving and giving away. He finds his true self by pouring out his life (cf. 2 Tim 4:7) and emptying himself of whatever is not according to the mind and heart of Christ.

Interiority and Heart
In each of the three best known prayers to the Holy Spirit, we ask that our hearts will be filled. In the short 'Come, Holy Spirit', we ask the Spirit of God to fill the hearts of the faithful and to enkindle in them the fire of divine love. In the Sequence that carries the same name, we invite the blessed light from the Holy Spirit to come and fill the inner recesses of our hearts. In the "Come O Creator Spirit," we pray that our hearts will be filled with grace from on high. The result of all this filling of our hearts is that there are moments when each of us can say that, in the words of one of the Advent prefaces, our hearts are filled with wonder and love. It is from this inner filling of the heart that we can develop true interiority. Interiority can have a bad name. The interior person can be caricatured as withdrawn, isolated from the realities of the lives of ordinary mortals in a world which God loves and for which Christ died. But the truly interior person is a man or woman of real heart. The words and deeds of interior people come from the inner depths of their hearts, depths of reflection, depths of motivation, depths of conviction, depths of prayer. People of interiority speak and act in ways that really touch hearts. Their hearts speak to our hearts. St. Vincent de Paul and St. Louise de Marillac were two great activists in furthering human well-being wherever they saw human misery. After Louise's death, Vincent asked the Daughters of Charity what they saw as her greatest virtue. His own answer was interiority. Neither saint could have poured out so much love into people's lives unless they were continually emptying their hearts of all self-seeking and letting them be filled with God's love.

There is one area in which the church today is experiencing particular humiliation and being called to a lot of *kenosis*, a lot of emptying, a lot of need to be filled again. It is the area of what Balthasar called the humiliation of office. This humiliation has, in various forms, been with the church from the beginning. It began to show in Peter's betraying of the Lord. Rather than being a reason for discouragement, it is an urgent invitation to all the church's office-holders to look with real faith and real love toward the mother of all disciples and toward the disciple who kept experiencing the love of his only teacher and master. What Balthasar called the constellation comprising Peter who confirmed the disciples in faith, John who is the type of all disciples, and Mary the mother of disciples, must be continually interacting with each other. This is interiority in action, hearts in real communication.

Why the Resistance?

If priesthood and sacrifice are about hearts and what promotes their well-being, why are there so many people today who say they are tired of the language of priesthood and mediation? There would seem to be as many answers as there are people. It is good to remember that there is a very real sense in which Christians do not need mediators. The great work of mediation has been done, once-for-all, in Christ. The ministry of the ordained is a kind of immediate mediation. The task of all church ministry is to make transparent the work of our redemption, the work of our one and only mediator. Without this transparency, human mediators could give the impression that they are acting in their own right. This would be the negation of the ministry of mediation. Without transparency, the work of the ordained person, in particular, could seem like a brokering in one's own name. This happens when the ordained person exercises a kind of power and control that are the opposite of the style of the Lord who emptied himself so that we might be full. It happens when the lifestyle of the ordained person, the titles by which he expects to be addressed, the places of honor which he expects to be offered, the kinds of salutations he expects to receive in the market place (cf. Mark 12:38-39) are more reminiscent of those who live in royal palaces (cf. Matt 11:18) than of the dwelling which Jesus invited prospective disciples to come and see (John 1:39). It happens when the servant-leaders have, without their realizing it, been coming across as a caste, an elite, a chosen few who have forgotten that they were chosen only to be of self-emptying service to the many.

God's Way of Being and Doing

All the emptying which Christ willingly underwent was done so that we may be filled. His emptying is his expression of the love that has been poured into our hearts through the Holy Spirit that has been given to us (Rom 5:5). This is why the language of Christian prayer has much to say about filling and pouring and other activities that remind us of these. It was by emptying himself that Jesus poured the fullness of God into us (cf. Col 1:19). His emptying was dramatically expressed in his descent into hell. Out of that hell he was enabled to ascend again to his Father's right hand. In his emptying and in his descent, he gave himself and allowed himself to be given away, for the sake of us and for the many. All Christian ministry is an invitation to empty, to descend, to give.

All authentic ministry is a continual call for the kind of emptying that will help people to be filled with all the fullness of God (Eph 3:19). This will often call for an emptying of church ministry of baggage from another culture, another age.

All authentic ministry is a call to ask the 'love divine' to descend so that people can keep ascending to where true love is. This continual ascending and descending is beautifully symbolized in the story of Jacob's dream in which he saw a ladder set up on the earth, the top of it reaching to heaven, with the angels of God ascending and descending (Gen 28:10-17). The symbol was used by Jesus in his promise to Nathaniel that he would see the heavens laid open, with the angels ascending and descending upon the Son of Man (John 1:50, 51). It was the realization that God's ladder links heaven and wherever the believer is now that made a poet say that Jacob's ladder is pitched between heaven and Charing Cross (Francis Thompson, "In no Strange Land"). The image of the ladder is complemented by St. Thérèse's desire to find an elevator that would lift her to Jesus, since she was too small to do any climbing.

All authentic ministry is a call to give and to be given away. In a priestly ministry that is continually giving and being given away, there will be room for priests who will risk being called trendy, if that helps the flow of the good news of the gospel. There will be priests who are reluctant to have their identities expressed in the forms of garb and title that have passed their sell-by date, and there will be those who are convinced that even garb and title can sometimes be gospel reminders. There will be priests who have a high profile socially and those who are determined not to. The church is, in many senses, a church of particularities. Each of its ministers is called, like its founder, to help people to recognize the presence and action of God in this particular place, with this particular people at this particular time.

The Counsels

In the continual program of emptying and filling, descending and ascending, giving and being given away, Balthasar saw the centrality of the place of the evangelical counsels as expressing the radical call of the gospel. In line with some other recent writers, he saw chastity, obedience and poverty not as the preserve of the few but rather as somehow a program for all disciples. Celibate priesthood and the vowed religious life are two particular expressions of what was intended as an agenda for all. In this perspective, Balthasar saw no need for an apologia for priestly celibacy. He saw obedience in terms of continual self-giving and self-emptying. He saw a specially privileged place for evangelical poverty which expresses our relationship with Father, Son and Spirit who hold on to nothing. To those who would say that this upstaging of the counsels might tend to blur the lines of demarcation between the call to religious life and the call to diocesan priesthood, he would calmly say that this blurring is good if it focuses us all on the person and mission of our one and only Savior who gives us true fulfillment as we join him in his self-emptying. For him, the vocation of the diocesan priest is in what he called a delicate medial position between religious vocation and lay vocation.

Truly Fulfilled?

One may well ask whether priests and those vowed to live the evangelical counsels really come across to us as truly fulfilled people, people who have key roles in a great symphony, a great drama. An honest answer may be that we have had glimpses of such fulfillment but that we would not like to say anything more definite. More disturbingly, we might look back at some of the model seminarians and religious whom we have admired and the straps of whose sandals we didn't feel worthy to loose, people whose every thought, word and deed was gospel-inspired and who now, sadly, walk no more with us and have, perhaps for long, been victims of disillusionment, breakdown, or dysfunction of one kind or another. And there is good reason to think that many of those who have recently been in the news in connection with various forms of human abuse started their priestly or religious lives with the highest ideals and the loveliest dream of total discipleship. Here we are dealing with mystery indeed, and any judgment of individuals is certainly not in order.

One line of thought suggests itself. Jesus emptied himself and, in so doing, he was filled. The deeper he descended, the more he was helped to ascend. In giving all away, he was given the name that is above every other name (Phil 2:9). He invited us to leave all but he promised to reward us a hundredfold, even in this life (Matt 19:29). There is a kind of giving in priestly and religious life that is impoverishing rather than enriching. There are communities who serve the poor but who themselves become very impoverished in the process. They become physically tired, emotionally drained, dried up in terms of human conversation, with no leisure to appreciate the beautiful. It is significant that, like many other documents on priestly formation, the post-synodal document of 1992, *Pastores Dabo Vobis,* dealt with spiritual, intellectual and pastoral formation. But it gave considerable prominence to a fourth element, human formation. In fact, it placed this element first (par. 43–45). It stated that the whole work of priestly formation would be deprived of its necessary foundation if it lacked a suitable human foundation. It stated that the priest should mold his human personality in such a way that it becomes a bridge and not an obstacle for others in their meetings with Jesus Christ. It talked of and listed the human qualities that future priests should cultivate. It talked of affective maturity. It talked of the urgent need for properly understood sexual education. It talked of a training in mature and responsible freedom and about authentic realization of self. It saw the intimate connection between this responsible freedom and the education of the moral conscience. It talked of human formation being carried out in the context of an anthropology that is open to the full truth of what it is to be human. In the context of this openness, it saw human formation as leading to and finding its completion in spiritual formation.

The Journey Ahead
We have a long way to go before the implications of this section of the post-synodal document will be fully appreciated and

before its vision will become a reality. It may well be that it is here that all the secular models and paradigms for leadership in church ministry will really come into their own. Balthasar was clear that these should always be secondary in our understanding of the implications of the priesthood of Christ. He was convinced that some writing had put them at center-stage. But he in no way believed that they are unimportant. There has been a variety of assessments of the strengths and weaknesses of his arguments. The tension will remain in our continuing search for a holistic approach to priestly formation and to all Christian formation, initial and ongoing. One hopes that we will do full justice to both the Christ-form of emptying and filling and to whatever history teaches us about what is true and good and beautiful and healthy in human experience.

In going back to the great gospel foundations for the Christian vocation, about the religious vocation, about priestly vocation, we are building on a rock. In doing so, we keep our eyes fixed on Jesus, the Word of God who emptied himself by becoming one flesh with us so that we might be one body with him, filled and fulfilled in God's way.

CHAPTER 21

Discerning the Body

When I was being introduced to the study of theology, there was much talk about the Mystical Body of Christ. It had been only a short time since Pope Pius XII had written his great encyclical of which that was the title. Many people were joining the Legion of Mary which gave and gives a good deal of prominence to the doctrine. In our theology courses, and not just in the ones that dealt directly with the topic of the church, the idea of the Mystical Body seemed an inexhaustible source for new approaches. Up to the time of the Second Vatican Council, it provided a lot of nourishment for the prayer life and apostolic life of many. When the Council came, I was one of the many who took it for granted that the Mystical Body would receive a new prominence. I was particularly sure that it would form the backbone and the leitmotiv for not only the Council's direct teaching on the church but for all its teaching. In fact, I expected that the teaching of the Council would be a development of what the Pope had said so well in his encyclical. He had said that there was "no more noble name" for the church, "none more excellent, none more divine than the Mystical Body of Christ." It was, he said, "a name which blossoms like a flower from numerous passages of sacred scripture and the writings of the fathers of the church."

As the contents of the new *Constitution on the Church, Lumen Gentium,* began to become public in 1964, it was clear that the assembled bishops had decided to take a different line. The first of the eight chapters was on the mystery of the church, the unfolding in time of the secret and eternal plan of the three divine persons. In the second chapter, the Council fathers had sought for an overarching image for an understanding of what constitutes the church. They did not choose in favor of the "Mystical Body of Christ." They chose the title "the People of God." But already, in the chapter on the mystery of the church, they had given much prominence to many of the biblical images that help us to understand the church. They had stated that, by communicating his Spirit, Christ "mystically constitutes as his body those brothers and sisters of his who are called together from every nation" (par. 7). This long and rich paragraph pointed to many of the implications of the body image. It is interesting that, in the paragraph itself, the expression "Mystical Body of Christ" does not appear. The continual reference is to "the body," "Christ's body," "his body." Pius XII had clearly distinguished between the physical body of Christ and his mystical body. In the intervening years, there had been a search for new ways of expressing the vital union of believers with and in the one body of Christ. There was also a growing awareness of an old and venerable usage according to which Christ's glorified body present in the Eucharist was seen as the Mystical Body. There can be no denying that the Council fathers paid attention to the new and old understandings of our being one body with Christ. It would be far from correct to say that all their teaching on the church as the body of Christ is contained in the *Constitution on the Church.* And still some people were disappointed with the fact that the image of the body did not receive anything like as great a prominence as it did in the teaching of Pope Pius XII. However one assesses this issue, it is certain that the body image has, from many directions, received a new prominence since the days of the Council.

A New Prominence
In the great search for new ways of imaging God and God's relationship with the universe that followed Bishop John A. T. Robinson's *Honest to God* (in 1963) a good deal of prominence was given to the image of the body. In some writings, the whole of creation was imaged as being somehow the body of God. The image has had considerable influence. At the same time, there has been a lot of writing about Christian attitudes to the human body. On the one hand, there have been suggestions that, in spite of the healthy understanding of the unity of the human person that prevails in the Bible, some Christians came to make strong divisions between "soul" and "body." They had been influenced, it was said, by various dualisms that tend to divide the human person. These divisions were attributed to many sources. Much as we would all acknowledge the great and good influence of the philosopher Plato, many saw him as the source of much of the dualism that was to color a lot of Christian thinking. Many

writers have detected a variety of forms of Platonism and neo-Platonism at work over the Christian centuries. What is perhaps much more serious is that there are many signs in Christian history of the influence of Manichaeism which, in essence, looked on matter as evil and, by implication, saw the human body as evil. There is still some writing on priestly celibacy which suggests that, at least in some of its aspects, it is an articulation of some Manichaean influences. The same applies to the whole topic of Christian, and especially Catholic, attitudes to human sexuality in general.

It would be easy to attempt simplistic and defensive answers to the many historical questions about Catholic approaches to the body. Indeed, one cannot deny the reality of many of the not so noble influences that colored our tradition. One can be grateful that, allowing for all the ways our tradition has been colored and discolored, we have continued to proclaim, with some pride and joy, that everything made by the hand of God is good (cf. Gen 1). One is also grateful that, for centuries, we have been saying that, just as every being participates in the oneness and truth of God, every being is privileged to participate in the very goodness of God. One can be grateful, too, for what the very influential St. Thomas Aquinas contributed to our understanding of the whole human body. Though he was careful to distinguish between body and soul, he did not separate the two. He saw the human being not as body only or as soul only but as body-soul. Though he learned much from Plato, the philosopher who most helped him to articulate his understanding of human unity was Aristotle in whose language of matter and form he kept finding new resources.

A Growing Emphasis

In the teaching of the Second Vatican Council and in all the official church teaching that followed it, there has been a growing emphasis on the unity and goodness of the human body-soul. Catholic writers generally have been at pains to situate every aspect of human sexuality in the context of this unity and goodness. Even when they speak of the disorders to which human sexuality is prone, they very rarely lose sight of this perspective. Some have cynically described this as a making up for lost time. Ironically, it is often in the defending of the human body and of human sexuality that official Catholic teaching meets up with opposition. Since the promulgation of the encyclical *Humanae Vitae*, "On Human Life," in 1968, Popes have found themselves in positions in which they felt called to defend the rights of every human body. In a sense, the great question has become "What think you of the human body?" Much papal teaching has focused on what is special about the human body, at conception, before birth, at birth, at every stage of life, at death—all in the perspective of what Christians see as the destiny of the human body after death. Sometimes it has been an uphill struggle. Pope John Paul II's encyclical *Evangelium Vitae*, "The Gospel of Life," could be called a charter for the human body. In writing it, the Pope was well aware of the weaknesses, the limitations and, in a sense, the worthlessness of the human body. But it is precisely in this weakness, this limitation, this worthlessness that he asked us to see the loving wisdom of God at work, just as it was at work when his Son's body was most frail and most apparently worthless.

A Prophet of the Body

The prophet of the human body in our time has been Mother Teresa. Shortly after her death, one of her young Missionaries of Charity was asked on a television program why she had joined the community and why she had stayed. In her reply she said that, as a university student, she had been moved by the continual news of Mother Teresa's concern for the poorest of the poor. She described how, on the morning after she was accepted into the community, she attended Mass with the other sisters. Later in the morning, there was a period of eucharistic adoration. Later again she and another prospective sister traveled with Mother Teresa to a very poor part of the city. On the way, they noticed a man in a most degrading condition. Mother Teresa insisted on stopping and seeing to it that the man got every possible attention and loving care. Later that day, she said to the two aspirants, "Wasn't it beautiful this morning when we were asked to take the body of Christ and eat it? And wasn't it beautiful that we were able to adore the Lord's body on the altar? The body of the man we attended on the way is one body with the one we received and adored." "After that," said the young sister, "I couldn't look back."

The life and example of Mother Teresa captured admirably the core of what Christians, at their best, think and feel about the

body, about their own bodies, about the bodies of others, about
the body of Christ. The more we reflect on the teaching of St.
Paul, a teaching that is closely linked with his own experience of
being asked "Saul, Saul, why do you persecute me?" (Acts 9:4),
the more we realize that being baptized into Christ means
becoming one body with him and with each other. While we appreciate Pope Pius XII's clear distinction between the physical
body of Christ and his mystical body, we keep looking for new
ways of expressing the mystery of our identification with
Christ's body as a result of baptism and the fact that our bodies
become a kind of continuation of his body. The emphasis on
baptism should not leave the bodies of the unbaptized out in the
cold. The chapter on the People of God in the *Constitution on the
Church* groped for words to express how all other people of
goodwill are, in various ways, "related to" and "joined to" the
church that is the body of Christ (par. 15, 16). Naming these re-
latings and joinings has been part of the work of ecumenism and
inter-religious dialogue ever since. The identification of the baptized with the body of Christ is the basis for our belief that, just
as we depend on Christ, he allows himself to depend on us. In
religious circles and outside them, much has been made in recent years of the story of the broken statue of Christ that spoke
and said, "I have no hands but yours; I have no feet but yours."

Eating and Drinking Worthily

In the light of all this, there is an urgent task for Christians to
recognize the Lord's body whenever and however it manifests
itself. The most powerful expression of this urgent task is in the
first letter to the Corinthians which could be called the letter on
the body. In the eleventh chapter, St. Paul describes a group who
thought they were fittingly celebrating the Eucharist and were
told bluntly that they were not really celebrating the Lord's
Supper (v. 20). Having outlined the activity of the group, Paul
said, "You are eating and drinking unworthily" (v. 27). They
were not discerning the body (v. 29). Paul told them that, before
they did eat and drink, they should "examine" themselves (v. 28).
I, for one, was brought up in the belief that this lack of discerning consisted in not being sufficiently reverent toward the consecrated species. I was taught that "examining" oneself meant
what we would today call going to confession before receiving
Holy Communion. I am now convinced that the examining

means a whole change of outlook whereby one realizes that the poor who were humiliated at the eucharistic gatherings in Corinth were the body of the Lord about which Paul was talking. The examining that Paul called for was the opening of the eyes of the rich in a way that would make them say, "He is a member of the body of the Lord; she is a member of the body of the Lord; we receive the body of the Lord; we are the body of the Lord."

In the widespread interest in spirituality today, there are so many voices that people often don't hear each other. Even within the community of the baptized, there is a good deal of fragmentation. Some look for a spirituality in which all Christians will feel equally at home. Some seek for a new spirituality of marriage. Some seek for a distinctive spirituality of diocesan priesthood. Some seek for a deeper spirituality of religious life and, within religious life itself, they talk of the myriad shapes of spirituality that take into account the different charisms and traditions of different institutes. It is all a worthwhile search, but there will be no real headway until there is a greater deepening of our understanding of the baptismal call of all Christians. This is a call to be body. It is by baptism that all of us become one body with Christ. We are "plunged" into the Lord's living body.

One Spirituality?

It is in this context that we can best answer the question as to whether there is one Christian spirituality or whether there are several Christian spiritualities. The prevailing way of speaking would seem to favor the second view. One hears, for example, of a spirituality of marriage, a spirituality of sexuality, a spirituality of leisure. The possible list is endless. But this way of speaking encourages a new fragmentation. A strong case can be made for saying that there is only one Christian spirituality and that it consists in being disciples of the Christ into whom we are all baptized. It is here that the multiplicity finds its place. Rather than speak of a spirituality of marriage, it would be better to speak of the particular ways in which discipleship is expressed in the living-body-to-living-body relationship that is unique to Christian marriage. Rather than speak of a distinctive spirituality of diocesan priesthood, the focus should be on the paths of discipleship which the person authorized to say "This is my body" is asked to walk. Rather than talk of a special spirituality of the body, it is better to keep asking what light Christian discipleship throws on our attitudes to the body. I believe, in fact, that this is the question that best unifies all our understandings of Christian spirituality. I believe that the clarion call of all Christian spirituality is summed up in two words—the body.

As a Christian, I am called to have a unified vision of all the aspects of my body, physical, psychological, psycho-sexual. As a Christian, I cannot fully understand my own body except in relation to the bodies of others. As a Christian, I cannot understand human bodies in isolation from the whole universe which, according to one metaphor, is the body of God. As a Christian, I cannot see my body and the bodies of others in isolation from the body of Christ, with which all of us have become somehow identified at baptism. So the call of St. Paul to discern the body has many implications. It has implications for every moment of my existence. It has implications for how I approach the celebration of the Eucharist and how I see my place in the universe, for the life of which the Eucharist exists. It is all very well expressed in the Christmas homily of Pope St. Leo the Great: "O Christian, be aware of your nobility...Think of the head, think of the body of which you are a member...."

Corporal and Spiritual

Over the centuries, Christians have managed to concentrate many of their convictions and beliefs around the number seven and around the numbers three and four that add up to seven. One powerful list of seven is the list of the corporal works of mercy:

Feeding the hungry
Giving drink to the thirsty
Clothing the naked
Sheltering the homeless
Visiting the sick
Ministering to prisoners
Burying the dead.

This is the program that grows out of St. Paul's call to discern the body. The list has an astounding freshness. As a call to discern the body, it is a beautiful context for all that is involved in the preferential option for the poor and the many calls to justice and peace which we have been receiving in recent times. The corporal works of mercy cannot be separated from the spiritual works of mercy:

Converting the sinner
Instructing the ignorant
Counseling the doubtful
Comforting the sorrowful
Bearing wrongs patiently
Forgiving injuries
Praying for the living and the dead.

Does the distinction between spiritual and corporal works of mercy tend to perpetuate a dualism between body and spirit that would be better abandoned? It all depends on how we use words. If spirituality is about the human spirit in tune with the divine spirit and interpreting all created and uncreated reality, it should be clear that concern with the spiritual should in no way take away from the importance of discerning the body. To talk about the human being in terms of body, mind and spirit is not to divide the corporal from the spiritual. The human spirit does not inhabit a world somehow superior to the world of the body. Body and spirit are one. And to talk about works of mercy is not a call to be condescending. It is a call to participate in the nature of the God who is forever merciful and true.

The call to practice the corporal and spiritual works of mercy is a good context for understanding the seven sins that are variously called capital and deadly. All of these are deadly in that they can contribute to the destroying of both body and spirit. The works of mercy flow healthily from three virtues called theological and they are further enlivened by the four cardinal virtues, the hinge virtues of prudence, justice, fortitude and temperance. After an eclipse for some decades, there is a new interest in all virtues today. Virtue literally means strength. To keep discerning the body of the Lord we need much strengthening, especially when we realize that we carry our treasure in the clay jars that are our bodies (cf. 2 Cor 4:7).

From Motive to Motive
The call to discern the body keeps finding a new motivation and a new perspective in each of those topics that make up the contents of all of these chapters. It finds new motivation in our relationship with the three divine persons and in our learning to sit at each of the many tables to which they invite us, and in the program for daily living to which they are calling us. It finds a new motivation every time we realize that we are called to be

members of a saving church, a sacrificing church, an interceding church. It finds a new motivation every time we realize that we are called to make our home in God's word. It finds a new motivation every time we realize that we are living stones in a living temple in the building up of which all those consecrated in baptism, all those consecrated in religious life, and all those consecrated in ordination need each other and support each other. It finds a new motivation whenever we are called to be present, to be emptied, to be filled. It finds a new motivation when we are called to be members of or work with various groupings that make visible the compassion of God. It finds a new motivation every time we are called to be and to do something beautiful for God.

CHAPTER 22

Preached or Directed?

When I had been a priest for ten years, my provincial superior asked me to prepare to give a retreat to a group of diocesan priests. I was both honored and awed. I was honored because I knew that this work was near to the center of what we now call the charism of our community. I was awed because I was being asked to enter closely into the lives of men whose daily ministry was far removed from the seminary walls behind which I was working. But my provincial gave me every encouragement; he gave me a full year to prepare; he told me that such retreats lasted for about four days and that there were normally three or four lectures a day as well as a few other shorter inputs. He admitted that preparing the lectures might be hard going, but he consoled me by saying that the notes would stand me in good stead for the rest of my life. The priesthood, he said, doesn't really change and the topics that priests need to hear about at retreat time do not change. He didn't suggest a list of topics, but he advised me to talk to a few diocesan priests and the list would take shape as the year went on.

Over the year, I did a lot of reading on priesthood and on priests' retreats; I reflected a lot on what I was reading; I remembered the good preached retreats that I had experienced in my own community. I took to heart the words of a wise and elderly colleague who had doubts about the value of preached retreats and who assured me that the very idea was a relative newcomer in the Vincentian tradition. I talked to quite a few diocesan priests and I was particularly fortunate to be able to drink at the wells of the wisdom of a few priests who had preached quite a few diocesan retreats. I went through my own notes of retreats I had given to religious women and, though I was keenly aware of the difference between the daily life of a sister and the daily life of a diocesan priest, I found myself seeing clearly that we cannot talk convincingly about Christian ways of holiness unless we are clear on what is the one Christian way of holiness.

As the months went by, the topics fell into place. I managed to compose two lectures each month. By Christmas I was about halfway through; by Easter all the foundations had been well laid; from Easter on, I was able to cross many t's and dot many i's; by summer, I had all the lecture material assembled in a large, handsome copybook. I knew that I hadn't written in stone or in iron, but I was confident that I had assembled something that would last, if not for my lifetime, at least for many years.

First Rumblings

The retreat came and went. The priests were encouraging in their words of thanks. I had decided to go against the wise advice I had received in my student days that one should never say, "This is my first time preaching to a group like you." Our mentor had told us that, if we spoke like that, the listeners would quickly conclude that they were dealing with an amateur who had book knowledge only; I had a feeling that my retreatants would come to this conclusion anyway. Be that as it may, they were generous in the ways they said "Well done!" But a few of them who were both discerning and courageous told me, in the most courteous of ways, that though my lectures were fine for a first-time attempt, they would need a good deal of reshaping. I took their words to heart; I purchased a new and smaller copybook and I wrote in a number of additions, corrections, and modifications. In one instance I canceled a whole lecture and wrote a new one, but the foundations were laid. I was ready and willing to give another retreat next summer. The work involved was minimal compared with the workload of the previous year. This was to be the pattern of things for a number of years to come.

It took me quite a while before I saw any new light. But there were flashes on the way. One of these came in a conversation with a priest-friend who, shortly after the Second Vatican Council, was invited by Cardinal Heenan to preach the annual retreat for the priests of Westminster. The Cardinal himself took part in the retreat. After the retreat, he wrote a letter to the preacher. It was full of glowing tributes but the last paragraph contained a gem—"I would advise you, Father," wrote the Cardinal, "to tear up all your notes for the retreat. The word of God is so important that a priest should not preach the same sermon twice; above all, he should not preach the same retreat sermon twice." As we discussed the Cardinal's letter, my priest-friend and I had a few good laughs. But we were agreed that the preached word should always be fully alive.

More to Come

In the early 1980s, I was appointed full time to the Damascus House retreat and conference center in North London. I discovered that the number and variety of retreats and retreatants was quite mind-blowing. The retreatants included lay people, religious and priests. Some asked for a completely solitary and silent retreat, with no fixed retreat exercises. Some looked for the kind of preached retreat that I had been used to. But a growing number of retreatants were from Christian communities that were coming to terms with the call of the Second Vatican Council to return to the living sources from which their communities had originally come into being. The largest number of these were, in various ways, living and working in the tradition of St. Ignatius. Many of them had been rediscovering the treasures of that tradition. Some of these treasures were in the constitutions of the Society of Jesus. The rediscovery of the riches of *The Spiritual Exercises of St. Ignatius* was having an impact that one could best describe as explosive. Here was a gold mine providing riches not merely for the body of the Society of Jesus but for many other men and women who were seeking help and light in their journey into God. Already one was hearing about the great pioneering work being done in places like Guelph in Canada, St. Beuno's in North Wales, Manresa in Dublin. Many of those coming to our retreat house had, in various ways, tasted the rich fare on offer at such centers. Significantly, a growing number of them were lay people.

The impact of all this left me with a number of perplexing questions. Was there a future for the kind of retreat that I had presumed to be the norm? Was it too late to try to learn new ways? In my questioning, I went to talk to an experienced Jesuit. His advice was good. "Do what you feel most confident in doing," he said. He was, I think, telling me that there was and would be a place for every kind of retreat, and he seemed clear as to what my place might be. But I still felt the need to be basically literate in the directed form of retreat. I signed on for a six-day directed retreat and I was fortunate to have a patient and wise director. This gave me confidence to sign on, shortly afterwards, for a thirty-day retreat in Guelph, and for the days that led up to it and that followed it. Of the forty-eight participants, a third were lay people, a third priests, a third members of religious communities. After some further experiences of directed retreats, I was accepted as a member of a team of men and women giving a directed retreat. Through all of this time, I had to endure the teasing of some of my colleagues who wondered when was I going to join the Society! I remembered my very fine novice master who, not too approvingly, used to describe some religious practices as "a bit Ignatian!" Around the time of my Guelph experience, he was persuaded to do the full thirty-day Exercises. We all waited with bated breath for his verdict. "Wonderful," he said, "very Vincentian." Interestingly, our community historian pointed out that when St. Vincent was providing for the best possible formation for his first novices and students, he thought it wise to send a very gifted priest away for a year to be trained by the Jesuits.

New Vistas

Even in my years in the London retreat house, I continued to be invited to preach retreats to priests. But it was clear that something new was happening. The number attending the retreats was diminishing. On making discreet enquiries, I was to learn that, in many dioceses, the priests were being offered a choice of different kinds of retreat. They could go to the official preached retreat or they could go for a directed retreat. Even among those opting for the preached retreat, a good deal of questioning was going on. While they all liked the social aspects of being together with priests from all over the diocese, many wondered whether the days together really deserved the name of retreat. The questioning was becoming more and more acute as the more rigid structures of the older form of diocesan retreat were breaking down. Word was going round that priests who had had one experience of directed retreat were saying that they would never again take part in a preached retreat.

What was happening at the diocesan level was replicated for me as I went to preach retreats to various church groupings, lay, religious and clerical. The change was particularly noticeable in religious communities of women and men and, all the time, I was myself engaged in a search. Just a year ago, I was one of a team of directors with a group of seminarians. The practice of the seminary in question has, in very recent years, been to alternate between an annual directed retreat and an annual preached retreat. I became convinced that the directed retreat has come to stay. In preparing for the retreat, I wondered whether I should carefully follow the model that has become common in many directed retreats today or whether I should follow the basic dynamic of the Ignatian exercises and allow myself a good deal of scope, especially in the choice of scripture texts. One reason why an adaptation seemed called for was that the retreat was to last for less than four days. This seemed to call for a special work of adaptation. I had to make my own decisions.

Which is the Greater?

My search goes on. As I prepare now for yet another preached retreat to priests, there are many questions on my mind. I have decided, in fact, to open the retreat with a question. I intend to ask what, in the light of all the unforeseen developments in recent years, is the best kind of retreat for baptized persons, whether they are lay people, religious or priests. My answer will not, I think, be in terms of preached or directed. It will be something like this: the best retreat is the one in which the retreatant allows himself or herself the greatest space to speak to God and to listen to God. I have a growing conviction that, for this to happen, the directed retreat needs elements from the preached retreat and the preached retreat needs elements from the directed retreat. If I feel drawn in favor of one rather than the other, it remains toward the preached retreat. My basic reason is somehow situated in St. Paul's conviction that "faith comes from what is heard" (Rom 10:17) and his question, "How are they to hear without someone to proclaim?" (v. 14). In this I am supported, I think, by St. Ignatius in his stress on the importance of the right kind of knowledge and the right kind of knowing. I am also encouraged by his allowing for much flexibility and scope for different ways of praying and for human freedom in the making of the Exercises. I know that, in the recent renewal in the giving of the Exercises, there is a very strong movement away from any preaching of the Exercises to the giving of one-to-one direction. But there is preaching and there is preaching. Good retreat preaching is not the giving of lectures. The retreat director is there for only one purpose, to facilitate the flow of communication between the retreatant and God. He or she is there to provide prayer-aids, communication aids, hearing aids, seeing aids, speaking aids. In the search that this entails, there is much to be said for various forms of what I would call "the Heenan principle." What is suitable for this re-treatant, this year, may not be suitable for the same person next year. In the movement from preaching the Exercises to one-to-one direction, there is room for many forms of preaching and directing, as heart speaks to heart.

A Clear Dynamic
The basic dynamic of the full Exercises is now well known. The thirty days are divided into four "weeks," some "weeks" being longer than others. The exercitant/retreatant begins with the "principle and foundation," the realization that we are created "to praise, reverence, and serve God, Our Lord" and thereby reach our salvation.

In the first week, the retreatant is alerted to the reality and implications of sin in all its dimensions.

The second week concerns the "election," the choice of a way of life or the renewing or reforming of the way of life in which one finds oneself already. In this week, all that concerns decision is important. The focus is on the kingdom of Christ the eternal king. This is the week to meditate on the two standards under which one can live one's life. This meditating provides a kind of x-ray of what is really going on in one's mind. Meditation on "the three kinds of persons" provides a similar x-ray for what is influencing our wills and our decisions. Consideration of the "three kinds of humility" brings the x-ray into the deep recesses of the "heart." The retreatant, immersed in the mysteries of Christ's life from the beginning to the Last Supper, keeps con-templating him and praying to know, love and serve him better.

The third and fourth weeks are taken up with "confirma-tion,"a word that concerns strengthening and consolidating what was decided and chosen in the course of the second week. The retreatant desires to be deeply with the Lord as passion moves toward resurrection. The decision of the second week is plunged into these.

The third week can profitably be given over to recognizing the ways in which God, up to now, has been leading and strengthening us toward the great goal of salvation. We are en-couraged and strengthened by immersing ourselves in the mys-teries of the passion, crucifixion and entombment of the Lord in the spirit of a prayer dear to St. Ignatius: "Passion of Christ, strengthen me; within thy wounds hide me."

In the fourth week we seek the kind of confirmation that will lead us in the future into the final sharing of the glory of the Lord. In the "contemplation to attain love," we are encouraged to enter into the joy and gladness of the mystery of the Lord's risen life. This is the real setting for finding God in all things.

Most retreats that one is called to preach or direct last for from three to eight days. It is difficult to deal with the substance of the Exercises in three days. Much can be done in five or, better still, six days. I have come to see that, in both the preached and directed retreat, the basic dynamic and the substantial content of the Exercises cannot be surpassed. For both, I have recently been trying to work out a program for a five-day retreat. In the shorter or longer retreat, suitable adaptations can be made. This is the skeleton outline:

Day 1: Why do I exist? For me, asking and answering this question is always reminiscent of a retreat preacher who influenced me profoundly during my novitiate days. He startled us in the way he asked us, "What are you for?" He asked us and asked us again. I believe it was his version of the "principle and foundation." Nowadays, the topic deserves a whole day in a five-day retreat. It situates the retreatants in the network of the related words *creator, creation, creature*. It helps them to keep looking in the direction of their final destiny and to order their desires and decisions in that direction.

Day 2: What is keeping me from giving glory to God?

Day 3: Deciding or re-deciding to give greater glory to God by knowing, loving, serving.

Day 4: Who and what has confirmed and strengthened me in doing this in the past?

Day 5: Who or what will confirm and strengthen me in doing it for the rest of my life? A final call to "love the love that loves you."

The Place of God's Word

At the risk of generalizing, it can be said that entering into the full liturgical life of the church has not been a prominent feature in the Ignatian *Spiritual Exercises*. The Exercises have not been famous for encouraging the retreatant to enter deeply into the Common or Proper of the Mass of each day or into the psalms or readings of the Office of the day. There have been good reasons for this. It would appear that the principal reason was the difficulty in harmonizing two dynamics, the dynamic of the liturgy and the dynamic of the Exercises. A feature of the giving of the Exercises, at least in recent years, has been the providing by the retreat director of daily scripture readings to match the movement of the four weeks.

In my own attempts to wed the basic dynamic of the Exercises with various elements of the tradition of spirituality in which I was formed, and with the contemporary searching for ways of balancing personal spiritual growth and communal spiritual growth, I find myself searching directly in the liturgy itself for suitable scripture readings. I now see my main preparation for the retreat as a careful searching into the Masses and Offices of the five days. Each time, I find texts admirably suited for the topic for each of the five days. A result is that I might find myself suggesting for the first day a scripture text that will be coming up on the fifth day. It is one of my ways of contributing to the renewal of *lectio divina* which has much in common with St. Ignatius' second method of praying. It helps me in the search for a spirituality grounded in the word of God at a time when we are being encouraged to subject all spirituality to gospel spirituality and to find new ways of absorbing the daily word that seems to pass by the heads and hearts of many of those who half-hear it. I like to draw, in particular, on the gospel of the evangelist of the year and on the continuous readings. I have no qualms in sometimes going outside the scriptural readings and drawing on spiritual writings from the tradition in which the retreatants have been nourished.

The search for suitable scriptural and other texts keeps leading me back into the dynamic of the Exercises. Part of this dynamic is the very language of the Exercises. Here indeed we have something bordering on an infinite treasure. There is a continual opening up of new vistas in words and expressions like the following, which I choose at random but I don't use at random:

what I want and desire
interior knowledge
praying for a particular grace
not to be deaf to God's call
dispositions
application of the senses

repetition

finding God in all things, actions and conversations

enjoying the Lord in many places and duties rather than in one only

interior understanding and savoring.

All of this is in the perspective of "the greater glory of God." Perhaps we should more correctly speak of the greatest glory of God. Here the word *greatest* is not a question of quantity. We are talking of the glory that has its source in a human being fully alive, in mind, in will, in feelings, in affections, in desires. It is the glory that comes from the depths of a person who prays, "Take, Lord, and receive all my liberty, my memory, my understanding, and my entire will, all that I have and possess."

The Questions Remain

In my transition from the lecture form of preached retreat to new blendings of new things and old, I am still left with many questions. Can you expect the person used to the older form of preached retreat to do daily the three, four or five hours of prayer that are taken for granted in the directed retreat? My answer is that it can be done but that we are dealing here with a process that demands patience and time and that one can have too much of a mystique of measurement by hours. With a large group of retreatants, how can we provide for the one-to-one communication between retreatant and preacher? One answer is to say simply that it cannot be done. But there are other possibilities. One possibility is to ask each retreatant to find one person, whether a fellow retreatant or somebody on the staff of the retreat center, with whom the retreatant will talk daily in a heart-to-heart way about what is going on in his or her heart in response to the word of God. One should not bargain for seeing this as a poor second-best. Some of my own experimenting has been encouraging. It has been most encouraging when I keep pondering the contents of the Ignatian Exercises.

I have found that some of the new blendings keep overflowing during the year into the lives of the retreatants. One example is in the use of the new forms of examen of consciousness which pick up many of the best elements of the examinations of conscience that had gone threadbare by dint of unimaginative usage. I have met people who shape their own private "five days" at suitable times during the year. I have met people who are making new sense out of the rather staid language of purgation, illumination and union which they had heard of in the older textbooks of ascetical theology. I have met people for whom retreats had become a wearying experience but who, with the help of new blendings, have found a new heart and a new spirit. And that is surely what all retreats are about.

CHAPTER 23

At the Shrine of the Lamb: Knock Calls

The day I received my first Holy Communion, my mother gave me a very precious gift. She handed me a small silver locket and she asked me to treasure it all my life. She explained to me that the locket was called an Agnus Dei and that the words meant Lamb of God. On one side of the locket was the figure of the cross of Christ. On the other side was the image of a lamb. Later I was to learn that the locket contained wax from a paschal candle and the relic of a saint, presumably a martyr.

My first communion day was a lovely introduction to the Lamb of God. Over the years I have heard of many beautiful representations of the mystery of the Lamb. There is none more thought-provoking and prayer-provoking than the one at the gable wall of the parish church in Knock, County Mayo. It tries to capture the experience of a group of people who had a vision of the Lamb in 1879. There is a sense in which the shrine at Knock is just one more shrine of Our Lady, but this time our attention is drawn to her Son who is the Lamb of God taking away the sins of the world.

Hard Times
The original vision took place during hard times. They were the times of a second famine in Ireland. My mother was born about seven years later. From the accounts she gave me of her childhood, I can only conclude that, along with her neighbors, she had her share of hard times. Having completed her primary school education, she was one of thousands who emigrated from Cobh to Boston to earn a modest fortune. The years that surrounded my first introduction to the Lamb of God were the hard times in which people experienced the grimness of an economic war in the years leading up to the Second World War. All of this would seem to indicate that the Lamb of God is particularly close to people at any times that can be called hard. Indeed,

our principal introduction to the sacrificial lamb in the Bible is in the descriptions of the annual ritual of the slaying of a lamb in the celebrations of a people going out of a land of bondage. In these celebrations, there was a delicate combination of spring festival and religious sacrifice.

The Lamb of God who takes away our sins by his blood continues to have a strong prominence in our celebrations of who we are as Christians. The church has come to see the Lamb as identical with the suffering servant of God who was crushed with pain for the sins of the many and was like a lamb led to the slaughter (Isa 53). It is significant that we give prominence to the Lamb not just in some Masses but in every Mass, not just once but twice. Shortly before holy communion we call on the Lamb of God who takes away the sins of the world and we ask him to have mercy on us and to grant us peace. A moment later, we look up at the same Lamb and we declare ourselves blessed because we are called to his supper now, in anticipation of that great final supper at which the Lamb will be our host in heaven. In Masses in which we say the Gloria, we ask the Lamb to receive our prayers. The whole of the Easter liturgy is steeped in variations on the theme of the Lamb who was slain but who is now fully alive. The innocent Lamb is seen as atoning for our lack of innocence. We praise the genius of God who brings life where there seemed to be only death. Drawing on such sources as the Book of Revelation, the Easter church gives almost daily expression to the paradoxes of a divine plan in which the Lamb gathers the sheep and God keeps turning the tables for those who thought that human ingenuity is better than God's wisdom.

Hard Times Again

The Lamb once slain continues to be the supporter of all those who are going through hard times. Nobody would claim that we live in the kind of hard times that prevailed in 1879 and intermittently through to the Second World War and after. We are living not in a time of economic war but in a time of an economic boom that would have been unimaginable in the not too distant past. But it is a hard time to be a Christian and to follow the Lamb "wherever he goes" (Rev 14:4), not just along the ways that are humanly attractive. In Europe generally, Christians have been experiencing many forms of decline. In Ireland, the decline has sometimes been steep. There are times when we cannot help recalling the Lord's question: "When the Son of Man comes, will he find faith on earth?" (Luke 18:8).

In this situation, one could speculate as to whether our society today is more or less sinful than what prevailed in the economically hard times of the past. It is a largely futile question. What is certain is that a sinless society has never existed and that the Lamb has been slaughtered from the foundation of the world (Rev 13:8). What is certain too is that the sins of our society, past and present, are coming into the open today in a way that they did not get a chance to do in the past. We are experiencing a striking expression of the Lord's words that nothing is hidden that will not be disclosed (Luke 8:17). One is reminded of the work of the good housewife who boils the local berries and removes the scum that comes to the surface before she gives us something that delights our taste. In the various boilings over of present day anger about the secret sins and hypocrisies of our society, much scum has been coming to the top. This is good for us. But we often find ourselves uncertain as to what to do with the scum. We know that we must at the same time reject it and love our fellow-sinner in whom it surfaces. We feel a new urge to cry out to the Lamb of God who alone can take away the sins of the world, who alone can bring us God's mercy, who alone can give us peace.

The Help of Two Evangelists
In interpreting the message of the silent figures in the Knock apparition, figures that are now represented in marble in the Church of the Apparition that highlights the original gable wall, we are particularly helped by the perspective of two evangelists, John and Matthew. John the evangelist, who is in some way identified with the apostle John, was himself one of the figures in the apparition. He is holding the book of the gospel in his hand and he is dressed as a bishop. The key to what he is telling us must surely be the first chapter of his gospel. He tells us about the Word that was in the beginning, about another John who was sent by God to bear witness to the light, about the Word becoming flesh and living among us, about John the baptizer recognizing him as the Lamb who takes sin away, about the call of some of the first apostles, about Nathaniel who was told that he would see heaven opened and the angels of God ascending and descending upon the Son of Man. The episcopal dress is a

clear indicator that it is the call of those who continue the mission of the apostles of the Lamb (cf. Rev 21:14) to teach the whole mystery of the Word made flesh and to be witnesses of the same Word. For John, the Word made flesh is identical with the innocent Lamb who alone can undo the damage done by our lack of innocence. The gospel according to St. John contains no infancy narrative; neither does it contain an explicit invitation to become as little children. One could say that the equivalent of these is the identification of the Word made flesh with the sinless but sin-bearing Lamb. We have the foundations here for the images of the Lamb in the Book of Revelation and in such compositions as the Easter sequence, *Victimae Paschali*. We are given a key to the Christian understanding of victimhood, of sacrifice, of God making Christ to be sin so that we may become righteous (2 Cor 5:21), of the just one dying for the unjust (1 Pet 3:18).

In and Out of Bondage
The second evangelist who can help us to interpret the Knock vision of the Lamb is Matthew. He is the only evangelist who tells us about the flight of the Holy Family into Egypt and about their return from there. All the Knock figures are standing. One cannot help thinking that they are expressing their readiness to go, to enter into hard times in the alien land associated with the ancient bondage of the house of Israel. Their reason for going was that Herod was searching for the child to destroy him (Matt 2:13ff). This search was followed by the massacre of the innocents. The stay in Egypt was to last until those who were seeking the child's life were dead. As we read the story of the holy family's flight into Egypt and of the new exodus from there, we cannot miss the resonances with the original story of the going down into Egypt and of the exodus that was to be annually celebrated by the festive sacrifice of the lamb. It is easy to see the message for the people who were experiencing hard times when the gable wall at Knock was lit up by the vision of the Lamb. There is an unmistakable message here for the church and for the whole human family in new forms of exodus, exile and desert that we have been recently experiencing. Words like *massacre* and *abuse* make frequent appearances in our daily news. The prophets of our day alert us to ways we can find the presence of God in new testings, new deserts. People like the late Dom Helder Camara have told us that preaching justice and peace in

today's society calls for a new willingness to live in the desert and to listen to what the voice of God is saying to us there.

A Call to Family
The Holy Family at the gable wall at Knock has a message for the whole human family in whatever bondage or freeing from bondage in which they find themselves. They help us to come to the Father who alone knows the Son and to the Son who alone knows the Father and reveals him to anybody he chooses (Matt 11:27). The Father to whom the Holy Family leads us is the Father from whom all fatherhood, all motherhood, all sisterhood, all brotherhood in heaven and on earth takes its name (cf. Eph 3:15). Each time we look at the family we call holy we are encouraged to wish and to pray that something of both the sinlessness and the courage that held them together will pervade our families, our church communities, for the building up of which St. Matthew, in his gospel, gives us so many detailed prescriptions.

Matthew has something very special to tell us about each of the persons to whom so many devout people give their hearts and their souls, from whom so many devout people seek assistance in their last agony, in the peace of whom so many devout people hope to breathe forth their souls. He encourages us to look at the "righteous man" (Matt 1:18) who was given the impossible task of getting up, taking the child and his mother and fleeing into Egypt for an indefinite period of time (2:13). He encourages us to discover again the very valid reasons why the church has, in various times, given Joseph the titles of protector, guardian, custodian. He helps us to appreciate the validity of the instincts of St. Teresa of Avila who, when she set out on journeys outside her own community, placed the statue of St. Joseph on her chair and asked him to look after the house in her absence as he did when she was present.

Matthew invites us to look at the woman who is the mother of the child with whom we must identify if we wish to enter the kingdom of heaven (18:3). This is the child who is the Lamb of God. This is the child whom the wise men found after they followed the star. They were overwhelmed with joy as they entered the house, found the child with Mary his mother, knelt down, paid homage and offered gifts (2:7-11). As we look at Mary in the Knock perspective, we cannot help recognizing her as the mother of pilgrims, ready to be part of the sorrowful mys-

teries as well as of the joyful and glorious ones. This mother of
pilgrims is identical with the woman whom the evangelist John
portrays as the mother of disciples (19:26, 27).

The Child at the Center
The Jesus of the Knock vision is the Jesus who is at the center of
the holy family and who alerts us to whatever destroys the child
in ourselves and in others. He wishes to be at the center of every
family along all of life's journey, all our entries into the land of
bondage and our exits out of it. For Matthew, he is the child. For
John the baptizer and John the evangelist, he is the Lamb of God
taking away the sin and the scum of the world. As we contemplate him on the first page of the gospel which John the apostle-
evangelist is holding in his hand, the gospel which is the life-
program for all those who continue the mission of the original
apostles and evangelists, we recognize him as the one who was
in the beginning with God and who was himself God. We recognize him as the Word who became flesh and set up his dwelling
place among us. We recognize him as the one who still wishes to
set up his dwelling place wherever people are. As Christians, we
can never see our earthly dwelling place as a "lasting city" (Heb
13:14). It is more in the nature of a temporary lodging place. The
playwright Jerome K. Jerome wrote a beautiful work called *The
Passing of the Third Floor Back*. It is the story of a disgruntled
group who find themselves together in a lodging house. Their
relationships with each other are very far from what one would
wish to find in an ideal human group. They are, in fact, characterized by hatred and mutual criticism. Into the motley compa-
ny comes an unknown stranger who is more than content to oc-
cupy the least attractive room in the house. His loving and un-
selfish presence soon transforms the group and makes them recognize each other as brothers and sisters building each other up
in mutual concern and love. The Christian interpretation of the
play is plain for all to see. Here indeed is a glimpse of the Word
who has become flesh and who, under many guises, keeps
dwelling among us.

Agents of the Lamb
All Christians are called to be agents of the Lamb who keeps
taking away the sins and the scum of the world. Each of us is
called to cooperate with the Word in his becoming enfleshed

and accompanying people into and out of the many forms of human bondage. Each of us does this in the perspectives of a particular tradition and a particular charism. It is good for us to name these perspectives from time to time. The lenses through which I interpret the Knock apparition are the ones that have been passed on by St. Vincent de Paul. St. Vincent looked out at a world that was experiencing hard times. It has been said that the experience of hard times can lead any of us to do one of four things. We could decide to ignore, or to deplore, or to restore, or to explore. The ignorer decides not to face the reality. The deplorer laments the passing of better times. The restorer sets out to bring back the way things were in the better times. The explorer asks what can be done now and how it can best be done. The Vincentian charism is one of exploring for action. As St. Vincent saw the hard times in which his beloved France found itself, and as he heard of hard times in other countries, he asked what could be done. He got others asking the same question. With people like St. Louise de Marillac, whom Pope John XXIII was to declare patron of all Christian social action, he set in motion a whole series of practical projects that earned him the title apostle of charity. A hundred and fifty years later, the young academic Frederic Ozanam saw a variety of shapes of poverty and of hard times. He was not content to theorize as to what might be the reasons. He became one of the founders of the society that placed itself under the patronage of St. Vincent de Paul.

Angels Ascending and Descending

The witnesses of the apparition at Knock saw angels hovering about the Lamb. As I pray in the new chapel at the gable wall, I come to realize that the angels of God are still "ascending and descending to where the Son of Man is" (John 1:51) and that the risen Son of Man is close to both our right hand and the Father's right hand. It helps me to realize that the angels are God's messengers ever active in our two-way communication with God. It helps me to realize that there is still light on the whole church's gable wall and that the light continues to be "the light of people" (John 1:4). It helps me to realize that "the marriage of the Lamb" (Rev 19:7) has not broken up. It helps me to keep washing myself white in his blood (cf. Rev 7:14). It reminds me that I am part of and an agent of the beautiful plan of a beautiful God who keeps bringing triumph where there seemed to be nothing but failure.

The Cross

The cross of the Lamb was prominent in the Knock apparition. The cross and Lamb continue to throw light on each other. The figure of the Lamb standing on the sacrificial altar, under the shadow of the cross, assures me that, in spite of all the glooms that might encircle us, the sin of the world is continually being taken away. The piece of wax between cross and Lamb in my first communion gift is a continual assurance to me that the Easter candle is always lit, in Paschal time and outside it. The relic of the martyr is an assurance to me that the various forms of martyrdom which the church has to endure throughout the ages are not in vain. It helps me to interpret the message of Oscar Romero and of the lifeblood of the many other martyrs of our time. It invites me to look up at the cloud of witnesses that intercede for us as we try to persevere in running the race (cf. Heb 12:11). The unchanging good news is that the Lamb, though slain, is alive and calling us all to be fully alive.

CHAPTER 24

Miraculous Indeed: A Medal Speaks

Early in the 1990s, I was invited to direct the Miraculous Medal Novena in a church long associated with that devotion. I was pleased to have been asked and I said yes. But I had two secret reservations. I had directed the novena three years earlier and I wondered whether I had anything fresh to say. More seriously, I wondered whether I was continuing to encourage a form of devotion that had had its day. And I had a feeling that I was not alone in my wondering and that there are many good Catholics today who look on such novenas as a kind of holy lavender from the past. Rather than support a marginal devotion, they would prefer to give their energies to serving marginalized people and to promoting the liturgical renewal that is not marginal but central to the life of the church.

At the very time that I was musing along these lines, I was engaged in what looked like a different kind of search. I was looking for the reasons why Jesus performed his miracles of healing, of exorcism, of power over the forces of nature. In the learned books I was told that the miracles were, largely, acts of compassion. They were also expressions of the power of God at work in Jesus as he preached the good news of the kingdom; they were invitations to faith. Seen in this way, the miracles are not a kind of appendix to the teachings and ministry of Jesus. In a real sense, they are his teaching and ministry. They are the good news of the kingdom.

My Conversion

As I reflected on this, I had my moment of conversion. I redis-covered the obvious. The right use of the Miraculous Medal is a continual invitation to see, touch, kiss and put on the compassion of God, the power of God, God's loving invitation to faith. It reminds us that we can be nourished by sacramentals as well as by sacraments. In the early days of the medal's history, it was not called miraculous. But, as those who wore it came to be blessed with many heavenly favors and consolations, they sensed that they were back into the world of the miracles of Jesus. The result was that they could find only one apt name for the medal. As they wore it in faith, they experienced countless rays of light coming down into their world through the hands of the woman whom Christians have at various stages come to know and love as mother of the Lord, mother of God, mother of the church. They knew well that, unlike the serpent, this very special woman never obstructs or distorts the daily coming of God's dawn from on high. They looked with love on the two pierced hearts that resonate with all the needs of every human heart. They saw that the queen of apostles is closely linked with the church's twelve foundation members who point us toward the stars. They saw the healing cross on which Christ was raised up as the special sign of the compassion of God, the power of God, God inviting us to faith.

Compassion, Power, Faith

The generations of people who have worn the medal ever since did not need to be told that the miracles of Jesus are daily occurrences rather than past events. The medal helped and helps people to open their eyes to the many signs in their own lives of the compassion of God, the power of God, God's continual invitations to faith.

In pastoral ministry, we are both receivers and dispensers of the compassion of God. The invitation of Jesus to "be perfect" (Matt 5:48) is made very concrete for us by St. Luke's "be compassionate" (Luke 6:36). It is by compassion that the God who again and again keeps offering us a covenant wishes to be best known. In the medal we recognize God's mother-love as well as God's father-love. It is a love that is ever kind and true, strong and faithful.

The power of God is the power we cry out for when we recognize our helplessness. It is the "power greater than ourselves" that we resort to in all life's "addictions" when it dawns on us that we are powerless in the face of all the many old and new forms that sin, sickness and death can and do take in our lives.

The invitation to faith is the gradual opening of our eyes and ears to the continual action of a loving God in a world that we can so quickly dismiss as secularized. We need this opening especially in our ministry to the young whose faith needs new supports at a time when many of the old ones are collapsing.

Breathing Gospel Air

The medal of the miracles helps us to get all the gospel miracles into focus and to see them as wonderful works of God. It is a gateway to the whole ministry of Jesus. It helps us to breathe the wholesome gospel air. It is a daily assurance that the Jesus of the gospel miracles has identified with human flesh and that he still dwells and walks among us, not merely in the occasional dramatic miracle but in the favors with which God blesses us every day.

Even after my conversion, I allowed myself one more scruple. Why did Mary choose a member of a group of women, Daughters of Charity, whose cloister is the streets of the city and the wards of hospitals, to promote a devotion that seems to be far more at home in the cloisters of convents or churches? As I looked again at my own medal, I felt compelled to say "Surely, all human life is here too!" This makes me wonder whether the medal has been too much pietized over the generations. There certainly is a need to keep reassessing the ways we present it, pray it, preach it. We need to keep building new bridges between church-cloister and street-cloister. To help us do this work of building, it would, I think, be good to keep looking on the medal as a group of symbols throbbing with life.

Symbols

Wherever you go today, people are fascinated by symbols. Whatever the situations they are in, you can offer them, in the medal, a mirror that will help them interpret the story of their lives. Mary could have given St. Catherine Labouré a message in the form of a series of statements. By now they would have been forgotten. Instead, she gave her a collection of five pictures, each of which can touch hearts in every age. That is what symbols do. They touch hearts; they stimulate our memories; they affect our imaginations and emotions; they invite us to dream and to do; they help us to communicate. Could there be a richer and more basic set of symbols than the ones on the medal? We would miss the point if we asked for the exact meaning of any one of them. They all speak for themselves. Each of them represents a common experience, a common memory, a common hope. The lovely thing is that each disciple of the Lord, in each new situation, sees something new in each of them. I suppose we will never quite know the detail of what Catherine saw, what she experienced, or how she interpreted what she experienced. But she got enough to set her heart aglow and to be single-minded, even dogged, in carrying out her mission. In the months when the format of the medal was being finalized and when it was changing its name to "miraculous," people must have interpreted what they saw in a variety of ways. Both the simple and the sophisticated wearers of the medal today have a whole range of ways of reading its message. The scriptures have been described as waters in which an elephant can bathe and a small child can paddle. It is somewhat similar with the medal. Each of its symbols comes straight from human experience. For that very reason it has many links with the Bible. The medal's symbols, and those of the related image of Our Lady of the Globe, are like pictures on the pages of the gospels in which miracles are the sure signs that the kingdom of God is here. Could we have more basic symbols than the globe itself, the stars, the heart, the cross, the maternal face?

The great globe itself; earth, sun, moon, stars. A thousand years before Abraham was a boy, our ancestors looked in awe and fear around the part of the earth which they inhabited. They were in awe and fear of the sun, which shone brightly at midsummer but which had virtually disappeared by the time of the winter solstice. This was the very time they invited it to shed its rays into the world of the dead, an invitation that it graciously accepted. They must have been equally in awe and fear of the different faces of the moon at various seasons of the year. Their symbol of the triple spiral was a search to make sense of, and even control, the movements of the three orbs, the earth, sun and moon. A thousand years after Abraham, the people of God were assured that it was the loving and faithful God who had made the greater light to rule the day and the lesser light to rule the night (Gen 1:16). After another thousand years, a Christian visionary at Patmos saw a woman clothed with the sun, with the moon under her feet (Rev 22:1). The church, who is that woman, has come to recognize Mary as the special embodiment of the vision. It is this Mary who is portrayed on the medal and in the image of the Virgin of the Globe which is inseparable from the medal. At the beginning of a new millennium, we look at her gracious hands, and she assures us that all creation is safe in the strong hands of her Son in whom "all things hold together" (Col 1:17).

The stars in the medal are symbols of the apostles, but they are more. Look up any dictionary of the Bible and you will be reminded of their rich symbolism, not all of which is religious. When scientists explore the stars and tell us that the dust from which the first human bodies came was stardust, we see why the first stars in God's creation said "Here we are" (Bar 3:25). They were preparing the way for the sun-star and moon-star and all of us human stars. Is it any wonder that the designers of the European Union flag drew inspiration from the stars of the Miraculous Medal?

The rays from Mary's hands are about graces. More important, they are about Jesus who, for the whole world, is a lamp brighter than the sun (Rev 21:23). He is also the morning-star (Rev 22:16), a name that Mary has come to share with him. He keeps helping us to be attentive to the good news as to "a lamp shining in a dark place, until the day dawns and the morning star rises in your hearts" (2 Pet 1:19).

The heart. The God of the medal is the God who seeks a heart-to-heart relationship with each of us and whose Son has taken a heart of flesh. God's heart is a fathering heart and a mothering heart. The purity that features so much in the novena prayers is about chastity, but it is also about the whole range of purity of heart which, according to the Beatitudes, enables us to see God (Matt 5:8), and which is embodied in the woman conceived without sin, the woman who alone was undamaged by the world's sin and who keeps banishing sin by her example and her gracious intercession. It is significant that the original name of the medal was the medal of the Immaculate Conception.

The cross. A cross, as we are learning these days, is an attractive symbol in its own right. Its very shape is appealing. It reminds us of life's many crossroads. It points to the four corners of the globe. For believers, it overturns all human values. It is the sign of shame become the great symbol of the redemptive work of the Lord of love who, by dying, destroyed our death and, by rising, restored our life. It keeps standing while the world goes round. Its saving influence reaches out in all directions. We have in it, and in it only, the key to an understanding of the many dyings to which we are called and the seeds of life that lie hidden in the most senseless of deaths, until the Lord Jesus comes in glory.

The maternal face. The Savior of the world was "born of a woman" (Gal 4:4). There is a search today for a rightful under-standing of the feminine, in God and in humankind. It is a very deep search and, though we do not know where it will lead, it is bound to enrich us. How fortunate we are to have a medal that discloses the riches of God in the name, the face, the heart, the hands, the feet of a woman. The serpent under her feet is a sym-bol of fertility gone badly wrong. The medal is an assurance that what has gone badly wrong is, by the grace of Mary's Son, being continually set right. The victory of his grace is assured.

The Same Mary

The Miraculous Medal devotions, like all other devotions in which Mary is invoked, can, when well celebrated, help draw our attention to all that the church has been learning about Mary for the past two millennia. Each celebration can give us a glimpse of the reasons why every age found new reasons for calling her blessed.

The full portrait of Mary was not completed by the composi-tion of the fourth gospel, but a dynamic had been set in motion whereby Christians came to give her titles that express her close-ness to Jesus in the work of our salvation. Her cousin, Elizabeth, had greeted her as "mother of my Lord" (Luke 1:43). At the Council of Ephesus (431) she was given the stunning title of *Theotokos* (God-bearing). At the end of the Second Vatican Coun-cil (1965), Pope Paul VI declared her "Mother of the church." In various ways, Christians, individually and in groups, have ex-perienced, through her, both the mothering qualities of God and the saving qualities of her Son who is her only Savior and our only Savior. In the Miraculous Medal prayer, we do not ask her to give us favors. We ask her to pray for us to the one who is the source of all favors. She is happy to remain the servant of the Lord (Luke 1:38) and our servant.

Mother in God's Family

The revelation of God as Abba, Father, is the basis of the great religious revolution whereby Jesus changes the meaning of all family words. In the family that is the community of disciples, everybody is brother, sister and mother, but the mother of the Lord has a key position. Every human being is made in the image of God (Gen 1:27). In the powerful language of Psalm

139:1, God "searches" and "knows" every one of us. It is God who "knits" every person together. As we come to recognize Mary as the perfect disciple, we see such words as applying in a unique way to her. Behind all Marian dogma is the conviction that the hands of the Creator God were specially at work in shaping and preserving the body, mind, spirit and hands of the woman who is "God-bearer."

Because the church is the family of God, it is well described as a household. In the family that is the church, Mary powerfully expresses the mothering qualities of God. Who can put boundaries to the influence of the mother in any good family? Who can do it in God's family? Who can limit the number of miracles that our Savior can, through Mary's intercession, perform for those who go to the throne of grace? These are some of the questions prompted by good celebrations of the ongoing novena of miracles.

We Are All Mediators

In the miraculous medal devotions, Mary is experienced as praying for us, interceding, mediating. Because all believers form one living body with Christ, our one mediator, we are all mediators. By our prayers and good works, we are all cooperators in the work of our salvation. The reason is that, as the Eastern Church has always emphasized, and as we are reminded in the mixing of water and wine in every Eucharist, we have all been divinized. The Second Vatican Council did not stop us from calling Mary a mediator. But it stated strongly that her influence "rests on" Christ's mediation, depends entirely on it and "draws all its powers from it" (*Constitution on the Church,* par. 60).

In an article which he wrote over thirty years ago, and which he significantly called "One Mediator and Many Mediations," Karl Rahner throws much light on Mary's work of mediation. He makes it clear that Christ's mediation, Mary's mediation and our mediation make sense together. As a result of and by virtue of the unique mediatorship of God's Word made flesh, he says, every one of us depends on everyone else and is significant for everyone else. Every one of us has a task subordinate to Christ. Because we have received salvation, we are carriers of salvation.

Three words which Rahner uses and which are much used in our own day are crucial to our understanding of the network of salvation in which we are all actively involved and in which

Mary plays a particularly active part. They are "interconnected," "interdependent," "intercommunicating." The words speak for themselves. In the household of salvation set up by the Abba-Father, there is no end to the ways in which the three words keep getting new and richer meanings. They throw much light on the role of the woman who is mother in the house. The same three words help us to keep tracing our relationships with those outside "the family of faith" (Gal 6:10), with people of other religions, with the whole of the human family, and indeed with the whole of creation. According to the Letter to the Colossians, all things "hold together" in Christ (1:17). One could also say that, in him, all work of mediation holds together, including the ongoing work of his interceding mother.

Heart to Heart

It has been suggested that, rather than standing beside Christ facing us, Mary should be seen as standing beside us, facing Christ. I suggest that neither image is really helpful. In the medal, Mary is heart-to-heart with her Son. The hearts of all the circle of the Lord's disciples will one day be at one with both hearts, in the house where the Lord himself will move around among his friends. He "will fasten his belt and have them sit down to eat, and he will come and serve them" (Luke 12:37). This image is about both the present and the future. The medal of the miracles keeps reminding us to stay in the circle of disciples. It keeps reminding us to be active in the circle of mediators, in tune with the desires of our one Mediator.

CHAPTER 25

Old Oak, New Branches: St. Vincent Lives

One of the great experiences of my life was my visit to the birth-place of St. Vincent de Paul, near Dax in the south of France. The place has come to be called the Berceau. This is not the name of a town. It is a simple, descriptive word and it means "the cradle land." It is an evocative and emotion-filled word, as are many of the words that recreate for us our childhood experiences. We can all find personal resonances in it, as we do in a poem like "I remember, I remember the house where I was born." I had often heard and read about the Berceau of St. Vincent. But it was a different experience to browse around the place and take in its atmosphere. I got a new appreciation of why words like *place* and *space* and *pilgrimage* are so important in the Christian vocabulary. As I watched people praying in the house, and as I observed them writing down the deep desires of their hearts in the visitors' books that left plenty of space for personal comments and intentions, I had a strong feeling that many birthings had taken place here. It was clearly a place of blessings where, over the centuries, many desires have come to birth in many hearts.

The two great symbols that comprise the Berceau are the house and the oak tree. The six-roomed house stands on the spot where stood the house in which St. Vincent was born. It has been constructed with the kind of meticulous care that makes it like the farmhouses in the Landes country in the seventeenth century and that makes it a faithful reproduction of the house of the de Paul family. Some of the oak beams may have been taken from the original house. The oak tree has been standing for about seven hundred years. It has withstood the ravages of time and of people who wished to graft new life from it.

The House
The house has been well cared for ever since its construction. But, of course, you could not call it a home. With so much family

breakdown today, we know but too well that not every fine house is truly a home. We know that not all the elegant new houses that surround us today are places where people are at home. We also know that the word *home* does not automatically spell happiness. Recent events have disclosed for us the sad deficiencies of some public places called "homes." The Berceau house replaces what was the home of the de Paul family. The house as St. Vincent knew it was the one in which children were conceived and born and in which they experienced a father's love and a mother's love as they grew together from childhood, through adolescence into adulthood. In that network of loving relationships that make family, they learned to worship a homely God.

One could say that the essence of the apostolate of the members of the Society of St. Vincent de Paul, whom we often simply call Vincentians, is to ensure that, though nobody has a "lasting city on this earth" (Heb 13:24), everybody lives with love and dignity in a house that is truly home, that every home is truly a cradle of love. In the original ideal expressed by Frederic Ozanam, it is clear that he saw each member of the Society as attending to the needs of one poor family. The family was to be visited once a week. The work to be done was primarily a work of compassion, a work of trying to understand, a work of what we would today describe as calling for a lot of empathy.

What are Vincentians expected to bring into somebody else's house today? In the words of the prayer at the regular meetings, they give their time, their possessions, themselves. Could I suggest that, in terms of easiness, the order is possessions, time, themselves.

There are still families, perhaps many families, who are lacking in food, in clothing, in essential money. In assessing the urgency of the need of these, the Vincentian visitor can never take the risk of being judgmental. It is a safe principle that those requesting help should always be believed. Once you begin to wonder and to ask whether a particular family is really in need, it is difficult to show the face of the prodigal God who, as the Bible keeps telling us, could not bear to see the stranger, the widow and the orphan receiving a raw deal. The strangers, widows and orphans of the Bible were real people, but they were also symbols pointing to the needs of anybody lacking in anything required for the maintaining of human dignity.

It is easy enough to give some of our possessions. But these can be substitutes for something that is more difficult to give. I have heard it said that it is often the parents who can least afford it who buy the most expensive toys for their children. This can indeed be an expression of their love. It can also be an unrecognized attempt to cover up for their inability to engage in the kind of conversation and communication that would help the children to grow through the various stages in life's journey. There is, I think, a message in this for Vincentians. True Vincentian giving requires time, prime time, quality time: time to talk with all the members of a family, to understand them, to ensure that there is never any semblance of condescension, time to make it clear that the one you are visiting is truly your brother or sister with whom you share a common human fragility, a common need of God's mercy, in a way that helps all concerned to see what is real poverty and is real wealth.

Possessions, time, yourself. By giving your time, you are learning what it is to give yourself. What does it mean to give yourself? It seems to me that the giving of yourself means the giving of your undivided attention. To give somebody your undivided attention means that you keep listening, you keep trying to understand the other person, you keep trying to refrain from quick judgments, you keep learning to communicate. It means that you learn to deal with each person as if nobody else on earth mattered. It means you are fully present. Is it any wonder that, as the church was coming to birth out of his pierced side, Jesus entrusted to the attention and care of the attentive woman the needs of all disciples, all those who would be learners and teachers in the school of God's love (cf. John 19:26, 27)? Attention is an attitude that all of us need to keep learning. It is possible to get absorbed in the giving of material goods, whether in the form of food baskets for the poor or in a more complex form, in a way that blurs the gift of real attention. I have always been full of admiration and regard for Vincentians who beautifully combine both forms of giving. They can speak two languages well, the language of meeting material need and the language of meeting the needs of the heart.

Building a Civilization of Love
It is in this heart-to-heart communication with the person in need that one learns the call to the Christian love that will be the

only topic of examination when we appear before the judgment seat of God. St. Vincent de Paul is on record as saying that unless we love them, the poor will never forgive us for the bread we give them. He would be the first to recognize that there is nothing romantic about giving to the poor. He painted very powerful word pictures of the ignorance, the physical ugliness, the coarseness and crudeness, the ingratitude that one often finds in people who are experiencing any poverty that is degrading. But he invites us to see beyond all this, to reach the heart of the poor person, to recognize that Jesus is in the poor, to keep discerning the body of the Lord (cf. 1 Cor 11:29). In searching for Christ in poor persons, one finds qualities that make them amiable in their own right. The search is ongoing. I am truly communicating with the poor person when I feel in no way superior and the poor person feels in no way inferior.

The search leads us on to an appreciation of the unique dignity of each human person. The Vincentian who keeps trying to be attentive and loving gets more and more glimpses into what Jesus meant when he said, "Life is more than food and the body more than clothing" (Luke 12:23) and when he asked, "What will it profit you to gain the whole world and forfeit your life? Indeed what can you give in return for your life?" (Mark 8:37, 38). To adapt a line from Rudyard Kipling, the heart of Judy O'Grady is no less attractive than the heart of her sister under the skin, the Colonel's lady. In the many dwelling places in the Father's house (John 14:2), there is no upstairs-downstairs. With this clear vision, St. Vincent was able to help the Ladies of Charity, some of whom at first found it very difficult to give love and care to the foundlings, to see that they were no more precious in God's sight than the foundlings and those who had fathered them and given them birth. I believe that the recent "scandals" in the church and the fact that the contemporary moral chaos is affecting "respectable" families as much as it is affecting families from the lower echelons of society is God's opportunity to help us see what Kipling was saying, what St. Vincent was saying, and what God keeps saying.

In inviting us to build up "a civilization of love" and in directing us in so many ways to the God who is rich in mercy, recent popes have been drawing us into the perspective of the God who sees beyond the face into the heart and whose covenant name is "faithful mercy." All of us, not just the members of the

Society of St. Vincent de Paul, are called to be agents of God's love and compassion. Without God's loving initiative, we can do nothing (John 15:5) but with it we can "do all things" (Phil 4:13). We are like the mouse in Aesop's fable who, against all accepted wisdom, managed to do a life-saving good deed for the lion. We are often told these days that people like Vincentians shouldn't be satisfied to keep doling out "charity" and that they should tackle the roots of injustice. It is wise advice, but in tackling the roots of injustice we should get back to gospel roots. A Christian is one who is "rooted and grounded in love" (Eph 3:17). For the Christian, this is what it is to be "radical."

The Oak

Searching for roots brings us back to St. Vincent's great oak tree. Frederic Ozanam visited the Berceau in 1852. It is clear that the experience put him very much in touch with gospel roots and Vincentian roots. Of what he experienced on December 2, 1852, he wrote, "I send you, my dear friend, a leaf from a blessed tree. It will dry out in the book where you leave it, but charity will never wither in your heart...I saw in it a symbol of the foundations of St. Vincent de Paul. They never seem held to the earth by anything human, and they nevertheless have been triumphing for centuries and growing amid revolutions."

The parish priest in St. Vincent's homeland realized that in Ozanam he had met a man who was no ordinary sightseer. He cut off a whole branch of the tree and saw to it that it was brought to the headquarters of the Society of St. Vincent de Paul in Paris. One is reminded of the oak tree of Mamre which features so prominently in Rublev's icon of the Trinity and which forms a piece with the house and the table. At a time when many priests, religious and members of societies like that of St. Vincent de Paul are aging and graying, we can take consolation from the fact that aging can have its advantages. In our search for new and younger members, our greatest "promotion work" will come from the fact that, old or young, we "still produce fruit ...always green and full of sap" (Ps 92:14). Ozanam himself never reached a ripe old age, but he did die a very ripe man. His entry into the pain of the poor helped him cope with the sad moments in his own marriage and in the illness that was to claim his life. In this ripening, he produced much fruit, fruit that remains.

The Few for the Many

The members of the Society of the St. Vincent de Paul are not an elite group. They are called to be and to do what God wants all to be and to do. God expresses through the few what the many are intended to be. Liberation and deliverance cannot be optional words in the vocabulary of any Christian. The Society is like a sacrament, an outward sign helping to advance the "peace and salvation of all the world" (Eucharistic Prayer 3). This makes it into a true expression of the church which is the universal sacrament of salvation. Jesus came that all "may have life and have it more abundantly" (John 10:10). Every group of Vincentian brothers and sisters is called to be alive and to be life-giving. Vincentians are called to be bearers of news that is always good and always new. It is the news of Jesus Christ. It is good to keep reminding ourselves that the word *Jesus* means the one who saves, and that *Christ* means the anointed one. In the time of Jesus, people were anointed for four principal purposes: to grow in strength, in healing, in beauty, in well-being. Jesus the Christ assures us that he is with us always (Matt 28: 20), strengthening us, healing us, beautifying our lives, making us well. He is with us as a physician looking out for the sick (cf. Matt 9:12), and as an itinerant searcher for those on the margins.

Look Out for the New Starvations

The branch taken by Frederic Ozanam from the Berceau tree has brought blessings to many people. I benefited from it myself at an early age. The evening my mother died, the neighbors began to come to our house, as good neighbors do, to bring words of sympathy and consolation. Later in the evening, we had a visit from two pleasant-looking gentlemen who were strangers to me and to the rest of the children. They brought a basket of lovely food. My father looked ill at ease. He thanked the two men politely and he saw them off. When I got him on his own, I asked him who they were. He looked around rather guardedly, to ensure that we were truly alone, and he said in a low voice that they had come from the St. Vincent de Paul Society. I was taken aback. It was wartime. It was the time of ration books. At every Mass we were hearing a prayer that began with the words, "Dismayed by the horrors of a war which is bringing ruin to people and nations." That night, I loved the prospect of delving into the basket, but I couldn't ignore the fact that the men of St.

Vincent de Paul come only to those who were starving. The only time I had heard of St. Vincent de Paul was in the song that was the current rage and that became the local signature-tune during the war:

Bless them all, bless them all, bless all the men in the Dáil;
The long and the short and the tall.
Bless de Valera and Sean McEntee,
They gave us brown bread and a half ounce of tea
And they rationed the cocoa and all
That they shouldn't have rationed at all.
So look out for starvation in our little nation
And join up the Vincent de Paul.

On that evening in 1941, I was old enough to know that there are rich families and poor families. Our family never thought of itself as rich. But we certainly wouldn't have regarded ourselves as a poor family, much less as a starving family. In our parish there were some families who were known to be poor. In the church in town, there was a "rich side" where you paid two-pence and a "poor side" where you paid a halfpenny. There was a difference even between twopence and a halfpenny, those who were and those who weren't worth tuppence! There was a big difference between fur coats and the trendy swagger-coats that were making their appearance at the time. May the Lord forgive us all our little snobberies!

In the words of our war prayer between 1939 and 1945, St. Vincent was "dismayed by the horrors" of the wars going on in France and in other parts of Europe in his time. He "looked out for starvation" and he was quick to recognize its many forms and to do something to relieve every one of them. His great genius was to see through accepted attitudes and to recognize who was truly poor and who was really rich. In a parish called Chatillon, he was shocked to find many families suffering from real starvation. Not merely did he come to their aid, but he organized people's voluntary help in such a way that the people themselves began to see the forms that hunger and starvation were likely to take in the future. He mobilized the goodwill and the talents of many men and many women. At the estate of a wealthy lady called Madame de Gondi, he heard the confession of a dying man. The experience alerted him to the spiritual starvation of countless neglected people who, in the words of the gospel (Matt 9:36), were "like sheep without a shepherd." Out of his dismay at the many horrors of many wars that were bringing ruin to his own nation and to places as far away as Ireland, which was then wartorn, and out of his compassion for people in any form of poverty of body or soul, he founded the priests and brothers of the Mission who share the name of Vincentian with the Society of St. Vincent de Paul, the Sisters of Charity whom we now know as the Daughters of Charity of St. Vincent de Paul, and other groups of women dedicated to all kinds of works of charity.

Diagnosing Real Poverty
Did St. Vincent himself come from a poor family? The Berceau house is certainly much bigger and more elaborate than my twentieth-century family home. It is the kind of house that the members of the Society of St. Vincent de Paul would see no need to visit! I rather think that the de Pauls always went into the rich side of the parish church! But as St. Vincent went on in life he became more and more convinced that he himself was the poorest person on earth. He kept saying that he was "wretched," a word that translates the title of the great musical that many of us find hard to pronounce. Some simply call it *Les Mis*. To say I am miserable and wretched is to say that I am in need of divine mercy. In the prayer after each decade of the Rosary, we sometimes say "especially those most in need of your divine mercy." St. Vincent would say "That's me!" He would have loved the story that Cardinal Jaimé Sin of Manila often tells about himself. The Cardinal comes from a large family. When he was small, his mother always hugged him good night and said, "Jaimé, I love you more than I love any of the others." One night, he asked her why she kept telling him this. She paused and replied, "Jaimé, you're the ugliest of them all; that's why!" St. Vincent would have well understood why we sometimes say, even of wealthy people, "poor man!" or "poor woman!" or even "poor devil!" He saw clearly that Madame de Gondi and her poorest servant were sisters under the skin. In his long hours of prayer, he came to see very clearly that the Holy Eucharist is the body of Christ but that the poor are also the body of Christ. He found new ways of recognizing where true poverty and true wealth are.

New Poverties
Every time I visit my home place, I am impressed by new prosperity—new houses, new educational and social facilities, a

dramatic rise in the general standard of living. And still, we are told on good authority that large numbers of our people are living below the poverty line. It doesn't always mean that they have no bread or low wages. But there are many new poverties, new starvations and new and subtle forms of stigma. Many members of the Society of St. Vincent de Paul could list them for you. They include the kinds of poverties that breed crime and drug abuse; the poverty of people who have access to a lot of money but don't know how to use it; the poverty of those who have nobody to advise them well on how best to avail themselves of educational and social opportunities. The fruit of poverties such as these is a new set of "horrors" in our society, the horrors not of war but of a time of alleged peace.

What has St. Vincent got to tell us in all of this? He is telling us:

• to look out for new starvations and be quick to recognize those starved of the spiritual values that sustained us in past times of hardship;

• to be a good neighbor to anybody in any form of human need. For this, you don't have to "join the St. Vincent de Paul Society." Its members alert us to what all of us should be doing all the time;

• to recognize our own poverty before God, that without God we can do nothing, but that with God's help there is no limit to what we can do;

• to realize that God is a rich God, rich in mercy. God dearly wishes that each of us be rich in the same mercy. This is the wish of St. Vincent for each of us as he invites us, in the words of his special Mass, to love as he loved and do as he did. The oak tree is alive and well.

CHAPTER 26

A Beautiful Millennium

The new millennium has dawned. Its coming was heralded by many plans and programs and its arrival was celebrated with the sound of many trumpets. We were all encouraged to dream dreams of what we would like the millennium to be. Christian leaders have thought it important to remind us that the start of the new millennium was primarily a religious occasion. We were celebrating two thousand years of God among us in the form of our own flesh and blood. This special and continuing presence of God dwelling among us must surely be the basis for the dream of all believing Christians.

In the shaping of the dreams of Catholic Christians especially, two people deserve to be listened to with special care. Both of them had for over twenty years been preparing us for this great moment in history. From the early days after his election as Bishop of Rome, Pope John Paul II invited us to look toward the year two thousand. At first, some thought they detected a darkly apocalyptic note in what he had to say, as if he was preparing the world for a bleak *Dies Irae,* a day of wrath that would bring new ominous expressions of the judgment of God. But it became clearer and clearer that he saw the beginning of the new millennium as a time of jubilee, with all the rich biblical connotations of that word. Like the Lord himself at the beginning of his public ministry, he talked in terms of a special year of the Spirit of the Lord being upon us, a year of new anointing, a year of good news for the poor, a year of release for captives, a year in which the blind would recover their sight, a year in which the oppressed would go free, a year in which the Lord's favor would be proclaimed (cf. Luke 4:18, 19). His special letter on the coming of the third millennium could be described as a whole program of how to be fully human and fully Christian. He invited us to become a people of the Trinity into whose name and life we were baptized.

Another Christian teacher who prepared us well for the jubilee year and who invited us to dream dreams as to what might follow it is Cardinal Martini. Through his pastoral letters and pastoral programs, and his proclaiming God's word in season and out of season, he has been a prophetic voice for many Christians and he has continually expressed a wish that the experience of the two disciples on the road to Emmaus (Luke 24:13ff) would be replicated wherever new disciple meets new disciple.

A Call to the Beautiful

If one were to distill the jubilee message and the millennium message of these two Christian teachers, one could say that it is an assurance that it is never too late to love the "beauty so old and so new" (St. Augustine, Confessions, X, 27), and that, in fact, now is the acceptable time. The message is expressed very well in the Pope's letter to artists which, significantly, he signed on the Easter Sunday of the last year of the second millennium. It is addressed "to all who are passionately dedicated to the search for new 'epiphanies' of beauty so that through their creative work as artists they may offer these as gifts to the world." The number of us who are artists in the strict sense may be very small, but we would all give a wonderful millennium gift to our sisters and brothers if we were to become passionately dedicated to give new expressions in our lives to the beauty that is both old and new. It is significant that, as saints of the beautiful, the Pope chose St. Francis who, having received the stigmata of Christ, said ecstatically, "You are beauty...you are beauty" and Fra Angelico who painted for others what he himself had contemplated as a Dominican friar.

Cardinal Martini's pastoral letter for 1999–2000 is entitled "What Beauty Will Save the World?" He took his title from an incident in a novel by Dostoyevsky whose own religious sense had been nurtured to a great extent by what is beautiful in Russian literature and icons like Rublev's on the Trinity on which the rest of Europe has been feasting in recent years. The novel is entitled The Idiot. In it there is a prince who is looking with loving compassion on an eighteen-year-old youth who is dying of tuberculosis. An atheist asks him, "Is it true that you said once that beauty would save the world?... What sort of beauty will save the world?" Like Christ before Pilate, the prince gives no answer, but the obvious answer lies in the love that shares in the world's pain.

Both Pope John Paul II and Cardinal Martini are inviting us to share their dream for new epiphanies, new expressions of God's beauty, new signs for all to see that God's beauty is new every morning. They are inviting us to be like St. Joseph who became the patron of the whole church by dreaming dreams and ensuring that the dreams would come true. They are helping us to see why the *Catechism of the Catholic Church,* unlike older catechisms, pays such prominent attention to the topic of beauty.

A Noble Tradition
Over the centuries, Christians have given a variety of expressions to the beauty of God. The prayer (Saturday morning, Week 2) for the pouring out of God's Spirit on artists, craftsmen and musicians is both a thanksgiving for the past and a program for the present and future. In searching for the beautiful, Christians have been helped by philosophers like Plato who helped us see how the beautiful things that surround us, and for the welfare of which we are nowadays seeing ourselves to be more and more responsible, are participations in ideas that go far beyond us, and by people who, in his spirit, searched for the *kalokagathon,* that which is both beautiful and good. The distinctive Christian vision sees created beauty at its greatest in human lives well lived. Perhaps the best compliment we have been paying to beauty is that we have for centuries been describing it in terms of what transcends any known categories. We talk of it in the same breath as the three transcendental properties that belong to God and that, by analogy and participation, belong to every created being. We say God is one, God is good, God is true. It is for this reason that we dare to say that every being is one, every being is good, every being is true. It is here that beauty comes in. Some would put it on the same level as the other three and say, simply, that every being is beautiful. All would agree that beauty is an epiphany, a manifestation, of the one, the good, the true.

Nobody has written so helpfully about beauty as did St. Thomas Aquinas. He pointed to some of the implications of the fact that all created unity, truth and goodness is a participation in the unity, truth and goodness of God. He saw beauty as the splendor, the shining forth, of what is true. He taught that those things are said to be beautiful which please, give pleasure, when we see them. He wrote of the incarnation and the unfolding of its mystery in the life, death and resurrection of Christ as the great manifestation to us of the beauty of God. He taught us to look for beauty wherever there is integrity, good proportion and clarity. His emphasis on the incarnation as the splendor before human eyes of the mystery of God was to influence Catholic devotion in the way people came to pray to Jesus Christ. The Litany of the Holy Name, which took its final shape a few centuries after the time of St. Thomas, addresses Jesus as the splendor of the Father, as the clarity of eternal light, as the king of glory, as the sun of justice.

A Biblical Word

If we look at the scriptures for the foundations for the thinking of people like Aquinas, we could, at first reading, be disappointed. The word itself is not all that central. But be ready for some surprises. It is as accurate to say that Jesus is the beautiful shepherd as to say that he is the good shepherd (John 10:11); his style of shepherding has the quality which Raymond Brown saw best interpreted as attractive loveliness. It is as accurate to report Peter's words on Mt. Tabor as "It is beautiful for us to be here" as it is to report him as saying "It is good for us to be here" (Mark 9:5). It is as accurate to say that Jesus praised the woman's anointing of his feet as a beautiful deed as to say that he called it a good deed (Mark 14:6). It is as accurate to say that the steward at Cana kept the beautiful wine till last as to say that he kept the good wine till last (John 2:10). It is as accurate to describe as beautiful the works by which Jesus introduced the kingdom of God as to describe them as good (cf. John 10:32, 33).

And still it is true that the scriptures do not often speak about beauty. But they do speak about its equivalent. That equivalent is glory. In a sense, the whole of the scriptures are about the glory of God. Of all the many wonderful things that the Old and New Testaments have to say about the glory of God, there is nothing more glorious, more beautiful than St. Paul's description of the Christian life in terms of being "transformed from one degree of glory to another" (2 Cor 3:18). One could paraphrase this as a call to move from one beautiful stage of life into another beautiful stage. To give glory to God is to let God make new epiphanies, new manifestations of the divine unity, goodness and truth through the way we live our daily lives. This means knowing, loving and doing in the way the Father, Son and Spirit know, love and do. It was all put very profoundly and very simply by St. Paul when he said, "Whether you eat or drink, or whatever you do, do everything for the glory of God" (1 Cor 10:31). It was put pithily by St. Irenaeus when he said that the glory of God is a human being alive. It was put equally well by St. John of the Cross who said that one sole thought in a human being is worth more than the whole world and so God alone is worthy of it. It was behind the thinking of the wise person who advised us that if something is worth doing at all it is worth doing beautifully.

Nobody has written so extensively of the glory and beauty of God as did Hans Urs von Balthasar. In his eight large volumes on the subject he has shown us that beauty is indeed a many splendored thing. He removes any of our illusions that beauty might be about what is pretty, about tinsel, about what is gaudy. While he recognized vestiges of beauty in everything created, he admitted that we have sometimes to look very hard before we can find anything that pleases. He was well aware of the reality of sin and ugliness in the world. His words are most effective when he shows that God's glory was at its best in what to all appearances was the most inglorious of events, the suffering and dying of Jesus and his descent into hell. Here we are somehow at the heart of the good news to which we hope to give new epiphanies as makers of the new millennium. In the journey ahead we have such icons of beauty as Mother Teresa who was single-minded in her desire to do "something beautiful for God" by recognizing God's image and icon in people who are living in the rawest and the most off-putting of conditions. We have similar icons in communities like L'Arche that help us recognize the beauty of the human form behind what is deformed. In icons like these, we learn that the many calls to a preferential option for the poor are calls to the heart of the gospel.

A Time of Many Calls
The Greek word for beauty comes from the verb *to call*. The call to manifest the glory and beauty of God is a call to make use of all our senses. It is a call to taste and see and to help others to taste and see, that the Lord is good (cf. Ps 34:8). It is a call to be and to help others be a fragrant offering to God (cf. Phil 4:18). It is a call to be members of communities that have looked at God and touched God incarnate with their hands. It is a call to tell

others about what we ourselves have heard and we have seen with our eyes (cf. 1 John 1:1).

The call of the gospel is, first of all, a call to hearing and to seeing. Disciples are learners. Daily Christian living is a series of exercises in learning the language of seeing and hearing, to help us be unlike the idols of the Gentiles who have eyes but cannot see and who have ears but cannot hear (cf. Ps 115:5, 6). We are called to learn a salutary lesson from those whom Jesus castigated for being hard of hearing and for shutting their eyes (cf. Matt 13:15). The call of the gospel is a call to have our eyes opened in a way that will help us take true pleasure in what we see. Jesus congratulated his disciples and he declared them blessed because they saw what they saw (Matt 13:16). Every new hearing of the word of life, which is the gospel, is an invitation to see, to behold. Jesus told prospective disciples to "come and see" (John 1:39). His miracles of restoring physical sight were symbolic of the many forms of new seeing to which he invited his followers. It was the experience of the Christian way of seeing that, centuries after the earthly ministry of Jesus, made a man (John Newton, 1725–1807) sing of the amazing grace whereby he had moved from being lost to being found, from being blind to seeing.

The risen Christ continues to invite us from vision to vision, until we enjoy what we have come to call the beatific vision. Our vision is a Christian vision to the extent that we try to see God in everything and try to see everything in the way that God sees it. When God first looked on the creation which had come into existence by his will, he saw that it was good (Gen 1). That great look of God is the basis for our belief that beauty is in the eye of the beholder. We are dealing here not with subjective likes and dislikes, but with the loving eye of God which is the source of all that is good, all that is beautiful. When we let God teach us to see in God's way, we have what Bernard Lonergan called the eye of love that is faith and this leads to the look of love that is contemplation. When we experience this eye and this look we know that the God whose eye saw that the created universe was good is still looking with favor on the lowliness of each of us his servants (cf. Luke 2:48) as we try to magnify the Lord by beautiful words and beautiful deeds. The loving look of the Father is most perfectly expressed in the call of his Son who by looking on those who wish to be disciples loves them (cf. Mark 10:21). When two people fall in love, we sometimes wonder what they see in each other. Maybe it is a variation of this kind of wonder that makes some people ask what Mother Teresa saw in those who were not obviously deserving of love. The truth is that everything in creation has been loved into being by God and it is the same loving look that keeps it in being and makes it continually worthy of love, of respect, of being cared for. It is no wonder that concern for the environment is getting an ever more prominent place in our Christian consciousness.

True Pleasure, True Joy

The call of beauty is a call to experience true pleasure, to find true joy as we enjoy the world on which God looked with creative love. It is a call to have moments in which we can experience true delight and to allow ourselves times of true leisure. There should be no conflict between our belief that we were created to know, love and serve God here on earth and the belief that we are to see and enjoy God forever in heaven. As we learn to know, love and serve, we can have many foretastes of the eternal seeing and enjoying. The variant reading of St. Luke's version of the Our Father (Luke 11:3) could help us here. In it, we pray not for our daily bread but for our bread for tomorrow. It is hardly a request that we will hoard up food for the rainy day. Perhaps it is an intimation that our daily table-fellowship is a foretaste of the seeing and enjoying that will be our heaven. It is in that fellowship that we learn to say "I see" and to taste the joy that is a sharing in the joy of God who, according to St. Thomas Aquinas, is happiness itself. We learn to drink from the river of God's delights (cf. Ps 36:8) and to rejoice in the Lord always (cf. Phil 3:1).

The Human Form

The call to beauty includes a call to appreciate the beauty of the human form. We often make use of the word *form* at a rather superficial level. We ask somebody "How is the form?" and we rarely expect a calculated answer. We very often identify form with shape. It is worthwhile to pause and remember the richer meanings of *form*. A favorite Latin word for the beautiful is *formosa*, which really means attractive in form. An older way of understanding the sacraments was in terms of matter and form. This way of speaking and teaching has been largely abandoned. There were good reasons for the change, but the older language had many merits. The search for the form of a sacrament was really a search for its essence, for its deepest meaning, for the heart of the matter. It is the form of baptism that makes a particular pouring of water into a sacrament of rebirth and of forgiveness of sins. It is the form of the Eucharist that makes a particular taking of bread and wine into the sacrament of the body and blood of Christ. Similarly, it is the human form that makes this blend of animal, vegetable and mineral into a human being in the image and likeness of God.

There are many ways in which we are called to be people of form. We are called to be con-formed to the kind of image of his Son that God the Father wishes us to be. We are called to be alert to the sins that de-form that image in us and that keep us falling short of the glory of God (cf. Rom 3:13-15). As we do so, we become more and more aware that we are members of the church that is in constant need of re-form. We seek for ways in which we can keep in-formed as to how this is to be done. It is all part of a program leading to the day when the Lord "will transform our humble body that it may be conformed to the body of his glory" (Phil 3:21).

The call to be people of form is a continual call to conversion. Conversion is a change in the way we hear and see. It is a call to new ways of knowing, of loving, of deciding, of acting. Above all, it is a call to fall in love, a call to change our way of loving the Lord our God and loving our neighbor as ourselves, as we get new visions of the marvels the Lord has worked both in our neighbor and in each one of us.

One of our greatest prayers and yearnings for the new millennium must surely be that our celebrations of the Eucharist will be truly full of form, full of beauty, truly *formosa*. This will happen to the extent that we keep inviting the risen Lord to appear to us at each Eucharist, to make our hearts burn as he opens the scriptures to us, to keep opening our eyes so that we can recognize him in the way we break bread (Luke 24:13-35).

Three Wishes

There are three areas in which the church is experiencing particular tension at the beginning of the new millennium. One hopes and prays that, with the passing of the years, there will be new injections of truth and beauty into each of these. While we puzzle over the meaning of John Keats's "Beauty is truth, truth is beauty—that is all ye know on earth and all ye need to know," it dawns on us that we will never make headway in presenting the truths of which we are convinced unless the beauty of these truths keeps flashing forth.

The first area concerns the original decision of God to create us male and female (Gen 1:27). We need new perspectives of beauty in the way we understand our sexuality and in our understanding of the relationship of male and female in our thinking and talking about God, about each other, about what makes or breaks Christian marriage, about church ministry.

The second area concerns what promotes true communion in the church and in the relationships of the church with people of other religions, and with the rest of the human family. We know that as we break eucharistic bread and drink the eucharistic cup we have a communion in the body and blood of Christ (1 Cor 10:16) and that, as a result, we are one bread, one body. But we also know that, over the centuries, the communion has been broken, indeed shattered. We are called now to find beautiful and perhaps daring ways of achieving the wish of the Lord "that they may all be one" (John 17:21).

The third area concerns our understanding of the world for which Christ died. We have been taught to share "the joys and hopes, the grief and anguish of the people of our time" (*Constitution on the Church in the Modern World,* par. 1). We have been encouraged to welcome and promote all that is good in contemporary culture. The practical working out of this can be difficult. In our search for new cultural expressions of the Christian faith and in revisiting older ones, we must make sure that we worship not the culture but the Lord whose teaching transcends all cultures, including the one in which his own human experience was shaped. There are forms of worldliness that cannot get Christian approval. There are aspects of the world for which Christ refused to pray (cf. John 17:9). There are ways of living and ways of ruling to which the Christian must say "no." To keep naming these will call, very often, for a wisdom from on high. To enable us to be a sacrament of salvation for the whole world, caring for all the earth and all its inhabitants, we need a continual discerning of how we can be the splendor of the true, the good and the one.

A Millennium of Grace

Perhaps our greatest desire should be that this will be a millennium of grace. God's grace is God's continual offer to us to share in God's own way of being, of knowing, of loving and of doing. May we keep responding generously to this daily offer. As graced people, may we be gracious in thought, word and deed. May we be mirrors of God's life, of God's glory, of God's beauty.

Index

Abba 7, 16, 22-26, 31, 48, 120, 161, 230
Abraham 13, 14, 16, 114, 228
All Hallows College 126, 127
Aloysius, St. 79
Alphonsus, St. 100
anam chara 181
anawim 117
Andrews, Eamon 131
Angelico, Fra 243
Anima Christi 43, 161, 213
anointing 44, 49, 126, 238, 242
Anselm, St. 35
Anthony, St. 116
argain ifrinn 23
Aristotle 200
Athenagoras, Patriarch 70
Augustine, St. 14, 18, 19, 95, 96, 110, 139, 167, 243
"baking" 130, 131, 133-142
von Balthasar, Hans Urs 23-26, 28, 29, 82, 98, 188, 190, 193, 195, 197, 246
"basics" 51, 52, 151, 158
beauty 242-251
Being-in-Love 28
Benedict, St. 125, 127, 139
benediction 148
Berceau of St. Vincent 233ff
Bernard, St. 136
big bang 111
Bloom, Archbishop 122
Bloy, Leon 114
body 78, 91, 101, 105, 118, 165, 178, 198-206

body and blood 34, 218, 225, 250
Bonaventure, St. 133, 181, 184
Bradley, Ian 108, 109
Breastplate of St. Patrick 12
Briege, Sr 117, 124
Brueggeman, V. 141, 171
Butler, B. C. 115
Calvin, John 96
Camara, Helder 220
Casson, Christopher 127, 131
Catechism of the Catholic Church 31, 99, 119, 224
Carmelites 123, 175, 176, 180
causes 60, 64, 108
Catherine Labouré, St. 227, 228
Catherine of Siena, St. 123
de Caussade, J. P. 65, 180
celibacy 76ff
Celtic 15, 23, 89, 92, 141
Chaplin, Charlie 67
de Chardin, Teilhard 103
chastity 78ff
Chesterton, G. K. 127
circles 14-16, 41, 162
civilization of love 26, 104, 235ff
Clare, St. 139
co-creators 135 and *passim*
Congar, Yves 137
consecrations 150-159
"consecrated life" 155-157, 160-168, 169-176
Constantine 72, 73
Constitution on the Church 97, 98, 167, 198, 199, 202, 231

Constitution on the Church in the Modern World 102, 250
Constitution on the Sacred Liturgy 178
Constitution on Divine Revelation 71, 138, 147
conversion 11, 20, 36, 70, 72, 119, 249
Craig, Mary 113, 114
"counsels" 172, 195
creation 11, 27-29, 32, 50, 54, 61, 63, 103, 135, 248
Cross 21, 189ff, 229
Cruise, Jack 136

Dalrymple, Jock 136
Damascus House 209
Danneels, Godfried 182
Dante 95
darkness 56, 57, 70, 83, 185
Daughters of Charity 26, 52, 144, 180, 192, 227, 238
Day, Dorothy 71
Dead Man Walking 188
de-Christianization 137
Dedication 152, 153, 156-158
Didache 134
Dies Irae 142
discernment 55-57, 65, 198-206
disciples 162ff, 243, 247
Dresden 93, 101, 105
Dostoyevsky 243
dove 54
Doherty, Catherine 165

eclipse 71ff
Ecumenism, Decree on 98
Eliot, T. S. 43
Elizabeth, St. 7
Elizabeth of the Trinity 12
emptying 23, 24, 27, 112, 187-198
endurance 113
ephipanies 73, 243-245
Eucharist 66, 88, 120, 134, 135, 148, 168, 202ff, 240, 249, 250
Europe 76, 95
European Synod 82
evil 99, 100, 103

examens 86, 215
evolution 61
Exodus 64, 140, 220
ex opere operato 138
Evangelica Testificatio 161

face of Christ 70, 71, 74
faith, hope, love 75, 76, 101, 125, 161, 185, 225ff
family 15, 20, 125, 221, 230ff
Father 11, 30-36 and *passim*
Feeney, Leonard 97
Fiddler on the Roof 121
filling 27, 187-198
fire and flame 29, 52, 75-83, 105
Florence, Council of 96, 98
forgiveness 56, 86ff
form 248, 249
Francis, St. 24, 130, 139, 144, 166, 243
Francis de Sales 96, 136, 144, 147, 148
freedoms 62

Gandhi, Mahatma 66
General Instruction on the Roman Missal 30
gift, giving 27, 53, 57, 107ff, 133, 194, 221
glory 8, 11ff, 103, 105, 215, 245 and *passim*
de Gondi, Madame 238, 240
grace 18, 247, 251
Grand Canyon 103
Gregory the Great 78, 79, 135
Guelph 209, 210
Guigo II 136, 148
Guinness Book of Records 111

Hades, hell 23, 100, 101, 190, 193
Hannukah 40, 157
Hopkins, Gerard Manley 47
harrowing 23, 24, 176
heart 19, 49, 50, 84-92, 191, 192, 227, 229, 232, 235
heaven 103ff, 127
Heenan, John C. 208, 212
holiness 34, 151ff

Holy Family 221
Holy Office 97
Holy Spirit 24-26, 45-54
home 125-132, 233, 234
hope 29, 98
Housman, A. E. 104

icons 12ff, 86, 189
Ignatius of Loyola 71, 77, 180, 181, 209, 211, 213, 214
images of God 31, 57, 119, 122 and *passim*
Imitation of Christ 92
intercession 9, 116ff, 231, 232
interiority 192, 193
Irenaeus, St. 105, 246
Iron Curtain 160
itinerant 41, 42

Jacobites 96
Jacob's Ladder 49, 191
Jansenism 96
Jeremias, Joachim 22, 31
Jerome, Jerome K. 222
Jesus Christ, images of 37-44
Jesuits 96
John of the Cross, St. 57, 83, 101, 113, 181
John XXIII, Pope 7, 31, 70, 223
John Paul I, Pope 35
John Paul II, Pope 23, 24, 31, 35, 70, 201, 242, 244
Joseph, St. 49, 221
Joyce, James 79, 100
judgment 29, 51, 242 and *passim*
Julian of Norwich 35, 64, 100, 108, 112, 141, 185
justice and peace 104, 105, 115, 179, 204-206

Kafka, Franz 35
kalokagathon 244
kataphatic 144, 181
Keane, J. B. 141
Keats, John 249
Kells, Book of 141
kenosis 111, 192
Killala 17

king, kingdom of God, *passim*
Kingsley, Ben 66
Kipling, Rudyard 236
Knock shrine 217-224
Kübler-Ross, Elizabeth 170

Ladies of Charity 236
Lady Macbeth 120
Lamb of God 217-224
L'Arche 33, 246
Lay vocation and baptism 17, 25, 80ff, 115, 150-159, 171, 175ff, 182, 197, 203
lectio divina 131, 133, 143-149, 214
Legion of Mary 119, 198
Les Miserables 240
Lewis, C. S. 125
Litany of Loreto 71
Litany of the Holy Name 68, 144, 245
Lonergan, Bernard 247
Louise de Marillac 51, 52, 192, 223
Louis of Granada 144
Lourdes 117
love 26-29, 34, 52 83, 192, 194

Maccabaeus, Judas 152
magnanimity 67, 68
Mamre 14, 227
Manichaeism 200
Manresa 209
marginality 40, 41
Martini, Carlo 35, 243, 244
Marmion, Columba 38, 139, 161
martyrdom 81
Mary 15, 22, 24, 47, 49, 50-51, 69, 71, 88, 116, 118, 119, 193, 198, 217, 221, 225-232
McQuaid, Archbishop 136
mediation 188ff, 231, 232
mercy 12, 56, 96, 204, 206, 217ff, 236, 237, 240, 241
messiah 38, 52
Michelangelo 95
millennium 242-251
Miraculous Medal 225-232
mirrors 71
mission 94f, 150, 152, 157